Making Government Work

About the Book and Editors

Relations between Congress and the executive branch have always been an uneasy mixture of mutuality and autonomy, cooperation and conflict. The U.S. Constitution required that the two branches of the federal government work in concert, but it also mandated a separation of powers. Inevitably, this situation has led to a clash of wills and a contest for power, but during the past 200 years the system has proved amazingly durable.

Recently, however, the two branches have been buffeted by a succession of political developments combined with institutional and technological change. The growing frustration of many policymakers has been increasingly evident in the process itself: fewer pieces of legislation actually become law, the budget process consumes ever-increasing amounts of time and effort, and the executive branch finds its foreign policy initiatives reshaped by an assertive Congress. Congress relied heavily on the legislative veto only to see the veto overturned by the Supreme Court. Officials in both branches of government and in both parties agree that the process has become excessively frustrating and time consuming. But what is to be done? There is agreement on the illness but little on the causes of each symptom and even less on the remedy. Each branch tends to blame the other for tensions and contends that the other should make the bulk of any reforms.

This book is a practical and realistic blueprint for change in the U.S. government. The contributors, a bi-partisan group of government leaders and academics, draw on their wide-ranging experience within Congress, the White House, and the bureaucracy. Using case studies that illustrate central issues in legislative-executive relations, the authors dissect key problems plaguing and often paralyzing the conduct of the government. Because this book emphasizes the viewpoint of practitioners responsible for getting government business done at both national and international levels, its recommendations for change are pragmatic and represent realistic opportunities for improving government.

Robert E. Hunter is director of European studies at CSIS and a contributing editor of *The Washington Quarterly*. **Wayne L. Berman,** a Washington lobbyist with the firm of Berman, Bergner, and Boyette, Inc., codirects CSIS's programs on Executive-Legislative Relations and National Elections Reform. **John F. Kennedy** is staff director of the Commission on National Elections and is assistant director of CSIS's European Studies Program.

Published in cooperation with
the Center for Strategic and International Studies
Georgetown University

Making Government Work

From White House to Congress

edited by
Robert E. Hunter, Wayne L. Berman,
and John F. Kennedy

Foreword by Amos A. Jordan

Westview Press / Boulder and London

Published in 1986 in the United States of America by Westview Press, Inc.; Frederick A. Praeger, Publisher; 5500 Central Avenue, Boulder, Colorado 80301

Library of Congress Cataloging-in-Publication Data
Making government work.
   Rev. ed. of: Making the government work/edited by
Robert E. Hunter, Wayne L. Berman. 1985.
   Published in cooperation with the Center for
Strategic and International Studies, Georgetown
University.
   Bibliography: p.
   1. United States—Executive departments. 2. United
States. Congress. I. Hunter, Robert Edwards, 1940–
II. Berman, Wayne L. III. Kennedy, John F.
IV. Georgetown University. Center for Strategic and
International Studies. V. Georgetown University.
Center for Strategic and International Studies.
Making the government work.
JK585.M33 1986   353.03′72   86-9218
ISBN 0-8133-0312-5

Printed and bound in the United States of America

∞ The paper used in this publication meets the requirements of the American National Standard for Permanence of Paper for Printed Library Materials Z39.48-1984.

6   5   4   3   2   1

Contents

Foreword

Since its inception more than two decades ago, the Center for Strategic and International Studies (CSIS) of Georgetown University has served as a bridge between the worlds of government, academia, and the private sector. It has been devoted to research and analysis into key problems facing our nation in foreign and defense policy.

In recent years, we have also recognized the importance of addressing the way in which policy is made—both the methods and the institutional structures of government. We have thus undertaken several important projects devoted to governance—the ways, means, and processes of government that make possible the foreign and defense policies that serve the country's objectives. Indeed, we have come to recognize that a proper understanding of governance is a prerequisite for developing useful policy recommendations.

Leading the effort to study governance of the nation has been the Center's project on legislative-executive relations, the results of which are presented here.

In embarking on this project, CSIS attempted what, for us, was a different kind of research. While we drew extensively upon the insights of many of America's leading academic authorities on legislative-executive relations, we also formed a special steering committee composed of seasoned practitioners of government. The committee's composition was carefully designed to provide a balance of perspectives and experiences; it was divided equally between Democrats and Republicans as well as between individuals who had served on Capitol Hill and those who had served in the executive branch—the White House in particular. To a considerable degree, the project was designed by the steering committee, which shaped the study's scope, methods, analyses, and recommendations according to what members judged to be the most salient issues in legislative-executive relations. Thus, in our view, this project brings together the best of both the academics' and the political practitioners' worlds—the latter largely setting the agenda and drawing conclusions, the former mostly adding special insights that illuminated the whole.

In this unique venture, we have benefited from having·the unstinting support throughout from the Prince Charitable Trusts of Chicago. Without that resource, this venture in understanding governance would not have been possible. With that support, CSIS has been able to complete successfully this central phase of its work on governance and to convince others of both the merits of the method and the results.

It is our hope at CSIS that the work begun here with the Legislative-Executive Relations Project will help to foster debate and decision within the United States about our basic institutions and governance processes. We have been gratified by the positive response from officials in both the Congress and the executive branch to the project's policy paper that was published and disseminated widely in 1985. We further hope that our work will help the nation to shape foreign and defense policies that better serve our common future.

Amos A. Jordan
President and Chief Executive Officer
Center for Strategic and International Studies
Georgetown University
Summer 1986

Acknowledgments

Neither the CSIS Legislative-Executive Relations Project nor its results would have been possible without the efforts of the practitioners of government on the steering committee and the observers of government who wrote the case studies. Their insightful analyses and judicious evaluations were indispensable to the project's success. The CSIS staff also has performed tirelessly and invaluably throughout the project. Among those who worked on this text, and without whom it could not have been completed, are Kazuko Campbell, Ann Eisele, Curtis Farmer, Jennifer Park, Martin Rust, and Linda Welch. The CSIS editorial staff also worked on the manuscript tirelessly and with great professional skill. Special thanks go to Terry Fehner, project rapporteur, whose reports and summations enabled the steering committee and project codirectors to bring everything together at the end.

Robert E. Hunter
Wayne L. Berman
John F. Kennedy

In all the changes to which you may be invited remember that time and habit are at least as necessary to fix the true character of governments as of other human institutions; that experience is the surest standard by which to test the real tendency of the existing constitution of a country; that facility in changes upon the credit of mere hypothesis and opinion exposes to perpetual change, from the endless variety of hypothesis and opinion; and remember especially that for the efficient management of your common interests in a country so extensive as ours a government of as much vigor as is consistent with the perfect security of liberty is indispensable.

George Washington
September 17, 1796

Introduction

Robert E. Hunter, Wayne L. Berman,
and John F. Kennedy

Relations between Congress and the executive branch have always been an uneasy mixture of mutuality and autonomy, cooperation and conflict. The Constitution required that the two branches of the federal government work in concert, but it also mandated a separation of powers—or what perhaps more accurately has been described as "separated institutions sharing powers." Inevitably, this situation has led to a clash of wills and a contest for power. In itself, this clash has not been a bad thing. It has been what the framers of the Constitution intended in order to preclude the exercise of arbitrary power and the tyranny of an overly centralized government.

During the past 200 years, the executive and legislative branches have fulfilled their constitutional roles more or less effectively. The Republic has survived and prospered under one of the most humane, enlightened, and stable systems of government the world has ever known. It is true that Congress and the executive have been at odds, sometimes bitterly, and that at times the balance of power has swung too far in one direction or the other. In rare instances, the process has threatened to come apart, but the system has proved to be amazingly durable. The inherent tensions between the executive and legislative branches have never resulted in the government's ceasing to function.

During the last two decades, however, the two branches and their ambivalent relationship have been buffeted by a succession of political developments combined with institutional and technological change. The rise of the so-called imperial presidency, the Vietnam War, Watergate, the congressional reforms of the mid–1970s, and the many ramifications of the computer and communications revolutions all have helped to exacerbate tensions in relations between the two branches. As though this were not enough, the issues and problems facing the president and Congress have grown increasingly complex and interrelated. Current issues, such as the budget deficit, social security, and arms control, indicate the demanding and at times seemingly insoluble nature of

1

today's problems. Rarely if ever before have so many factors come together at once to create strains in legislative-executive relations.

The growing frustration of many policymakers with the difficulties facing both the executive branch and Congress have been increasingly evident in the process itself. Fewer pieces of legislation actually become law. The budget process has come to consume extraordinary amounts of time and effort from both branches, rarely producing a result that has satisfied anyone. The executive branch has often found that its foreign policy initiatives have been reshaped by an assertive Congress. The Congress has come to rely heavily on the legislative veto to regain authority in its dealings with the executive branch, only to see the veto overturned by the Supreme Court. Members of both branches have pondered what the future will hold for the two institutions in this time of challenge and flux.

There is little doubt that a problem exists in the area of legislative-executive relations. Officials in both branches of government and in both parties agree that the process has become excessively frustrating, time-consuming, and at times even distasteful. A broad consensus has formed that something must be done.

But what? There is agreement on the illness but less on the causes of each symptom and little on the remedy. Each branch tends to blame the other for tensions and contends that the latter needs to make the bulk of any reforms. One side see the problem as excessive executive control, the other as excessive congressional interference. One person's travesty of the process is another's checks and balances. In addition, solutions offered have often been too simplistic or too difficult to implement. Thus returning to the "good old days"—when there was a strict congressional hierarchy and when a handful of powerful figures controlled Congress—will not work. Neither will turning the Constitution on its head and instituting a parliamentary system. There are many nostrums, but true solutions are difficult to discern.

In response to widespread concern about the way our system of government has been working, in 1983 the Center for Strategic and International Studies of Georgetown University undertook a two-year study of legislative-executive relations. To ensure that the project would have practical application and focus on issues relevant to the concerns of individuals directly engaged in the business of government, the CSIS Legislative-Executive Relations Project formed a bipartisan steering committee of former and current senior policymakers who possess an intimate knowledge of the way the executive branch and Congress work. From the outset, the steering committee was pivotal in determining the goals of the project, focusing the scope of inquiry, and providing critical analyses of the issues being considered.

During the next 24 months, the study explored the evolution of the executive and legislative branches, analyzed factors that will affect legislative-executive relations during the next several years, and formulated suggestions for improving the process. The project's goal was to identify practical procedural changes that could improve legislative-executive relations and make the public policy process more effective. The project began with the premise that the system is essentially sound—that major revisions to the U.S. Constitution would be both unnecessary and unwise. In fact, the steering committee recognized that any recommendations of such magnitude—and over the years there have been many—ultimately would fail to generate the political support needed to implement them. The project would thus risk being irrelevant even if it served to be educational.

The Method

In conjunction with the CSIS project codirectors, the steering committee defined the project's basic guidelines. Several case studies were commissioned—each designed to examine one or more issues and problems that illuminate or directly affect relations between the legislative and executive branches. These studies were written by those expert in their fields and served as the focus for interpretive analysis. Renowned practitioners of government, in some instances members of the steering committee, then were asked to prepare commentaries on the case studies. Each of these commentaries reflects upon the recent evolution of key institutions and practices in legislative-executive relations. Each also prescribes practical steps for improving the ability of the two branches to function effectively in the future. Together, these studies and commentaries have formed the core of the project. Both sets of presentations were analyzed and refined by the entire steering committee.

The process has led to three separate products: First, the CSIS Legislative-Executive Relations Project staff developed a short, high-impact briefing to communicate key findings to senior members of the executive branch and members of Congress. Second, with the assistance of the steering committee, the project codirectors wrote and edited *Making the Government Work: Legislative-Executive Reform*, a policy paper of the CSIS Legislative-Executive Relations Project (Washington, D.C.: CSIS, 1985). It summarized the project's analysis of problems in legislative-executive relations and identified possible changes in the political process, each aimed at improving legislative-executive relations. This paper has been distributed widely to senior political figures, local governments, state political parties, Capitol Hill, and the executive branch.

Third, this text, *Making Government Work: From White House to Congress* contains the materials—both case studies and commentaries—on which the project based its conclusions and recommendations, its briefing, and its policy paper. It is intended for use by students, professors, researchers, and scholars in the field. The structure of the book reflects the broad reach of the research project and provides a detailed review of the project analysis. Each chapter in the text highlights an issue or aspect bearing on legislative-executive relations.

Chapters 1 through 7 consist of case studies with their corresponding commentaries. Richard Rivers's "The System CAN Work" (chapter 1) chronicles the highly successful multilateral trade negotiations (MTN) of the 1970s, culminating in the Trade Act of 1979. The MTN negotiations were an example of the cooperation and productivity that have been possible in legislative-executive relations when the process has been mastered and manipulated effectively. The executive branch—before, during, and after the actual negotiations—cultivated and worked with Congress so that it became a partner in the entire process. Congressional implementation of the trade agreement was thereby assured. In his commentary, Robert S. Strauss, U.S. Special Trade Representative under President Carter, suggests that the procedures used in this instance can be applied to other issues.

Joseph Cooper's "Congress and the Legislative Veto: Choices since the *Chadha* Decision" (chapter 2) analyzes the Supreme Court's 1983 decision limiting congressional use of the legislative veto. The *Chadha* decision severely curtailed employment of a mechanism on which Congress has relied increasingly to curb what it perceives to be inordinate or improper executive branch activity. Both Mr. Cooper and Paul Findley, in his commentary, agree that the *Chadha* decision was a mistake, and they express optimism that eventually the Supreme Court will reverse itself. In the meantime, however, they advocate that Congress continue using forms of legislative veto that have not been declared unconstitutional.

Allen Schick's "The Many Faces of Congressional Budgeting" (chapter 3) focuses on the demands of the budget process. The procedures implemented in the Congressional Budget Act of 1974 gave Congress greater control over the budget as a whole. At the same time, however, they further complicated an already complex process by adding a third set of committees—the Budget Committees—to the Authorization and Appropriations Committees that had been performing budgetary functions. The budget process, which consumes 60 to 65 percent of all congressional activity, threatens to engulf not only the Congress but also the executive branch. It demands so much effort and energy from executive appointees and their staffs that they have little time left to perform other administrative tasks. Mr. Schick suggests that the current difficulties with the budget process can be attributed primarily to the economic environment, such as high budget deficits. But James Woolsey, in his commentary, argues that positive action is needed for the budget process to become manageable and workable.

Frederick S. Tipson's "The War Powers Resolution: A Continuing Constitutional Struggle" (chapter 4) looks at the contention and confusion that have marked legislative-executive relations over the question of war powers. The War Powers Resolution, passed by Congress in 1973, tried to restrain, in law, the executive branch's discretion to commit U.S. forces to hostilities. Although the executive branch viewed the resolution as an illegitimate effort by Congress to rewrite the Constitution, the issue caused only minor skirmishing between the branches until 1983, when in rapid succession the Supreme Court's *Chadha* decision limited Congress's use of the legislative veto, U.S. troops were sent to Lebanon, and the United States invaded Grenada. These events again highlighted the question of war powers. Little was resolved, however, and differences continue between the executive branch and Congress over various aspects of the war powers question, including the constitutional role of each branch, the definition of hostilities, and the relative lack of executive branch consultations with, and reporting to, Congress. In his commentary, Melvin R. Laird, who has served in both branches of government, argues that the War Powers Resolution must be maintained. The War Powers Resolution itself is reprinted as an appendix to chapter 4.

Alton Frye and I.M. Destler (chapter 5) focus on defense and the foreign policy process—areas traditionally reserved for executive management but in which Congress has become increasingly involved. Mr. Frye's "The MX and Strategic Policy" examines a decade of legislative-executive interaction on the question of the MX missile. It concludes that, in this case, Congress entered the struggle over strategic weaponry in large part because of executive branch indecision and change of mind. In spite of executive branch complaints, therefore, congressional intervention has produced beneficial results. Mr. Destler's "The AWACS Sale to Saudi Arabia" analyzes the 1981 agreement to sell Airborne Warning and Control System (AWACS) aircraft to Riyadh. It argues that the executive branch initially did not handle the arms sale well and thus precipitated a confrontation with Congress. The executive branch was able to recoup its position, but at great cost in terms of time, effort, and international prestige.

In his commentary on both the MX and the AWACS debates, Representative Richard Cheney notes that in both instances the executive made problems for itself, partly because of defects in its own organizational structure and partly because executive branch foreign policy making tends to divorce politics from policy.

Alvin Paul Drischler's "Foreign Policy Making on the Hill: A Search for Perspective" (chapter 6) examines the enhanced role of the Appropriations Committees in the realm of foreign affairs. The power of the Appropriations Committees has increased at the expense of the authorizing committees. This has happened largely because of a shift from traditional free-standing foreign assistance authorization and appropriation bills to continuing resolutions and supplemental appropriations. Mr. Drischler contends that, while this shift has had some positive effects, the decreased role of the authorizing committees is detrimental to both the executive and legislative branches. In short, long-range policy analysis and the oversight function of Congress are thereby impaired. In his commentary, Clarence D. Long, former chairman of the Foreign Operations Subcommittee of the House Appropriations Committee, disagrees with this argument. He insists that the enhanced power of the Appropriations Committees has not signaled the end of the deliberative process in Congress. According to Representative Long, the problem is not the balance of power in Congress but the fact that the executive branch resents any involvement by Congress that does not give the executive a free hand in foreign affairs.

Norman Ornstein's "Interest Groups and Lobbying" (chapter 7) looks at changes that have taken place in lobbying and interest group behavior since the late 1960s. The move in Washington from a closed to an open political system, particularly as Congress has democratized and decentralized, has resulted in an explosion of interest group formation and activity. Mr. Ornstein analyzes the effect of these changes on both the executive and legislative branches, and he concludes that there is now in the open system more tension between the two institutions. This tension exists regardless of who is president or who controls Congress. In his commentary, Kenneth M. Duberstein agrees that, although the new, open system demands more skillful management and hard work and involves greater frustrations, it is also functioning exceedingly well. The system provides more opportunities for presidents, lawmakers, and interest groups that otherwise might be excluded from the process.

Chapter 8, the text's final and most important chapter, consists of the policy paper produced as part of the CSIS Legislative-Executive Relations Project. Prepared by codirectors Robert Hunter and Wayne Berman, it includes the project's conclusions and proposed adjustments. It does not, however, call for radical changes, such as would require amending the Constitution. Most of the 43 steering committee members whose input shaped the policy paper work daily in and with the system and are familiar with both its strengths and weaknesses. The recommendations, which gained bipartisan consensus from individuals with either Hill or executive branch experience, are preeminently practical. They are suggestions that can be implemented by one branch or the other, rather than simply forming the basis for theoretical discussion.

The policy paper and its recommendations are thus directed toward the day-to-day workings of the political process and the behavior and responses of participants within that process. Central to the policy paper is the steering committee's conviction that nothing would enhance the quality of legislative-executive relations more than would improvement in the communication, confidence, and understanding between the two branches. Achieving these goals, however, will require basic changes in attitudes at both ends of Pennsylvania Avenue. The policy paper suggests ways in which these changes can be fostered, as well as adjustments in process and procedure that will increase coherence in policy-making and expedite the process of legislative-executive relations.

1

The System CAN Work:
The Trade Act of 1979

Richard R. Rivers

Executive-Legislative Partnership
In International Commercial Policy

Within most democratic governments, the conduct of international commercial policy is the joint responsibility of the executive and legislative branches. This division of powers exists in varying degrees in most Western political systems. Nowhere, however, is this joint responsibility more evident than in the unique governmental system of the United States. This case study discusses the partnership between the president and Congress for the conduct of U.S. trade policy, how this partnership became strained during the 1960s, and how it was renegotiated with apparent success during the 1970s.

Under the U.S. Constitution, Congress is vested with the power to regulate foreign commerce. The president is the country's chief negotiator and representative in the international arena. Throughout U.S. history, Congress and the president have carried out these mutual and interacting roles diligently, if not always harmoniously.

This system has gradually given rise to open rivalry as the two branches have undertaken to carry out their constitutional roles and respond to their different constituencies in the conduct of foreign economic

Richard R. Rivers is a partner in the law firm of Akin, Gump, Strauss, Hauer & Feld. Before entering private law practice, he served as general counsel of the Office of the Special Representative for Trade Negotiations in the Executive Office of the President. Rivers has also served as international trade counsel of the Committee on Finance of the United States Senate, participated in the preparation and enactment of the Trade Act of 1974, and subsequently served as a congressional staff adviser to the U.S. Delegation to the Multilateral Trade Negotiations in Geneva, Switzerland.

policy. Presidents, for example, have occasionally tried to exercise international trade powers properly reserved to Congress. And, on occasion, Congress has attempted to exercise the powers of the presidency.

At the same time, the nature of problems in international economic relations has become increasingly complex. The objective of trade liberalization has evolved from the reduction and elimination of tariffs to the negotiation of international rules on nontariff barriers.

The growth of economic interdependence during the postwar period has tested the existing political and legal mechanisms for governments in negotiating reciprocal reductions in the import duties they levy on imported goods at their borders. Yet, it is much more difficult for governments to negotiate international rules for nontariff barriers that indirectly affect trade and that may originate within state houses or even city halls.

For the United States, this trend toward economic interdependence and the proliferation of nontariff barriers has imposed a growing strain on the political and legal mechanisms for the conduct of international trade negotiations. These forces culminated in 1967 with the 90th Congress's express repudiation of an international code of conduct on antidumping that had been negotiated by executive branch officials during the Kennedy Round of trade negotiations. The antidumping code set the international rules by which governments must abide as they regulate imports sold in their national markets at prices below home market prices—a politically sensitive subject for Congress. In effect, Congress told both U.S. and foreign negotiators that, although they could negotiate and reach any international agreement they might wish, Congress could not be taken for granted, and the necessity for implementation in domestic law through legislation could not be circumvented.

This regrettable episode in executive-legislative relations created an atmosphere of suspicion and mistrust between the two branches and between the United States and its trading partners. Under such circumstances, the conduct of U.S. commercial policy became exceedingly difficult, if not altogether impossible. Foreign government officials, particularly those of The European Communities and Canada, came to doubt the credibility of U.S. negotiators and used that doubt as justification for not engaging the United States in negotiations on nontariff trade barriers.

In 1971, against this background of growing concern about the effects of nontariff barriers on trade and of mistrust between the executive and legislative branches, the Nixon administration began exploring ways to renegotiate the trade-policy partnership between the executive branch and Congress and to seek a renewed delegation of trade-negotiating authority from Congress. These efforts resulted in a negotiation between

Congress and the executive and the enactment of the Trade Act of 1974, which created an unprecedented statutory framework within which the branches could perform their respective constitutional roles. This unique "experiment in constitutional government," as the Senate Finance Committee termed it, resulted seven years later in Congress's passing the most comprehensive trade legislation of the postwar era, if not indeed the country's history, by an overwhelming margin.

The chain of events, which began with congressional repudiation of an antidumping code in 1967, led to the renegotiation and innovative redesign of the executive-legislative partnership in 1974 and resulted in the passage of the Trade Agreements Act of 1979, is often suggested as a model of executive-congressional collaboration in the field of foreign affairs. Without prejudging the validity of such a model, this chapter describes the modern evolution of the trade-policy partnership between the executive and legislative branches and its operation, which, in effect, broke down and had to be renegotiated by the parties during the Tokyo Round of Multilateral Trade Negotiations (MTN) from 1973 to 1979.

The Constitutional Base

The U.S. Constitution established a federal government with three branches, a separation of powers, a system of checks and balances among those branches, and the president as the chief executive. Inherent in the presidency is the foreign affairs power by which the president has emerged as the chief negotiator and representative of the United States in the international arena. The primacy of the president in the field of foreign affairs, however, is not without qualification, as the Constitution itself imposes several limits on presidential powers, such as vesting the power to declare war in Congress and requiring that treaties be submitted to the Senate for its advice, consent, and concurrence. Yet over the years the executive branch has developed various forms of executive agreements, which—depending upon their nature and content—may or may not be submitted to Congress for approval and/ or implementation.

In the field of international trade policy, the president's powers are strictly constrained by two powers the Constitution explicitly vests in Congress:

- the power to regulate commerce with foreign nations
- the power to lay and collect taxes, duties, imposts, and excises (Article I, Section 8)

As a practical matter, presidents may negotiate and enter into virtually any international agreement they desire. Such agreements may not be self-executing and may have domestic legal consequences, such as regulating foreign commerce by restricting imports at the border or raising revenues, which require congressional approval and implementation before having force and effect as domestic U.S. law.

The joint executive-legislative responsibility is a feature of most democratic systems, including parliamentary governments. The circumstance of a negotiator exceeding his or her legal authority and political capability is a potential problem for any government participating in international negotiation. These problems are manageable, however, for most parliamentary Western governments. In economic unions, such as The European Communities, they present difficult political, if not legal, problems. Because of the unique design of the U.S. constitutional system, these problems pose special challenges for the conduct of U.S. commercial relations—challenges that have not always been met or successfully overcome.

U.S. Commercial Policy

Prior to 1934, the tariff policy of the United States was set by Congress primarily to raise revenues and protect domestic production from import competition. Little, if any, attention was given to the consequences of U.S. tariff policy for the external relations of the United States or for the world economy.

In 1934, motivated by a desire to restore world trade and prompted by the exemplary leadership of then-Secretary of State Cordell Hull, President Franklin Delano Roosevelt requested and received from Congress advance authority to reduce tariffs in reciprocal negotiations with other countries from the levels designated in the Smoot-Hawley Tariff Act of 1930. This presidential action marked the beginning of the Reciprocal Trade Agreements Program and offers a modern example of executive-legislative cooperation in the field of U.S. commercial policy.

Following World War II, the United States took the lead in the design and construction of the postwar world economic order. At the 1944 international conference at Bretton Woods, and in later international conferences, the U.S. delegation proposed the creation of an international trade organization (ITO) and an international agreement for the regulation of trade among nations. Faced with growing opposition from a suspicious Congress, however, the executive branch abandoned its plans. The ITO never came into existence, and U.S. accession to the General Agreement on Tariffs and Trade (GATT) was accomplished by means of an executive agreement, which the Congress refused to recognize and never approved.

Despite this inauspicious beginning, the executive branch secured from Congress the authority to reduce U.S. tariffs in the context of reciprocal trade negotiations. Under the auspices of GATT, six rounds of tariff negotiations were held that steadily reduced tariffs, especially among the industrialized democracies.

As tariffs declined, the volume of world trade increased markedly in proportion to overall industrial production. As tariffs were lowered, however, more subtle and insidious barriers replaced them as the major obstacles to trade. Known as nontariff barriers, they came in such forms as subsidies, import licensing systems, customs valuation methods, discriminatory product standards, and government purchasing requirements. These governmental practices were deeply rooted in national laws and regulations and often served legitimate domestic interests, such as regulation of domestic industries, maintenance of domestic prices for international commodities, and the preservation of important industries for national security reasons.

Such governmental practices, however, seriously distorted world trade and created inefficiencies in the world economy. GATT, moreover, did not address many of these practices. Even those nontariff barrier practices that GATT restricted, such as export subsidies on nonprimary products, were addressed by rules that had proved vague, ineffective, and unenforceable over the years. In fact, many provisions of GATT had fallen into disuse and discredit, including procedures for settling disputes.

Although the reduction of tariffs was the principal object, during the Kennedy Round of trade negotiations, certain participating governments undertook to negotiate nontariff barrier agreements. In particular, the United States agreed to eliminate the highly protective American Selling Price system of customs valuation applied to imports of certain commodities and agreed to adhere to an international antidumping code regulating the responses of governments to imports sold below fair value. The decision by the executive branch to negotiate on nontariff barriers in the Kennedy Round was made in the face of express congressional opposition to negotiating such matters and was carried out under the general foreign affairs power of the presidency.

At the end of the Kennedy Round, Congress reneged on the executive branch commitments and declined to repeal the American Selling Price system. Despite the agreement of the U.S. negotiators to repeal the provision, the provision remained U.S. law.

Furthermore, Congress acted affirmatively to alter the terms of U.S. adherence to the antidumping code. In the first session of the 90th Congress in 1967, a resolution was offered in the Senate demanding that the international antidumping code be submitted to the Senate for its advice and consent. Later, in September 1968, the Senate passed an amendment that would have terminated U.S. adherence to the terms of the agreement. The House refused, however, to go along with the Senate action but agreed to a compromise, which provided for implementation only insofar as the provisions of the code were consistent with those of existing U.S. law and practice. Any conflict between the two was to be resolved in favor of the law as it had been administered previously. In effect, Congress took steps to nullify the antidumping code insofar as it differed from U.S. law.

The entire episode poisoned executive-legislative relations in the field of international trade. Senator Russell B. Long (D-La.), the chairman of the Senate Committee on Finance, published a law review article entitled "United States Law and the International Antidumping Code" in which he concluded:

> The international antidumping code was negotiated without advance authority by Congress, in the face of a strict admonition by the Senate not to change the antidumping act in any way. Apart from the question as to whether the President has authority to enter into international agreements with foreign nations in an area which the Constitution reserves exclusively to the Congress, it is settled law that when an agreement has the effect of changing existing domestic law, either directly or by indirection through giving the law a meaning and a result which Congress never intended, the agreement cannot be given effect until it has been submitted to Congress for implementing legislation.[1]

The Nixon administration entered office in January 1969 without tariff-cutting authority (the five-year authority granted by Congress in the Trade Expansion Act of 1962 had expired at the end of 1967). Moreover, both inside and outside of government it was thought to be imperative that nontariff barriers had to be subjected to the discipline of international rules. But there seemed little prospect, however, for obtaining the special authority required from a distrustful Congress, and, indeed, an attempt at trade legislation failed in 1971.

In July 1971, the Williams Commission, a commission on international trade and investment policy, reported "a growing concern in this country that the United States has not received full value for the tariff concessions made over the years because foreign countries have found other ways, besides tariffs, of impeding our access to their markets."[2] Slowly, a consensus began to evolve within the U.S. government that a new round of trade negotiations should be held. President Richard Nixon bluntly brought the issue to the forefront internationally and to the attention of U.S. trading partners with his actions of August 15, 1971—most particularly the closing of the gold window and the imposition of a surcharge on imports. These developments led to the Tokyo Declaration of September 1973, which called for a new international round of trade negotiations, to be known as the Tokyo Round, under the auspices of GATT. These multilateral negotiations would be aimed not only at further tariff reductions but also at nontariff barriers.

Although it was widely agreed that a new and ambitious round of negotiations on nontariff barriers to trade should be held, the problem of U.S. negotiating authority remained, with the executive branch needing to secure explicit and credible authority from Congress to engage in international negotiations on such practices. Work began within the executive branch on the design of a trade bill. The legislation that finally emerged contained a number of major executive branch initiatives, including a proposal to grant most-favored-nation (MFN) status to the Soviet Union. In many ways, however, the most significant provision of the 1973 Nixon trade bill was in the important and difficult area of nontariff barriers. In addition to seeking advance tariff-cutting authority, the executive branch sought a negotiating mandate on nontariff barriers and advance presidential authority to implement them in U.S. law, unless either the House or the Senate voted to override the president's proposal within a period of 90 days after notification—a one-House veto.

This unprecedented delegation of congressional authority to the president was approved by the House of Representatives and sent to the Senate in essentially the form it had been submitted to Congress by the executive branch. In the Senate, however, the administration's proposal predictably ran into strong opposition. Still angry about the Kennedy Round experience and believing that U.S. negotiators had turned deaf ears to congressional admonitions and private sector advice regarding the negotiations, key members of the Senate Finance Committee balked when briefed by committee staff on the provisions of the House bill.

During the 20 months of congressional consideration following submission of the trade bill much had occurred. In October 1973 the Organization of Petroleum Exporting Countries (OPEC) oil embargo darkened the world and, shortly thereafter, had plunged the world economy into a deep recession. In addition, President Nixon had resigned from office. His successor, President Gerald R. Ford, had renewed the previous administration's request for enactment of trade legislation, partly in an effort to head off spreading global protectionism. The legislation was being considered in the Senate in an entirely different political climate. Not surprisingly, given the passage of time and changed circumstances, the bill underwent major revision in the Senate Finance Committee.

In the judgment of the Finance Committee staff, the House bill proposed "the largest delegation of trade negotiating authority to the executive in history." In the view of Senator Herman Talmadge (D-Ga.), the House bill, with its legislative veto procedure, would establish procedures that were inconsistent with the traditional roles of the executive branch and Congress. "That's not the way our laws are made," Talmadge told Finance Committee staff persons. Instead he proposed that the president simply submit nontariff barrier trade agreements to Congress to be considered in the conventional manner. Executive branch officials took the position that such a procedure would leave them without credibility at the negotiating table.

Senator Talmadge asked the Senate Finance Committee staff to search for a compromise. The Finance Committee staff proposed that the House and Senate agree to amend their rules to provide for a mandatory up or down vote by Congress, without amendments, within a statutory deadline. The legislation would direct the president to negotiate on nontariff barriers to trade and to submit his agreements, and whatever implementing legislation was necessary or appropriate, to Congress for consideration under the new procedures. The procedures would pass muster under the Constitution because both House and Senate would act. The international agreements would not "enter into force for the United States" unless Congress approved.

The bill, as amended by the Senate, elaborated upon the provisions that the House had added to increase the participation of the public, Congress, and various governmental agencies in the negotiations. Extensive prenegotiation hearings and advice would be required. In addition, the legislation established an elaborate, private sector advisory system to include representatives of labor, industry, agriculture, and consumers to provide policy input and technical advice during the negotiations. These private sector advisory committees would be required to issue official reports during and at the conclusion of the negotiations. Private sector advisers were to be kept intimately informed during the course of the negotiations and, to the extent that the executive branch deviated from their advice, the president was required to inform Congress as to its reasons.

The Finance Committee also proposed that the capability of Congress to monitor U.S. trade policy during the negotiations be strengthened in the legislation. In addition to the procedures established for the approval of the nontariff barrier agreements, five members of the Senate and five members of the House were to be designated as official advisers to the U.S. trade delegation. Staff members of both the House Ways and Means Committee and the Senate Finance Committee would be given access to classified U.S. materials and kept abreast of the negotiations on a detailed and ongoing basis.

As amended by the Senate, close coordination and consultation on legislation formed an iron triangle between executive branch negotiators, Congress, and the private sector, with three types of advisory committees being established. The first would be an overall policy level advisory committee for trade negotiations to be composed of senior representatives of government, labor, industry, agriculture, service industries, consumer interests, and the general public. Second, by amending the House bill, the Senate gave the president authority to establish policy advisory committees for industry, labor, and agriculture to provide general policy advice to U.S. negotiators during the negotiations. Third, the Senate legislation provided that the president should establish such industry, labor, service, or agriculture sector advisory committees as he thought necessary for technical advice on tariff and nontariff barrier negotiations. Qualified experts from particular industries were to advise trade negotiators from the point of view of their personal expertise and not from the point of view of their particular employers. The advice they gave the trade negotiators would also be shared with Congress.

The Senate amendments were negotiated in conference with the House and sent to President Ford as the Trade Act of 1974. This legislation provided the basic charter for U.S. participation in the Tokyo Round and established the unique system under which the negotiated trade agreements would be approved and implemented into U.S. law.[3] Congress, acting in the light of its experience in prior negotiations, renegotiated with the executive branch the terms of their partnership for the conduct of U.S. trade policy. The result was a system of mandatory consultation and coordination so stringent that the executive could ignore it only at peril of losing all in a single vote.

The Negotiating Process

Although the Tokyo Round began formally with the Tokyo Declaration of September 1973, the negotiations did not commence in Geneva until Congress had passed the Trade Act of 1974 in January 1975. Two and one half years passed with few significant occurrences, however, largely because of global recession and the uncertain U.S. presidency. During this period the participating governments occupied themselves by preparing the technical basis for the negotiations. The Trade Negotiating Committee in charge of the Tokyo Round established the following seven negotiating groups to deal with specific subjects:

1. Tariffs Group
2. Sectors Group—intended to permit negotiations of all issues affecting specific industrial sectors (e.g., civil aircraft)
3. Agriculture Group
4. Nontariff Measures Group—including five sub-groups dealing with the following issues:

(a) government procurement policies (b) quantitative restrictions and import licensing (c) customs valuation (d) subsidies and countervailing duties (e) product standards

5. Safeguards Group—in charge of international rules relating to countries imposing temporary import restraint to prevent injury to a domestic industry caused by increased imports
6. Tropical Products Group—intended to permit concessions to the developing countries from the developed countries
7. Framework Improvement Group—intended to permit discussion of proposed changes in GATT rules, in particular, GATT rules governing dispute settlement.

It was not, however, until early 1977 that the negotiations began to show signs of life. In March 1977, President Jimmy Carter appointed Robert S. Strauss, the former chairman of the Democratic Party, as his special trade representative (STR), an appointment that apparently was made after consultation with key members of Congress and that was well received by the private sector. A lawyer and businessman, Strauss knew little about international trade, but he had a fine sense for domestic politics and Congress.

President Carter, early in his presidency, signaled his commitment to pursuing the MTN to a successful conclusion. At the Downing Street Summit, President Carter and Japanese Prime Minister Takeo Fukuda strongly supported continuing the trade negotiations in the face of recalcitrant European heads of state, particularly French President Giscard d'Estaing. Gradually the international negotiating process began to gather momentum.

By July 1977, the United States and The European Communities (EC) were able to agree on a timetable to complete the preparatory phase of the MTN. The negotiations of the Tokyo Round—in reality a hundred or more ongoing negotiations among a hundred or more countries—had begun in earnest and were moving ahead under the relentless prodding of Ambassador Strauss.

The executive branch and Congress had acted early in 1975 to implement the private sector advice and consultative provisions contained in the Trade Act of 1974. Periodic briefings of members of Congress and committee staffs by the STR, his deputies, and staff and regular access by the congressional committees to MTN documents had commenced shortly thereafter.

Congressional staff began traveling to Geneva in 1975 and preparing regular reports of the negotiations for senators and representatives. Senators and their staffs attended multilateral and bilateral negotiating sessions, met with officials of foreign delegations and of the GATT

Secretariat, and held regular consultations with STR officials in both Washington and Geneva.

These briefings of private sector advisers, members of Congress, and committee staff were anything but perfunctory. Private sector and congressional advisers insisted on being kept fully informed on the negotiations. Moreover, the government actively sought the views of the private sector advisers, and more often than not, incorporated their advice into U.S. negotiating positions. Senior STR officials often went from negotiating sessions with foreign governments to negotiating sessions with private sector advisers.

A negotiator on the sensitive and difficult Code on Subsidies and Countervailing Duties, for example, would spend two weeks in Europe negotiating with officials of The European Community. He would then return to Washington and participate in a round of interagency meetings and in the private sector advisory system where he was likely to run a difficult question and answer gauntlet. He had to read the draft Industrial Sector Advisory Report (ISAR) of each Industrial Sector Advisory Committee (ISAC) with whom he would be meeting and understand their particular objectives and concerns in the field of subsidies and countervailing duties. This process created a high degree of communication and consultation between Congress, its key trade committees and their staffs, the many private sector advisory committees, and officials of the special trade representative's office.

The office of the STR, headed by Ambassador Strauss and his principal deputies—Alan Wolf in Washington and Alonzo McDonald in Geneva—became a domestic and international clearinghouse in which tens of thousands of pieces of data—economic and political—concerning foreign and domestic interests could be processed and arranged. Transcripts of presentations by STR officials were available in private reading rooms at the Department of Commerce and in the special trade representative's office for all persons having appropriate security clearances. Ambassador Strauss was in daily contact with members of Congress and key private sector advisers, as well as with his negotiating counterparts. On occasion, foreign trade officials had direct contact with members of Congress and private sector advisers. These meetings were carefully monitored and coordinated with the STR officials.

Both domestically and abroad, Ambassador Strauss was perceived as having the confidence of both the president and Congress. He frequently made it clear that his effective function in office required serving two masters. There was no doubt that the STR spoke with the full authority of both the president and Congress.

Within the executive branch, the special trade representative enjoyed primacy in all matters relating to the trade policy of the United States.

Ambassador Strauss approached the negotiations with the perspective of a domestic politician, recognizing that there must be something in the package for everyone but that no single interest could have its way entirely. This was applied both internationally and domestically.

Internationally, Ambassador Strauss sought to convince participating countries that the negotiations would contain positive benefits to their economies and would present a balanced package that each negotiator could bring home for domestic approval and implementation. At the same time, in terms of domestic politics, Ambassador Strauss selected a combination of concessions to be given and gained that were not only in the national economic interest, but also struck an appropriate political balance between competing domestic interests—whether they were regional, agricultural or industrial, multinational or domestic exporter or importer, consumer or producer. For example, it might become necessary to trade away long-standing and important import protection for the domestic bourbon industry in order to gain valuable agricultural trade concessions from The European Communities. The bourbon concession could have negative consequences in such bourbon producing states as Kentucky, but, if the trade concessions gained at the expense of the bourbon industry included tariff concessions on tobacco, then the political damage in Kentucky would be offset or even overcome.

By the fall of 1978, the full scope of the Tokyo Round was apparent. There were hundreds of bilateral "request and offer" agreements on nontariff barriers between participating governments as well as tariff reductions as significant as those of the Kennedy Round on thousands of industrial and agricultural products. In addition there were the multilateral codes of conduct on the major nontariff barriers, the principal ones of which were:

- The Subsidies-Countervailing Duty Code—regulating the use of subsidies and the responses governments may take either unilaterally or through multilateral dispute settlement
- The Antidumping Code—revising and updating the code that regulates the actions governments may take in response to dumped imports
- The Government Procurement Code—liberalizing government procurement and eliminating discrimination
- The Customs Valuation Code—harmonizing national customs valuation laws and practices
- The Licensing Code—regulating governmental import licensing practices

- Civil Aircraft Code—a sectoral agreement eliminating duties on civil aircraft and parts and applying to a range of nontariff barriers on aircraft
- Framework Arrangements—relating to dispute settlement and other general GATT matters
- Safeguards Code[4]—relating to the measures governments may take to provide temporary import relief to industries seriously injured by imports

Concluding and Implementing the Tokyo Round

Winding down the negotiations in January of 1979, President Carter followed the procedures set forth in the Trade Act of 1974 and notified Congress of his intention to enter into the Tokyo Round trade agreements. This notice set in motion the intricate, bank-vault-time-lock procedures established under the Trade Act of 1974. Shortly thereafter, the STR office began sending detailed proposals for approving and implementing the trade agreements and for making other "appropriate" changes in the U.S. law to the Senate Finance Committee, and the House Ways and Means Committee.

Under an agreement initiated by the Senate Finance Committee staff, the administration had agreed to consult and work closely with Congress in drafting the implementing bill before it was submitted to Congress by the president and therefore became unamendable. The proposals that the administration sent to the House and Senate committees were contained in detailed papers setting forth the method for setting international obligations of the United States into U.S. domestic law. The staffs of both committees briefed their members in detail on each of the administration's proposals, and both committees held public hearings in February and April 1979. The administration's plans for implementing the Tokyo Round were shared with private sector advisers.

The Senate Finance Committee and the Subcommittee on Trade of the House Ways and Means Committee began holding closed mark-up sessions on the implementing legislation in March 1979, at which time the Senate Committees on Agriculture and on Commerce also met to consider the aspects that fell within their respective jurisdictions. A careful process of presentation and discussion was designed to identify and defuse any last minute political problems that might arise.

Only one serious political problem arose. The code on government procurement as originally negotiated would have opened federal government procurement to competitive bidding and eliminated the preference toward minority-owned businesses. When members of the House

expressed opposition, Ambassador Strauss immediately ordered negotiators in Geneva to make readjustments.[5]

Committee sessions continued throughout the spring. On April 12,
the United States concluded a *procés-verbal* with its trading partners in
Geneva. In early May, the Committees on Finance and on Ways and
Means met in a "nonconference" to reconcile their differences.

During this domestic implementation process, private sector groups
engaged in heavy lobbying of congressional committees and the executive
branch officials, as when STR officials met regularly with representatives
of domestic industries. These meetings produced a number of proposed
amendments to existing law, aimed at strengthening the unfair trade
practice statutes, in particular, the antidumping and countervailing duty
statutes. Although these amendments were not, strictly speaking, necessary for the implementation of the Tokyo Round agreements, they fell
into the category of "appropriate" changes provided for under the Trade
Act of 1974. The amendments did not contravene the international
agreements but made mainly procedural changes to appease the domestic
interests of those who had long been critical of import relief statutes.
The definition of material injury, which would be incorporated for the
first time into the U.S. countervailing duty statute, was a particularly
difficult issue.

As a practical matter, the negotiating sessions with domestic industries
added a new and strong source of political support for the passage of
the Trade Agreements Act. Whereas importers and exporters—who were
benefited by trade liberalization—had long supported the Tokyo Round
process, such domestic industries as steel previously had hoped to gain
little. As these industries saw an opportunity to improve the operation
of the unfair trade practice statutes, the Trade Agreements Act came to
have the support of both the weak and the strong in international
competition.

The actual text of the Trade Agreements Act was drafted by the
Senate and House legislative counsels in sessions attended by administration officials and committee staff persons.[6] The drafting group
produced a comprehensive committee print of the bill entitled "Office
of the Special Representative for Trade Negotiations Draft Proposal."
This draft was circulated among executive branch agencies for intensive
review, which resulted in very few changes in the actual legislation.
Thirty-three members of Congress wrote President Carter warning him
against making any changes in the implementing legislation. Another
congressional letter, signed by fewer, urged that he make whatever
changes were necessary to maintain a liberal trade policy.

The bill that ultimately was submitted to the Congress by President
Carter on June 19 contained minor changes from the bill that Congress

and the executive branch had agreed upon. It was immediately introduced in both the House and Senate and 34 days later was adopted by both bodies by overwhelming margins. The speed of the U.S. implementation process and the precision with which it faithfully implemented the international agreements astonished U.S. trading partners, particularly officials of The European Communities. Passage of the legislation was front-page news in all the capitals of the world but one: Washington, D.C. The passage of the Trade Agreements Act of 1979, probably the most significant trade legislation in U.S. history, received only slight mention in the back pages of the *Washington Post*.[7] The event had become an anticlimax to the process.

Notes

1. 3 *International Lawyer* 464 (1969).

2. Commission on International Trade and Investment Policy, *United States International Economic Policy in an Interdependent World*, A Report to the President (Washington, D.C.: USGPO July 1971), 22.

3. It is interesting to speculate on what would have been the fate of the Tokyo Round agreements had the Congress enacted the House version containing a one-House legislative veto, in light of the Supreme Court's decision in *Immigration and Naturalization Service v. Chadha* et al., 103 Sup. Ct. 2764 (1983); see also, *Consumers Energy Council of America v. Federal Energy Regulatory Commission (FERC)*, 673 F.2d 425 (D.C. Cir. 1982), and *Consumers Union of the United States, Inc. v. Federal Trade Commission (FTC)*, 691 F.2d 575 (D.C. Cir. 1982), aff'd per curiam sub nom. *Process Gas Consumers Group v. Consumers Energy Council of America*, 103 Sup. Ct. 3556 (1983).

4. Ultimately, the negotiation of the Safeguards Code could not be concluded during the Tokyo Round, and the code fell out of the final legislative package.

5. The readjustment was that the National Aeronautics and Space Administration procurement was made subject to the provisions of the code and therefore made available to foreign bidders.

6. The same procedure is traditionally followed in the drafting of amendments to the Internal Revenue Code.

7. In contrast, the conclusion in 1967 of the Kennedy Round of trade negotiations—basically a tariff-cutting exercise—had been the occasion for an eight-column banner headline in the *New York Times*. Annoyed by the lack of press coverage of the enactment of the Trade Agreements Act of 1979, President Carter wrote an unpublished letter of complaint to the editor of the *Washington Post*.

Commentary: On Trade

Robert S. Strauss

I offer a somewhat different perspective on the Trade Act of 1979 than does Richard Rivers. While his chapter is dispassionate and objective, rightly focusing on structure and organization, I will examine the process—how the negotiations were carried on during my term as special trade representative (STR) from 1977–1979. The manner in which the structure was used to achieve a successful outcome of the multilateral trade negotiations was as important as the nature of the structure, and the operation was as much political as technical.

Knowing very little about the intricate trade matters that would be subject to negotiation, I was uncertain whether or not to accept President Carter's offer of the STR position. Nevertheless, the special trade representative was one of the few positions in the new administration in which I had any interest, because it offered the opportunity to conduct negotiations, it was free of bureaucracy, and it was outside of the departmental chain of command.

I was convinced to accept the position when Senator Russell Long (D-La.), chairman of the Senate Finance Committee—whom President Carter had informed of my hesitancy—called me to say both he and Senator Robert Dole (R-Kans.), ranking Republican member of the Finance Committee, agreed that I was in their view the person most likely to engineer a successful trade agreement that Congress would accept. Senator Long said that he and Senator Dole strongly urged me to accept the position.

Assured of the bipartisan backing and support of the Senate Finance Committee, I told President Carter of my willingness to become the STR. The Senate Finance Committee had a vested interest in the negotiations process, and its seal of approval endowed the STR with a certain amount of leverage. I had enough experience to know how to use this leverage to good advantage and to know when to and when not to use it. The political muscle, visibility, and credibility that only Congress could provide was more important than that given by the White House.

Although congressional support was essential to the STR, the relative stature of the position within the administration was also critical. The

Robert S. Strauss is a partner in the law firm of Akin, Gump, Strauss, Hauer & Feld. He was chairman of the Democratic National Committee (1973–1976), U.S. special trade representative (1977–1981), President Carter's personal representative to the Middle East peace negotiations, and chairman of the Carter-Mondale Reelection Committee.

power and influence of the STR depends to a large extent on the individual who holds the office. In the early months of the Carter administration, I clearly was not in the White House inner circle. In fact, the Senate Finance Committee already had rejected several of the administration's choices for the position before it was decided that I was satisfactory to both Congress and the executive. The secretary of commerce thought that the secretary of the treasury had been involved in the Kennedy Round of trade negotiations and knew a great deal more than I did on the subject. Without an assertion by President Carter that the STR was in charge of trade, the position would be rendered largely ineffective.

To establish the special trade representative at the center of trade for the Carter administration, I insisted that I have direct access to the president and that I represent the United States on trade issues at the 1977 Downing Street Summit. Very early in my tenure, I sent a memorandum to the president that required a decision within 48 hours. After waiting four days with no reply, I contacted the president's secretary, who said the memo had not been brought to the president's attention but, rather, was still in the national security adviser's office. The national security adviser's office told me they did not consider the issue of sufficient importance to go to the president. I told them that, as a supposed member of the president's cabinet, I knew I had no control over the recommendations they might attach to my memorandum, but they should deliver my memoranda to the president or I would resign and publicly state the reasons for my resignation. With that I was assured direct access to the president without having to rely on the prior approval of the White House staff. To establish the STR as the spokesman on trade for the United States at the Downing Street Summit, I simply announced that, because the summit was specifically on trade, I intended to be there personally. As the STR, I would speak for the United States on trade issues and, if this were not the administration's understanding, it could get a new STR. I was then invited to the summit and to speak for the United States on trade.

The word quickly got around—both within the administration and on the Hill—that the special trade representative was in charge of trade. If the word had gotten around that I was not in charge, we would have had no chance to carry out our negotiating program. This is true of all cabinet positions. If the secretary of state, for example, is viewed as not having authority in foreign affairs, but rather that it resides with the national security adviser, then the secretary of state is in an extremely difficult position. The person in charge must establish his or her authority, whether it be in trade, foreign affairs, or arms negotiation.

Even after the authority of the STR was firmly established within the administration and with Congress, a domestic political constituency was also necessary. Authority and credibility without a power base have little efficacy when the time comes to pushing a negotiated agreement through Congress. Too many interests oppose change.

By courting a domestic constituency—the agricultural sector in this case—the STR can gain tremendous leverage on the Hill, when the constituency takes a major interest in the progress of the trade negotiations. Agriculture had been excluded from the Kennedy Round and was generally dissatisfied with the trade status quo. To woo agriculture, it was necessary to obtain decent press coverage. I began by making a speech in New York about agriculture's being on the "front burner," followed by a trip to the Midwest where I made several speeches to agricultural groups, repeating that front-burner assertion. Not only did we get good press in the *New York Times* and in the major midwestern papers, but every agricultural publication trumpeted the fact that the STR was putting agriculture at the top of his list, or, in the phrase that took hold, on the front burner. It did not take long for the agricultural constituency to get interested.

These moves—with the administration, Congress, and the agricultural sector—involved merely the preliminary shoring up of the STR's power base before entering into the main event—the actual trade negotiations. Authority and credibility were also issues, and one of the primary reasons I insisted on going to the Downing Street Summit was to ensure that our trading partners were well aware of who was in charge.

It was of the utmost necessity that U.S. trading partners become convinced that the special trade representative and his staff could deliver in negotiations. The trading partners were mindful of the 1967 repudiation by the United States Congress of the antidumping code negotiated in the Kennedy Round and its insistence on retaining the American Selling Price in chemicals. They had absolutely no confidence that the president could convince Congress to approve a negotiated trade agreement. It was common knowledge that Congress had rejected the Kennedy Round agreement because of its lack of involvement in the negotiation of that agreement.

To create both the impression and the actuality that Congress was thoroughly involved in the process and would support a resulting agreement, we began holding meetings on Capitol Hill, where we worked with staff as well as committees and their chairpeople. Stories began to appear in the press that President Carter had made a good choice in his appointment of the STR. Here is someone, it was said, who understood the political process and knew how to deal with Congress. Our trading partners did not fail to notice.

But gaining credibility with U.S. trading partners and getting them to negotiate seriously are two separate issues. By adjusting our tactics according to the audience—allaying European fears and exhibiting firmness with the Japanese—the STR and staff could proceed with the negotiations.

Due to the press that we had generated on the agricultural issue, the Europeans feared that the United States was seeking to destroy the Common Agricultural Policy of the European Community—a policy of subsidization and protection. They were unwilling to negotiate, so long as they thought that their agricultural program was at risk. To convince them that their fears were groundless, I gave them my word that we had no intention of destroying the Community's Agricultural Policy, but that we would see its modification. We wanted to open up the European agricultural sector, not to destroy it, I said. We knew that, for them, to alter the current agricultural system of subsidies was politically unviable, in the same manner that it was politically impossible to do away entirely with price supports in the United States. I had a reputation as a political animal, my argument made sense and was credible to them, and there was enough that they wanted and needed that, once their agricultural fears were laid to rest, they were amenable to serious negotiation.

Japan was a different problem. No one in the United States had confidence that we could negotiate successfully with the Japanese, and this expectation encouraged them to remain obdurate in their negotiating stance. We needed some evidence (once again the perception was of the utmost importance) that we could hold our own with the Japanese. Again, we needed good press.

The negotiating team's initial trip to Japan—which incidentally was led by Mr. Rivers—was scheduled for five days, and, because I knew little if any progress would be made in such a short period, I began looking for the opportunity to break off the negotiations and thereby gain some badly needed publicity. On the third day, having made no progress, the delegation walked out of the meeting. The resulting publicity worldwide was many times more than it would have been if the negotiating team had actually made some progress. Those who had doubted ability of the United States to negotiate with the Japanese were now saying the team had "kicked the hell" out of the Japanese. Admittedly, we did a rather demagogic thing, but it gave us credibility both in Japan, where the Japanese realized that the United States was going to be tough, and at home, where it convinced the doubters that the United States was going to negotiate competently.

The trade negotiations could now proceed with anticipation of a successful outcome. Concurrent with these negotiations, the special trade representative and staff were engaged in a constant effort to build and maintain domestic support for the prospective agreement. The STR sought to build a consensus within the administration, Congress, and, in particular, the private sector that the trade negotiation was necessary and its outcome beneficial. The scope of our domestic lobbying should not be underestimated.

Although the special trade representative was part of the administration, not everything we did at the negotiations necessarily had the administration's support. President Carter closely scrutinized the negotiations and had serious doubts about certain provisions, such as the ones on textiles, which had taken us six months to negotiate and was not a perfect reflection of the free-trade ideal. Although it was the best that could be achieved under the circumstances, the president was not initially satisfied. He did, however, trust the opinion of Richard Cooper, undersecretary for economic affairs at the State Department. So, to persuade President Carter to approve the textile provisions, I spent six weeks convincing Cooper.

Congress demanded even greater and more sustained attention. The staff of the STR and I spent a tremendous amount of time on the Hill, working both sides of the political aisle. What most helped the negotiating team was our ability to keep partisan politics out of the process. On an issue of this nature, representatives and senators vote their parochial interests. They pay very little attention to either the president or their own party. They must be approached in terms of their own self interest, whether it is price supports for milk in Wisconsin or grain in Kansas. We worked as hard mollifying and looking after the interests of Republicans as we did of Democrats. I cut television tapes and radio spots for representatives and senators, regardless of party, that stated how much help they had given us and what their support meant to the function of this governmental process. It helped them politically and enabled us to solidify support behind the trade agreement. Both parties gained from it, and neither lost.

We also worked diligently with with the staffs of the House Ways and Means Committee and the Senate Finance Committee. The interplay was constant, and the staffs were surprised that I, a rather visible member of the Carter cabinet, spent as much time and effort as I did with them. They had never experienced this kind of treatment, and, as a result, we were able to win their cooperation and support.

The private sector also received our constant attention. As already mentioned, agriculture formed the primary constituency behind the trade agreement. The most significant opponent was organized labor. The STR staff worked with the AFL-CIO's individual unions and their presidents, one by one. We gained their support by consulting with them on various aspects of the trade legislation in which they had special interests. Thus, when the executive union leadership attempted to align the individual unions in opposition to the trade agreement, we already had won our own block of union support and were able to constrain labor's executive group.

An important element in securing the private sector's support was the advisory committee system that Congress set up in the Trade Act of 1974. The advisory committees, composed of business people, various interest groups, and ordinary citizens, were structured in a pyramid. The Advisory Committee on Trade Negotiations was at the top, functioning over a period of five years in the same manner as the Greenspan Commission on the social security issue. Under the Advisory Committee on Trade Negotiations were advisory committees on labor policy, industry policy, and agriculture policy. Below them were approximately 100 technical and sectoral advisory committees. In effect, Congress was saying to the executive branch that because Congress itself could not be expert on all of the minutiae of every trade issue, the STR and his staff were to listen to the expert advice of these groups and to follow that advice, whenever possible. When the STR did not follow the advice of the advisory groups, Congress wanted to know the reasons why.

Congress intended for the advisory committees to check and balance the administration's latitude in conducting the trade negotiations, but Congress did not stipulate how the STR was to service advisory committees. We were able to make the advisory committees an integral part of the process, and thereby they served to everyone's advantage. They were consulted continually, encouraged to observe the actual negotiating process, and thus lined up behind the negotiating team, supporting the resultant trade agreement.

Agriculture, labor, and industry were involved intimately in the process through the advisory committees. By the time the legislation came before Congress, nearly every sector in the country had worked with the negotiating team on a monthly basis, had testified before Congress, and supported the trade legislation.

Even with the meticulous work that had gone into influencing the administration, Congress, and the private sector, the trade legislation would not have passed through Congress in its negotiated form had it not been for two aspects mandated by the Trade Act of 1974. First, the act stipulated that, once the trade package was introduced in Congress, it could not be amended. If amendments had been allowed, then a little bit more for one interest would have meant a little bit more for each of the others, thus chipping away at the agreement until nothing was left. But the genius of the procedure was that, once the trade package hit the floor, the entire package—as a whole—had to be voted up or down.

The second aspect ensuring procedural success in Congress was that, before the legislation came to the floor, a "non-conference conference" was held. In addition to both public and private mark-up sessions, there was a private, non-conference conference between the two houses in which the legislation was pretried and a positive verdict rendered by the "jury" before the Hill began official consideration of the trade bill.

Given these two aspects, there was no question that the trade legislation would pass, once it was introduced. We lost only four votes in the Senate and seven in the House. Of the 11 we lost, we could have had perhaps half in a close contest. Viewed from the outcome, the entire process was an overwhelming success.

The passage of the Trade Act of 1979 is one of the best examples of executive-legislative cooperation in our time. It shows us the potential for coordination and cooperation between the two branches and about leadership. The relationship between the executive branch and Congress inevitably involves a certain degree of disharmony. The amount and disruptive effect of this disharmony can be limited by active and intelligent effort by both branches, as was precisely the case with the Trade Act of 1974. The act "precooked" the procedural matters between the two institutions, and prior consultation was substituted for the usual after-the-fact review and changes. The results prove the advantages of the approach.

This case study of the 1979 act also reveals the effectiveness of cooperation and coordination between the executive branch and congressional staff. We gave constant attention to the staff and were rewarded with their backing and support. Often, the executive branch does not sufficiently relate to the congressional staff and bypasses it. Furthermore, this case study demonstrates that an undertaking of the magnitude of the trade negotiations must be bipartisan in nature. Without bipartisan cooperation and coordination and a willingness to spread responsibility and credit, the process would have disintegrated into a partisan conflict. Instead, we concentrated on parochial interests and were able to direct them toward a positive use.

The second area of executive-legislative relations that this case illuminates involves the question of leadership. On major issues such as trade negotiations, the president needs to find someone in whom both the Congress and the executive branch have confidence. This person has to be clearly in charge and prepared to offer his or her resignation, if necessary, to assert authority.

Leadership in itself, however, is not enough. An individual's talents and the requirements of the position must also be compatible. In my own case, I knew very little about trade when I accepted the position of special trade representative, and, in truth, I never did become a trade expert or specialist. I learned only what I needed to be able to converse intelligently on the issues. But trade was not my game. Politics was. Fortunately, above all else, politics is what is required of the special trade representative.

Many other jobs in the government would have suited me less well, and I no doubt would have been less successful in accomplishing the required tasks. But for the position of special trade representative, I was as well equipped as anyone in the country. I had a long history of successful negotiations in the private sector, long-standing connections on the Hill with both Democrats and Republicans, and more experience than most people in government—not in its substance but in how it functions and, in particular, how badly it can function. Such was the precise experience needed by the special trade representative.

One of these days, the country is going to elect a president who really knows how to form a government: one who will put six or seven hundred people in place who know how to make the government function. It does not matter from which party they are, or whether they are politically conservative or liberal. The nation will be better served. The relationship between the legislative and executive branches requires people who understand the process, for the relationship is more of a process than any single act, and it calls for a combination of skills accumulated through experience. It must be based on mutual trust and confidence.

The procedures used to negotiate and implement the Trade Act of 1979 can have broader application. The arms limitation situation demonstrates some of the same characteristics that were present with the trade issue. Arms limitation requires delicate negotiations with foreign powers, as well as with conflicting domestic constituencies. The executive branch needs a strong leader, clearly in charge of arms negotiations, who can bring together disparate voices within the administration. There are highly interested domestic constituencies that need to be mollified and placated. Congress needs to be included in the process, or it will repudiate any agreement reached as occurred in the trade area after the Kennedy Round. The administration should be certain that the proper people from the proper committees in the House and the Senate have been aligned in support. These lessons can also apply to the broader, day-to-day process of executive-legislative relations. Closer coordination and cooperation between the two branches can ease the friction in their work. Genuine leadership is not to be disdained, whatever the situation. The future of our government will depend on individuals who understand how effectively to use the process in order to make the system work.

2

Congress and the Legislative Veto: Choices Since the *Chadha* Decision

Joseph Cooper

One of the primary institutional developments in twentieth century U.S. politics has been the emergence and growth of the legislative veto. Admittedly, the process of growth often has been marked by conflict over the legality of the veto, the consequences of its use, or both. Nonetheless, from the 1930s through the 1970s, the history of the veto successfully combined both continuing controversy and expanding use.[1]

Conflict-ridden but expansionary, this era of the veto's history has recently been punctuated by two Supreme Court decisions. In late June 1983 the Court ruled in *Immigration and Naturalization Service v. Chadha* that one-House or simple resolution forms of the veto were unconstitutional.[2] Two weeks later it affirmed without comment two Appeals Court rulings against the veto, one of which outlawed two-House or concurrent resolution forms of the veto mechanism.[3]

As important as these decisions are, they have not foreclosed the need to examine the veto's constitutional merits and standing. Although Congress must obey the Supreme Court, members need to understand how much leeway the Court has left them and whether they have any sound basis for seeking to induce the Court to reverse or modify its position. The legal issues are not the only ones that need be addressed. However rigid or permeable the limits set by the Court, questions of

Joseph Cooper is dean of the School of Social Sciences at Rice University where he also teaches political science. He has served as a consultant for the Senate Rules Committee and the House Democratic Policy Committee. His publications include numerous articles on the legislative veto.

veto usage depend on the wisdom of relying on the mechanism as well as on its legality.The objectives of this chapter are thus twofold: to examine the legal and institutional statuses of the veto in the wake of recent Court decisions and, on the basis of this examination, to suggest strategies for Congress to follow as it seeks to cope with the actions of the Court.

Background Information

To begin, it is necessary to put the veto in more detailed perspective. This section defines the veto mechanism, outlines variations in its forms, and briefly reviews its history. Legal and institutional issues are addressed in the sections that follow, and the conclusions are applied in a final section to assess current options and strategies.

The Veto and Its Forms

The legislative veto may be defined as a statutory mechanism that renders the implementation or the continuing implementation of decisions or actions, proposed or taken in pursuance of the statute, subject to some further form of legislative consideration and control for a specified time. In other words, when veto review is included as part of an enabling statute, executive or administrative decisions or actions authorized by the statute cannot go into effect or remain in effect unless Congress approves or does not disapprove them within a specified time period.

All forms of the veto share this generic characteristic of rendering decisions or actions, authorized in an original enabling act, contingent on further legislative review and consideration. Nonetheless, before the recent set of Supreme Court decisions on the veto, the specific forms of the veto could and did vary greatly depending on the way choices along several dimensions of structure were made and combined.

First, a wide range of options existed with reference to the agent or agents charged with the exercise of veto power. Thus Congress has vested veto power in either or both Houses, committees, subcommittees, a committee chairperson, a blend of committee and House action, and even a blend of one and two-House action.[4]

Second, the manner in which the decision-making process operates has been and continues to be open in a number of respects. Two of the most important relate to whether veto review subjects decisions to approval or disapproval and whether veto review is after or before a decision has been implemented. In the first five decades of the veto's existence Congress preferred negative forms, though approval forms were also quite common. Reliance on after-the-fact rather than before-the-fact review has been infrequent, however.[5]

In addition, several other aspects of operation are important and have varied—whether veto proposals are submitted by or through the president, whether veto proposals are amendable once submitted, and whether veto proposals are protected by provisions that limit debate and ensure access to the floor.[6]

Third, until 1984 the formal mechanisms or instruments through which veto action was implemented varied. Approval or disapproval was expressed often by simple, concurrent, or committee resolutions—that is, by forms of action not subject to the president's veto power. From its beginnings, however, veto review also operated through waiting-period or report-and-wait procedures. In such instances the enabling statute simply requires that proposed decisions or actions lie before Congress or its committees for a specified number of days before taking effect. Although left unstated, formal congressional action to veto or negate the proposed decision or action has to take the form of a regular bill and, if passed by both Houses, be submitted to the president for his approval.[7]

Aside from these traditional instruments of action, Congress has invented several variants in response to criticism of the veto on legal grounds. In the 1950s Congress tied the committee resolution form to the appropriations process. Funds to implement executive decisions or actions were made contingent on securing the approval of designated committees. Since the 1950s, however, this form has been used only sporadically.[8] In the 1970s a new form emerged as both usage of the veto and criticism of it on legal grounds accelerated.[9] Under this form, authority to approve or disapprove is expressly stipulated in the statute, but it must be exercised through the passage of joint resolutions or bills. It should be noted that both are subject to the president's veto power. Finally, once the joint resolution form appeared, Congress began to blend concurrent and joint resolution forms of veto review in especially important areas of executive decision making.[10]

Growing usage of the veto combined with a variety of structural options has led to a profusion of forms. Students of the history of the veto have identified more than a dozen different forms. Our purposes, however, can be served adequately by a simple classification scheme, organized in terms of the factors the Supreme Court has found so critical to the veto's constitutionality—submission for presidential approval and bicameral consideration.

Thus we shall distinguish between congressional forms and law forms on the basis of these factors. Congressional forms are those in which veto action is not subject to the president's veto power and may be taken by portions of Congress, as well as by both Houses. Law forms are those in which veto action follows regular legislative procedures and involves both bicameral agreement and submission to the president for his approval.

Within these basic categories, congressional forms can be distinguished in terms of the agent or agents vested with veto power. Law forms are necessarily two-House forms but can be distinguished by whether approval or disapproval within a specified time period' is explicitly or only implicitly provided for in the enabling statute.

Table 1 is organized in the categories defined above. It provides summary data on the forms of vetoes embodied in veto provisions enacted into law in the period from 1932 through 1982. Shown are the three most noteworthy aspects of structural use: th heavy degree of reliance on various congressional forms of the device, 'h popularity of the waiting period form, and the increase in use of the joint resolution form as the 1970s ended.

Patterns of Veto Usage

In turning now to a brief survey of trends in the use of the veto, it is worth noting that the mechanism's rise to a position of importance in the operations of the federal government did not occur quickly or evenly. Yet, however sluggish and haphazard the process of development, the results by the early 1980s were impressive.

Only a few dozen veto provisions were enacted into law in the 1930s and 1940s. (See table 2.) Moreover, about two-thirds of them dealt with immigration matters and projects and contracts of various types. Perhaps the two most important uses concerned executive reorganization plans and the licensing of nuclear materials for production or use.[11]

In the 1950s and 1960s veto usage expanded. More than 100 veto provisions were passed. Project and contract uses continued to account for nearly half of all uses, however, and minor governmental operations uses for almost another quarter. Hence, important policy uses remained restricted in number and range, although they did include such matters as Department of Defense (DOD) and the National Aeronautics and Space Administration (NASA) reorganization, presidential action on Tariff Commission recommendations, the apportionment of highway funds among the states, foreign agreements regarding military uses of atomic energy, and termination of federal grants and loans for failure to comply with the Civil Rights Act of 1964.[12]

Although veto usage had grown in the 1950s and 1960s, in the 1970s it exploded. This also is shown in table 2, which reveals that roughly three-quarters of all veto provisions enacted into law over the last half-

TABLE 1. Veto Provisions Classified by Form, 1932–1982

Congressional Forms	1932–1978	1979–1982*
One House	71	28
Two House	65	33
Committee	69	31
Other	0	1
Total	205	93
Law Forms	**1932–1978**	**1979–1982**
Joint Resolution or Bill	9	11
Waiting Period or Advance Notification	238	no data
Total	247	11

Sources: Clark Norton, *1978 Congressional Acts Authorizing Congressional Approval or Disapproval of Proposed Executive Actions,* (Washington, D.C.: Congressional Research Service, 1979), V-VI (Report No. 79-46); Clark Norton, *Statistical Summary of Congressional Approval and Disapproval Legislation, 1932–1982* (Washington, D.C.: Congressional Research Service); Barbara Craig, *The Legislative Veto: Congressional Control of Regulation* (Boulder, Colo.: Westview Press, 1983), 18.
*As of August 5, 1982.

TABLE 2. Veto Laws and Provisions, 1932–1980

Time Period	Laws with Veto Provisions		Veto Provisions in Law	
	Number	*Percent*	*Number*	*Percent*
1930–1949	24	6.7	26	4.7
1950–1969	83	23.4	106	19.1
1970–1975	89	25.1	163	29.4
1975–1980	159	44.8	260	46.8
Total	355	100	555	100

Source: Barbara Craig, *The Legislative Veto: Congressional Control of Regulation* (Boulder, Colo.: Westview Press, 1983), 18–20.

century were enacted in the 1970s. Moreover, with this explosion in veto usage came scores of new applications in important policy areas. Some illustrative examples are provided in table 3.

It is not surprising that Justice Byron R. White, in his dissent to the Court's decision outlawing one-House vetoes, stated that the "prominence of the legislative veto mechanism in our contemporary political system and its importance to Congress can hardly be overstated."[13] "It has," he noted, "become a central means by which Congress secures the accountability of executive and independent agencies."[14] And, indeed, the Court decisions in mid–1983, outlawing congressional forms of the veto, affected more than 200 different vetoes in 126 different laws.[15]

The Legal Status of the Veto

The *Chadha* case is the only one in which the Supreme Court has issued an opinion on the legality of the veto. In addition, detailed opinions on the legality of the veto have been issued by lower federal courts in two other cases: *Consumer Energy Council of America v. Federal Energy Regulatory Commission*, 673 F. 2d 425 (D.C. Cir., 1982) and *Atkins v. United States*, 556 F. 2d 1028 (Ct. Cl., 1977). In examining the veto's legality our focus is on these cases, particularly on the *Chadha* decision.

The Chadha *Decision*

In *Chadha* the Court outlawed the one-house form of the veto on the basis of Sections 1 and 7 of Article I. These provisions require that laws be passed by both Houses and be presented to the president for his approval or veto. The scope of the decision thus extends to all congressional forms of the device.

For purposes of analysis, Chief Justice Warren E. Burger's majority opinion in the *Chadha* case can be divided into three parts. The first part of his argument concerns the inherent nature of legislative power. Burger admits at the start that not all acts of one or both Houses constitute exercises of legislative power in the sense understood and controlled by Article I. He states that the test of whether an action amounts to lawmaking rests not on form, but on whether it contains "matter which is properly to be regarded as legislative in character and effect."[16] Applying this test to the House's veto of an order of the attorney general suspending the deportation of Jagdish Rai Chadha, a Kenyan whose student visa had expired, Burger concludes that the House's action "was essentially legislative" because it "had the purpose and effect of altering the legal rights, duties, and relations of persons, including the Attorney General, executive branch officials and Chadha,

TABLE 3. Selected Veto Provisions Passed between 1970 and 1983

Defense Policy	**Consumer Policy**
War Powers (1973)	All Federal Trade Commission
Export of Defense-Related	Rules (1980)
Goods or Technology (1975)	All Consumer Product Safety
Arms Sales (1976)	Commission Rules (1981)
Foreign Policy	**Energy Policy**
Foreign Assistance in Violation	Rationing Plans, Strategic
of Human Rights (1975)	Reserves, and Oil Exports
Cooperative Agreements	(1975)
Regarding Nuclear Fuel,	Reimposition of Natural Gas
Facilities, and Technology	Price Controls (1978)
(1978)	Oil and Gas Bidding Systems for
	the Outer Continental Shelf
	(1979)
Trade	**Environmental Policy**
Presidential Proposals for	Sales and Withdrawals from
Import Relief, Waiver	Public Lands (1976)
Extensions, and	Environmental Protection
Nondiscriminatory Treatment	Agency (EPA) Rules regarding
(1974)	Hazardous Substances (1980)
Curtailment of Export of	EPA Rules Regarding Pesticides
Agricultural Commodities	(1980)
(1979)	
Education Policy	**Miscellaneous**
All Department of Education	Impoundment (1974)
Rules (1974, 1978, and 1979)	Federal Reserve Board Changes
Enrollment Periods in Veterans'	in Interest Rate Differentials
Educational Assistance (1976)	between FDIC and FSLIC
Schedule of Family	Banks (1975)
Contributions for Pell Grants	Farm Credit Administration
(1981)	Rules (1980)

Source: Appendix, 51 *United States Law Week* 4930–4933.

all outside the legislative branch."[17] Similarly, in the Federal Energy Regulatory Commission (FERC) case Senior Circuit Judge Malcolm R. Wilkey of U.S. Court of Appeals, D.C. Circuit, argued that a House veto of an incremental gas pricing rule constituted an act of legislative power because it was a discretionary policy decision that changed the law by negating an otherwise valid regulation and reducing the scope of FERC's authority.[18]

Critics of the legality of congressional forms of the veto, however, cannot reasonably base their case simply on the claim that these forms of the veto constitute acts of lawmaking or legislating because they are discretionary decisions that alter the law. Officials in executive or independent agencies also make discretionary decisions that alter the law. Somehow such discretion must be distinguished from lawmaking or legislating. In addition, of the veto's legality must deal more adequately with the argument that veto resolutions are distinguishable from statutes in that they are based on and derive their authority from prior enabling legislation. In short, the contention that veto action is an act of legislative power even when it merely negates or prevents implementation does not meet fully the broader claim that veto review is a condition imposed by Congress on the very exercise of delegated authority.

To handle these issues, critics of the constitutionality of congressional forms of veto amplify and extend their case against them. A second and more fundamental part of their argument emerges when what initially appeared to be an inherent function approach to legislative power becomes a procedural approach. Now character or substance is downplayed as a test of legislative power, and binding or controlling effect is highlighted. Concomitantly, legislative power is identified procedurally or sequentially so that the same decision may be considered "legislative" if undertaken by Congress in writing a statute and "executive" if undertaken by appointed officials in the process of implementing a statute. As a consequence, a new standard for judging decisions that are equivalent to lawmaking or legislating comes to the fore. The logical or inherent character of the subject matter provides no criteria for constraining congressional decision making in the regular legislative process; but Congress cannot exercise power over the implementation of its laws in a binding or controlling fashion except by returning to the regular legislative process.

Thus, in the *Chadha* decision, Chief Justice Burger argues that

> [d]isagreement with the Attorney General's decision on Chadha's deportation—that is, Congress' decision to deport Chadha—no less than Congress' original choice to delegate to the Attorney General the authority to make that decision, involves determinations of policy that Congress can

implement in only one way: bicameral passage followed by presentment to the president. Congress must abide by its delegation of authority until that delegation is legislatively altered or revoked.[19]

Similarly, in the FERC case, Judge Wilkey argues that the House veto of the FERC rule represented a congressional "second look" or "reconsideration" of its previously enacted policy.[20] He concludes, therefore, that the veto is illegal: "The president and both houses of Congress agreed on a policy when they took their 'first look.' Undoing their policy requires adherence to the same procedure."[21] A procedural approach to legislative power greatly facilitates the ability of the veto's critics to cope with the problems raised earlier.

First, once Congress has delegated authority, it is no longer "legislative," even if highly discretionary and even if vested in an independent agency. Chief Justice Burger thus states that the actions of the attorney general in the *Chadha* case were "presumptively" executive.[22] Similarly, Judge Wilkey argues that, although FERC is an independent agency, it performs executive functions in exercising its delegated rule-making authority.[23] Both judges acknowledge that the authority delegated to governmental officials must not involve unconstitutional delegations of legislative power. If the Article I requirements for the nondelegation of legislative power are satisfied, however, the only legitimate binding checks on the exercise of delegated authority are the terms of the statute, judicial review, and subsequent legislation.[24]

Second, the claim that veto review is merely a condition contemplated in the original enabling statute and not equivalent to lawmaking can be dismissed. If Congress cannot act legitimately to affect the exercise of delegated authority in a controlling or binding fashion except through the regular legislative process, then congressional forms of the veto represent an improper attempt by Congress to reserve power to itself. Thus, Chief Justice Burger can argue that negation through a one-house veto is equivalent to an amendment or a repeal of a statute and therefore that the device is unconstitutional because such ends properly can be achieved only through the regular legislative process.[25]

The third and final part of the critics' case against the legality of congressional forms of the veto involves linking particular arguments to general principles. The case against the veto cannot rest solely on a demonstration that specific constitutional provisions have been violated; what also must be shown is that these violations injure or harm the principles and goals of the separation of powers design of the framers of the Constitution. Both Chief Justice Burger and Judge Wilkey regard this as an easy task. They see no need to attempt any broad examination of the existing balance of power between the branches and the veto's impact in this regard. They simply point out that the framers regarded the presentment and bicameral requirements of Article I as essential, both to allow the president to protect his prerogatives and to ensure wise and balanced deliberation in the lawmaking process. If these requirements are violated, so too are the principles and goals of the framers' separation of powers design.[26]

The Merits of the Chadha Decision

The arguments of those who deny that congressional forms of the veto violate the bicameral and presentment provision of Article I can also be divided into three parts.

Their initial approach is to argue that the one-house form of the veto, involved in the *Chadha* and FERC cases, is distinguishable from a law or statute because the negation of proposed actions or decisions by resolution does not change the law but only maintains the legal status quo.[27] This argument, however, does not provide an adequate foundation for defending congressional forms of the veto. It does not apply to approval forms, and it does not come to grips with Chief Justice Burger's argument that veto action, even when negative, is equivalent to lawmaking because it accomplishes what could otherwise only be accomplished by law.[28]

Defenders of the legality of congressional forms of the veto, however, no more restrict their case to one level of argument than critics of these forms. Thus, in the *Chadha* decision, Justice White argues that the House's veto of Chadha's deportation suspension did not violate Article I because it existed as a condition on the exercise of delegated authority laid down in the original enabling act.[29] He recognizes explicitly that the linchpin of the majority opinion is the claim that Article I requires "all action with the effect of legislation to be passed as law."[30] He offers two broad arguments in opposition. On the one hand, he asks why the test must be more exacting in the case of Congress than in the case of officials in executive or independent agencies. After all, these officials make decisions with the force of law without bicameral approval or presentment to the president. Moreover, in both cases discretion is authorized by an original enabling statute and limited by the terms of the statute.[31] On the other hand, he argues that the Court has not been strict in controlling either the agents to whom authority has been delegated or the standards under which authority has been delegated. Thus, he finds it "odd" that a Court, which has allowed the nondelegation of legislative panel requirements of Article 1 to become a virtual nonentity and a group of farmers to veto marketing orders, cannot abide veto review as a condition of congressional delegations of authority under Article I.[32]

These are not the only or even the most cogent points that can be made in defense of congressional forms of the veto. The procedural premises and arguments of the veto's critics can be challenged more directly.

First, what line of reasoning or evidence supports the proposition that Congress cannot affect or limit the exercise of delegated authority in a controlling or binding fashion except through the regular legislative process? On their face the bicameral and presentment provisions of Article I do not prohibit Congress from conditioning its statutory grants of delegated authority to provide for veto review. Given this fact, the proposition rests more on conceptions of executive duties or prerogatives in implementing the law than on conceptions of legislating or law-making.[33] Thus, both Chief Justice Burger and Judge Wilkey argue that the instances in which one or both Houses of Congress can take binding action outside the regular legislative process aside from proposing constitutional amendments are few and specifically stipulated—impeachment and confirmation, for example.[34]

But this argument does not address the issue of whether veto review infringes on duties or prerogatives reserved to the executive. Rather it presumes to know the answer from the start. As Justice White points out, the fact that matters such as impeachment are stipulated "hardly demonstrates a limit upon Congress's authority to reserve itself a legislative veto, through statutes, over subjects within its lawmaking authority."[35] The claim that congressional forms of the veto violate the bicameral and presentment clauses of the Constitution, then, is not as clear and straightforward as it appears. Rather, on the basis of certain presumptions about executive duties or prerogatives, it assumes what it needs to prove—that Congress cannot exercise binding control over the implementation of delegated authority except through new legislation.

Second, proponents of congressional forms of the veto can provide substantive constitutional grounds in support of their argument that Congress has the power to make veto review a condition of granting delegated authority. The vertical effects of the necessary-and-proper clause of Article I are well known. This provision, however, not only endows Congress with the ability to employ all appropriate and convenient means to carry out its enumerated powers, it also endows Congress with the same ability with reference to the powers of all other governmental units. Hence, it can be argued that the necessary-and-proper clause has a horizontal, as well as vertical, effect: that the clause endows Congress with broad discretion over the means of implementation as long as they, too, are appropriate and convenient and do not violate any express provisions of the Constitution.[36] This was one of the main arguments in the Atkins case in which the Court of Claims upheld a one-House veto over federal salaries.[37] And it is an argument Justice White employs in the *Chadha* decision as well.[38]

Finally, proponents of congressional forms of the veto, like the opponents, appeal to broader constitutional principles. In the *Chadha* decision, Justice White does this in two mutually reinforcing ways. On the one hand, he denies that the one-House veto injures separation of powers principles or goals. His point is that, although veto procedures reversed the regular legislative process, the one-House form did not impair the ability of either House or the president to control results.[39] This is arguably true in the *Chadha* case and even more difficult to dispute in cases in which veto proposals must be presented formally by or through the president. On the other hand, he argues that congressional forms of the veto provide a means of readjusting the balance of power between the branches in an age in which circumstances have required and the Court has permitted substantial delegations of discretionary authority to governmental officials. They thus serve to preserve the separation of powers, not to destroy it.[40]

The Implications of the Chadha Decision

What, then, can we conclude regarding the constitutional standing and merits of the legislative veto?

One fact that is clear is that Congress retains considerable leeway. The Supreme Court, explicitly or implicitly, has outlawed the one-House, two-House, and committee forms of the veto. The same logic or rationale that accomplishes this, however, makes the joint resolution and waiting period forms difficult to challenge, even though in practice these forms often permit powerful committees and members to exercise as much leverage as congressional forms.[41]

If, as is argued in the *Chadha* and FERC cases, the hallmark of constitutionality is that Congress cannot alter the terms of delegated authority except through the regular legislative process, then forms of the veto that involve bicameralism and presentment are not objectionable. Even though these forms impose conditions on the implementation of delegated authority, they clearly do not violate Article I. Nor can a procedural approach to legislative power, as argued and relied upon in the *Chadha* and FERC cases, sustain an attack on these forms based on alleged infringements of executive prerogatives under Article II. A procedural approach, no more than an inherent function approach, can provide grounds for limiting Congress' authority to legislate within its enumerated powers in instances in which no express grants of power to the president are violated. Hence, the procedural approach cannot provide an adequate foundation for challenging law forms of the veto under either Articles I or II.[42]

Last, but not least, the rationale of the decisions in the *Chadha* and FERC cases widens the constitutional potential of one specific type of congressional form—House or committee vetoes tied to the appropriations process.[43] If the distinguishing line between legislative and executive power is procedural or sequential, then bars to the prospective appropriation of funds, whose passage is tied to the approval of simple, concurrent, or committee resolutions, can be strongly defended as internal acts of rule making or self-governance and integral aspects of Congress's historic right to appropriate or not appropriate as it alone sees fit.[44]

A second conclusion that may be drawn is that good and substantial reasons exist for disagreeing with the decisions in the *Chadha* and FERC cases.

As has been argued, the contention that congressional forms of the veto injure basic separation of powers principles because they violate the presentment and bicameral requirements of Article I is problematic and inconclusive rather than clear and undeniable. The contention that these forms of the veto violate executive duties and prerogatives under Article II is equally, if not even more vulnerable. This type of argument was employed by Judge Wilkey in the FERC case as a second and independent basis for invalidating congressional forms of the veto, and it is a frequent refrain among the veto's critics.[45]

Yet, unless one assumes either inherent executive functions or implied executive power, it is difficult to see why congressional forms of the veto violate Article II. These forms interfere with administration or execution, but so do all forms of congressional review, including authorization and appropriation.[46] Admittedly, they differ from informal forms of oversight and regular legislation in that they provide for binding control without presentment to the president and possibly without bicameral passage as well. This fact, however, is not a constitutional defect unless the presentment and bicameral provisions of Article I are violated.[47] If they are not violated, there is no legitimate difference between what Congress can accomplish regarding administrative control through congressional forms and what it can accomplish through regular legislation. Thus, the case against congressional forms of the veto on grounds of violating Article II rests on presumptions about Article I, just as the reverse prevails when Article I is the focus of attack.[48] This is the underlying reason law forms of the veto are immune to attack on grounds of violating Article II.

In sum, then, the case against the constitutionality of congressional forms of the veto is circular and unconvincing.[49] Presumptions alternate as needed to buttress different parts of the argument regarding the violation of constitutional provisions or arrangements. Indeed, only by assuming what they need to prove do the critics overcome the fact that congressional forms are not expressly barred by the Constitution nor equivalent to statutes in character or effect.[50] Given such fragile underpinnings, judicial claims that basic separation of powers principles and goals have been injured are unconvincing. Judicial fears that the veto involves open-ended possibilities for congressional aggrandizement exaggerate the dangers. Congressional forms of the veto can accomplish no more than law forms or regular legislation, and presidential power can be protected by structuring the device so as to require submission by or through him, nonamendability, and expedited legislative procedures. In truth, the weight of the evidence suggests that it is Congress that is most threatened by modern conditions of government, not the president and certainly not the bureaucracy.[51] The Supreme Court thus would have been better advised to have approached the veto with less confidence in its institutional wisdom and more humility toward the views of Congress.

The Institutional Status of the Veto

Although recent Supreme Court actions have highlighted legal challenges to the veto mechanism, opposition to the device has never been and is not now limited to legal objections. Throughout its history, and with growing intensity in recent years, critics have also charged that congressional forms of the veto severely harm the efficiency, effectiveness, and representativeness of governmental decision making at the national level.[52] The belief that the veto is bad or venal is so widely and intensely held by the veto's critics that one suspects it inspires their legal attacks on the device. Certainly, that belief reinforces powerfully whatever inclinations they do have to object to the veto on constitutional grounds.[53]

Most critics of the veto have not yet addressed the institutional merits of law forms of the veto. As we shall see in more detail, however, the logic of their argument against congressional forms of the veto applies to law forms as well. If these arguments are correct, there is little to consider in terms of options and strategies, no matter how much leeway Congress retains in the wake of *Chadha*. Rather, with the possible exception of the waiting period form, the device should simply be abandoned. Hence, the impact of the veto on governmental decision making and on the political system's need for the mechanism must be assessed before the question of how Congress can best adapt to recent Court actions can be addressed.

The Impact of the Veto

In recent years, as usage of the veto has increased, criticism of it on policy or institutional grounds has increased as well. Such criticism has been directed at congressional forms of the veto and has focused on the use of one and two-House vetoes to control the exercise of rule making power in a variety of important policy areas.

The character of the critique has been multifaceted, but its most significant aspect concerns the veto's impact on effective decision making in the public interest. Critics argue that all congressional forms of the veto provide congressional committees with a substantial increment in leverage over officials in agencies and commissions. The late Robert G. Dixon, a former assistant attorney general, for example, has called such leverage negotiating power "with teeth" because proposed rules go first to the relevant committees and may not go into effect if a committee opposes them.[54] According to the veto's critics, the consequences of conferring such leverage on committees are generally, or even necessarily, inimical to sound, democratic decision making. Such leverage, the veto's critics contend, is used to disrupt fair, open, impartial, and expert processes of decision making under the Administrative Procedure Act and to subject these processes, instead, to covert and intensely political pressures. The result, they claim, is both to promote ad hoc, arbitrary, and irrational decision making and to provide the special interests, which operate through committees, with excessive and unfair advantage.[55]

These claims not only have been made by a variety of authors, but also have been included in the amicus curiae brief submitted by the American Bar Association in the *Chadha* case and in articles in the *American Bar Association Journal* explaining the brief and "why the veto was bad."[56] In addition, they have been supported by case studies of veto control over administrative rule making; initially, in a classic formulation of the case against the veto by Harold Bruff and Ernest Gellhorn and more recently in a broader study by Barbara Craig.[57]

Some critics of congressional forms of the veto nonetheless favor the use of waiting period forms, and others have contrasted congressional forms and regular legislative procedures in attacking the impact of congressional forms on representative government.[58] Yet the logic of the case against congressional forms of the veto applies to law forms as well.

Joint resolutions of approval or negation also provide committees with substantial leverage. In contrast to one and two-House vetoes, they are subject to presidential veto. In addition, in contrast to one-House vetoes, they require bicameral approval. Although these requirements reduce committee leverage, they do not eliminate it entirely or prevent it from varying according to the politics of particular circumstances. Thus, under joint resolution forms, as under one and two-House forms, officials have to negotiate with committees and carefully heed both the short and long-run costs of opposing them. Indeed, it can well be argued that joint resolutions of approval provide committees with greater leverage than one and two-House vetoes, because in such instances officials must organize positive majorities in both Houses rather than simply avoid disapproval in one or both Houses. Moreover, it can be argued that the possibility of making amendments under joint resolution forms, whereas they were usually barred under congressional forms for reasons of constitutionality, increases committee leverage. In any event, the basic point is clear: the practical differences between one and two-House vetoes and joint resolution forms are not great enough to render these forms immune to the criticisms leveled at congressional forms.

The situation with respect to the waiting period form is similar. Formally, this type of veto is highly distinguishable from congressional forms, and it would appear not to have the same consequences as these forms. The waiting period form, however, flags matters for congressional attention and institutionalizes opportunities for intervention and negotiation. Given the continuing dependence of officials on committees for both authority and funds, such opportunities can provide substantial leverage whenever committees choose to exercise it. Thus, as shown even in case studies conducted by the veto's critics, the leverage exercised by committees under the waiting period form can approach—or match— the leverage exercised under one or two-House forms of the veto.[59]

If providing congressional committees with opportunities for intervention and leverage in the process of execution is bad, then the point applies to the law forms of the veto as well as to congressional forms. The issue is, however, whether congressional participation in the administrative process through the veto is as bad as the veto's critics claim. The answer is no. The veto's critics exaggerate the virtues of executive decision making and fail to appreciate the role and benefits of politics in a democratic order.

Two points may be made to counter the executive biases of the veto's critics. First, special interests are just as much at home in the process of execution as in the legislative process.[60] It is arguable whether more diffuse and less well-financed interests have easier access to agencies and commissions or to congressional committees. It undoubtedly varies with circumstances. Thus, black-and-white contrasts rest on bias and presumption. The claim that notice and comment procedures render the administrative process "open," while special interest domination renders committee operations "closed," fails to take account of the policy blinders and commitments that administrators bring to their jobs, the high costs in terms of time, attention, and money that participation in the administrative process involves, and the responsiveness of elected representatives to broad and diffuse interests, which crisscross large numbers of individual constituencies.[61]

Second, in areas in which important questions of public policy are at issue, it is not obvious that administrators are any wiser or more devoted to the public interest than legislators. The basic belief of constitutional democratic orders is that they are not. Their operative premise is rather that experts need to be told where the "shoes pinch," that the quality of decision making benefits from the assertion of interests or viewpoints that otherwise would not secure as strong a hearing. Moreover, judicialized procedures themselves are a mixed blessing when important policy decisions are involved, as they may narrow and inhibit full and responsive consideration of all the related factors and issues.[62]

Similarly, the antipolitical biases of the veto's critics are identifiable and may be countered. First, committees are not pathological entities in Congress but rather instruments of division of labor that contribute to institutional effectiveness. Otherwise, they would not have been invented and could not continue to exist. This is not to say that gaps or differences between the committees and the whole cannot and do not occur. Committees are responsive to the whole, however, and can be disciplined by the whole. With respect to the veto, under one and two-House forms, as well as all law forms, a committee's leverage rests in large part on the credibility of its capacity to induce the whole to accept the resolutions or bills it brings forward or might choose to bring forward.[63]

Second, because they are parts of Congress rather than the whole, committees are not primarily the home of special interests. Such reasoning is as fallacious in the case of Congress as it would be if applied to executive agencies. Thus, the arguments and case studies used by the veto's critics to indict committee participation in the process of execution often rest on a simplistic equation of constituent pressure and special interests. As a result, committee actions on behalf of the parents of middle-class college students, housing assistance for disadvantaged senior citizens, or women athletes in opposition to administrative policy inclinations and/or their reading of legislative intent become fights for special interests.[64] If so, one wonders what the public interest is and how it is to be found.

The equation of constituent pressure and special interests and the conclusions that result reveal something basic about the underlying assumptions of the veto's critics. They lack faith in politics and political processes of accommodation as the central means of locating and formulating the public interest. Rather, they see the public interest as some entity above politics that is best identified by judicious and expert administrators, at least once Congress has acted through law. Because the process of execution, as well as the legislative process, now involves highly discretionary and important policy decisions, any sequential or procedural distinction in this regard lacks relevance and persuasiveness.

Still, it is no accident that the arguments of the veto's critics against congressional forms apply to law forms as well. In truth, the arguments apply to the legislative process in general because committees have as great, if not greater, power vis-à-vis the whole in the regular legislative process. And the committees can and do use this power to influence both the content of administrative proposals for law and administrative choices in carrying out the law. One wonders whether critics of the veto understand, or simply choose to ignore, patterns of informal and nonstatutory control that have long prevailed between agencies and committees. These patterns facilitate comity between the branches, despite some costs and despite their variance with civics books conceptions. They are indispensable to viable government in a separation of powers framework.[65]

One final point remains to be made concerning the impact of the veto mechanism. Critics have focused on rule making uses and assumed that their critique is generally applicable. Yet, not only does rule making constitute only a portion of veto uses, in many other areas it is far harder to assume some yawning gap between committee preferences and the desires of the whole. Note, for example, impoundment, arms sales, war powers, federal pay, and reprogramming of agency funds. Even with respect to its uses for controlling various types of projects and contracts, the veto does not represent any strengthening of special interests, but rather a choice to give the executive more flexibility while still providing for congressional control.

In conclusion, then, my intent is not to argue that committees or political processes do not err. The legislative process is not without its problems. But then the administrative process is not the paragon of fairness, wisdom, and objectivity that the veto's critics assume either. The issue thus becomes one of balance and trust. Approached in these terms, the veto should be treated as an instrument, not an anathema. Wholesale strictures against its use do not accord with the basic faith, genius, or realities of constitutional democratic government in the United States.

The Need for the Veto

Treating the veto mechanism as an instrument, not an anathema, leads immediately to consideration of the need for the device. Critics of the veto do not avoid this question, but they treat it in a somewhat secondary fashion. Obviously, if the veto is venal, it is not needed.

Nonetheless, the veto's critics feel obliged to suggest alternatives to the veto. And well they should, given the number and importance of veto uses as illustrated in tables 2 and 3 and the growth of executive power since the 1930s.

All critics of the veto argue that Congress should abandon congressional forms of the device and do a more craftsmanlike job of lawmaking instead.[66] Many argue that better lawmaking plus reliance on traditional congressional oversight mechanisms will suffice to protect Congress' role and power in the political system.[67] The American Bar Association, however, has endorsed waiting period forms in selected areas of rule making, and Bruff and Gellhorn suggest greater committee involvement in notice and comment proceedings as an alternative to rule making vetoes.[68] In addition, Gellhorn argues that the veto is not needed because it is ineffective.[69] Finally, Antonin Scalia agrees that the veto is ineffective, but argues that the problem of combining executive power and congressional control is insolvable unless the nation resolves to have the federal government do less.[70]

In assessing these arguments, the first question to be considered is the need for greater congressional influence or control over delegated authority. The veto's critics do not deny the need to increase congressional effectiveness; virtually all admit that a serious problem exists. The issue therefore reduces to the alternatives to the veto and the veto's effectiveness.

All alternatives except better lawmaking are easily disposed of, often on the basis of considerations raised by opponents of the veto themselves. First, critics of the veto such as Bruff, Gellhorn, and Scalia understand the ad hoc character and limited reach of oversight through appropriations, investigations, and confirmation of personnel. They lack faith that increased reliance on these weapons would raise oversight to some qualitatively superior level of performance, and they understand that the constraints derive from time pressures, substantive complexity, political divisions, and career interests.[71]

Their judgments in this regard are powerfully reinforced by past experience. In fact, Congress has not stood still. In recent decades it has augmented substantially its capacity for oversight through traditional mechanisms. Congress has expanded its staff, established a host of oversight subcommittees, increased the number of provisos in appropriations bills, and required periodic review and reauthorization of programs in a variety of policy areas.[72] Nonetheless, such actions have not deterred it from expanding veto usage as well. Nor is this attributable simply to personal or institutional aggrandizement. Rather, it is largely attributable to the range of authority delegated to officials in agencies and commissions, to new and more conflictual patterns of politics, and to the difficulties of after-the-fact control through traditional mechanisms.[73]

Take, for example, the area that is most salient to the veto's critics: rule making. It is true that rule making applications of the veto exploded in the 1970s.[74] But note the following facts: In the years from 1955 through 1960 the number of new pages of public laws totaled 6,057, and the number of pages added in the Federal Register. totaled 4,569. The comparable figures for 1973 through 1978 are 11,338 and 32,337.[75] Similarly, whereas 37 new regulatory laws were passed between 1956 and 1965, 119 were passed between 1966 and 1975.[76] In short, there was an explosion in regulatory authority and administrative rule making as well, an explosion that could not be contained or controlled by adjusting fund levels, adding provisos, periodic reauthorization, or confirmation of personnel.

Second, Bruff and Gellhorn's suggestion that Congress encourage its committees to participate more actively in agency notice and comment proceedings as a substitute for the veto speaks volumes regarding their disdain for congressmen and bias toward executive or administrative officials. In effect, it asks members of Congress to become supplicants for the favorable judgment of supposed agents of Congress because these agents are assumed to have qualities of wisdom, objectivity, and fairness that representatives themselves lack.

Third, waiting period review in general does confer less leverage on Congress and its committees than one or two-House forms of the veto. It is, however, far from an innocent mechanism in terms of the preferences and presumptions of the veto's critics, and it is subject to the same objections they raise to congressional forms. Nor can the veto's proponents accept it as the single form of the veto mechanism upon which Congress should rely. From their vantage point it is not strong enough to merit such reliance.

Fourth, and last, Scalia's conclusions are insightful but hardly realistic. Undoubtedly, the volume and complexity of the responsibilities the federal government has assumed are a prime factor in expanding executive power and straining congressional control. Yet to ask the federal government to do less to a degree that would obviate the need for enhanced oversight capacity in areas where the veto has been used ignores realities that cannot reasonably be ignored. Is the federal government to refrain from arms sales, trade negotiations, aiding schools and students, regulating pollution and hazardous substances, using military force abroad, and regulating private use of public lands? If not, and if traditional means of control often are not adequate, then the problem recurs. In short, nineteenth-century solutions are not appropriate for twentieth-century problems.

The issue of alternatives thus reduces to the question of whether Congress can improve its lawmaking performance so as to make the veto mechanism unnecessary. At least some of the critics of the veto understand the substantive and political difficulties involved. They are not sanguine about the possibilities of any substantial increase in congressional control through better lawmaking. Nonetheless, they believe that the choice of this alternative is demanded by democratic ideals, and that the public has a right to insist on laws that provide clear and directive standards for executive action and a firm basis for holding officials accountable for results, no matter what the pressures or difficulties.[77]

Yet reliance on better lawmaking as an alternative to the veto is neither practical nor wise. This is not to deny that Congress can do a better job of clarifying its intent. What remains questionable is how much and to what effect.

First, in highly complex and turbulent areas of policy, it is difficult, if not impossible, to state intent except in broad terms because precise issues and problems cannot be anticipated. Arms sales provide a good illustration. Second, to the degree that clearer and more directive standards can be provided, sizable room for administrative discretion nonetheless remains, as Environmental Protection Agency (EPA) rules, for example, demonstrate. Thus, it is no accident that in recent decades the rate of increase in Federal Register pages far exceeds the rate of increase in statute pages or pages per statute.[78] The cure here is to try to write the laws in greater detail, because in the end, power lies in control of the concrete, not the abstract.[79] Yet, even if Congress had the time and the resources to follow this course in some general or comprehensive fashion, which is doubtful, the cure often could be worse than the disease. To limit authority by specifying details can well be to hamstring the executive, and in so doing, to vitiate Congress's ability to achieve the broader goals that led it to delegate authority in the first place. Third, given the current state of the congressional party system in which allegiance is weak, power decentralized, conflict intense, and alignments volatile, attempts to write clear standards or detailed provisions may well result in defeat of the legislation. The price of passage may be vagueness, but delegation of authority for action nonetheless may be vital to the national interest. Note, for example, gasoline rationing contingency plans in the late 1970s.[80]

In short, adherence to the critics' ideal version of the needs of the democratic orders does more damage to those needs than Congress's pragmatic willingness to delegate broad authority under veto control. The dilemma Congress confronts as it seeks to deal with its daily workload is simply not amenable to solution through better lawmaking, though admittedly the quality of lawmaking can be improved. To deny Congress access to the veto when it encounters one of the constraints outlined above is to restrict it and the political system to highly counterproductive choices:

- Congress can delegate the broad authority needed for effective action in vital areas of national responsiblity but without adequate control;
- it can refuse to delegate authority so as to preserve control through obstruction, though inaction may be only a temporary palliative that breeds more intense needs and even harsher demands for action in the future; or
- it can pepper the authority it delegates with detailed instructions and restrictions to protect its control, though such provisions may well vitiate executive effectiveness and Congress's ability to achieve its basic policy goals.[81]

In contrast, the veto frees Congress from such Hobson's choices. Its great virtue is that it permits the two essential yet conflicting needs of the modern democratic state—executive leadership and legislative control—to be reconciled and mutually satisfied. The mechanism is no panacea; it may be misused, and at times it may entice Congress into doing a poorer job of lawmaking than it would do otherwise. The point remains, however, that in a variety of policy areas the veto provides the only or the best means of maintaining the exacting balance between consent and action that the Constitution intends and upon which the continued viablity of our republic depends. Hence, some part of wisdom lies in accepting the limits of practical reality. Pristine notions of a legislature that legislates and an executive that executes were not fully descriptive or functional in the nineteenth century; they are even less so today.

Finally, let us consider the claim that the veto is not needed because it is ineffective. One part of the argument relates to time. With respect to rule making, the contention is that effective use of the veto requires more time and attention than Congress can devote.[82] A second part of the argument is more basic. The contention is that the veto, like other oversight mechanisms, is applied in an ad hoc, limited, and particularistic manner. As Gellhorn puts it, "The legislative veto, therefore, is unlikely to rescue Congress from itself."[83]

Ironically, the second contention counters the first. Selective and particularized use allows Congress to pick and choose in terms of political salience. It is quite practical and will require far less time than the critics' preferred alternative of better lawmaking across the board.

The more substantive objection is normative, not empirical. If Congress does not have the time, resources, or inducements for generalized or comprehensive oversight, why is picking and choosing particular topics in terms of political salience so bad? As noted in Gellhorn's quote, the answer really inheres in the Millsian presumptions held by the critics that proper legislative operations mean plenary power to the whole and a concentration on broad policy questions.[84] Thus, at heart, the veto is ineffective because it does not fit the critics' ideal view of proper legislative operations or oversight. If anything, however, the critique of the impact of the veto implies that it is too effective.

In the preceding section of this paper the validity of a view that equates committee leverage with special interest power has been questioned. Here its realism may be criticized as well. As suggested earlier, power over important policy issues more often lies in the control of the concrete facets of a question than abstractions. Equally important, how could Congress maintain its role and power in the political system if it did not delegate power to committees? This may create a tension between the whole and its parts, but it is a tension whose elimination in either direction would undermine prospects for representative and effective government in the United States. The Millsian presumptions of the critics are thus more appropriate to legislatures in parliamentary systems than to the U.S. government's separation of powers framework. Criticisms that rest implicitly on alternate ideals should at least be revealed for what they are. Then, the question can be focused on the real issue: whether preserving congressional power through the veto serves or advances representative government in the United States. For all the reasons outlined above, the answer is most decidedly yes.

Strategies and Options

If we conclude that the veto is neither bad nor unnecessary, this analysis of legal and institutional issues suggests two basic strategies for the Congress to follow, as well as some guidelines for selecting options within these strategies.

Extending Law Forms

Congress's immediate response to the *Chadha* decision should be to substitute law forms of the veto for congressional forms. In so doing, it should be attentive to the costs and benefits of different types of law forms.

Negation by joint resolution or by bill under waiting period requirements provides greater opportunities for the conservation of time and effort—two scarce resources in a late twentieth-century Congress of some 500 members. Issues can be selected in terms of their political importance and only cursory attention need be devoted to noncontroversial matters. The cost, of course, is the need for a two-thirds majority if the president and Congress disagree, which reduces the power of the mechanism and Congress's leverage in applying it. Approval by joint resolution provides greater legislative control. It requires Congress, however, to pass on each and every matter subject to veto review. The results are likely to be quite costly in terms of floor time, even if special calendars or procedures are invented to expedite consideration.

In addition, different types of law forms influence the contours of congressional pause for reasons beyond the size of the majority required to exercise control. Under negative law forms, proposed decisions or actions go into effect unless opponents can organize a majority on the floor to strike them down. Under affirmative law forms proponents have to organize the floor majorities. Negative law forms thus provide the president and other officials with greater leverage.[85] Such leverage is even greater under waiting period forms than joint resolution forms because waiting period requirements typically do not provide for limitation of debate and discharge, whereas resolution forms of the veto frequently do.

Congressional leverage thus tends to increase as one moves from waiting period requirements to negation by joint resolution to approval by joint resolution. Time costs also increase, however, which constrains veto use in terms of flexibility and range of control. These effects do not operate in isolation. They are the primary effects associated with different law forms, but they may be augmented or depressed by secondary aspects of structure, which are also matters of choice.

I have referred to such aspects, and their impact, in discussing differences in leverage between waiting period and joint resolution forms. As suggested in my initial discussion of forms of the veto, however, structural variation can occur around a variety of foci. These include whether expedited procedures are provided to facilitate access to the floor and to limit debate, whether provisions for amendability are permitted, whether the submission of proposals is vested in the president or required to be forwarded through him, and the length of the time period. The primary effects of the main law forms and the secondary effects of choices among remaining structural options are outlined in table 4.

This is not to suggest that the range of possible variation in law forms exceeds that in congressional forms. Although amendability was usually not included in congressional forms for reason of constitutionality, the ability to vary the congressional agents who exercise veto power

TABLE 4. Law Forms of the Veto: Primary and Secondary Effects of Various Designs

Primary Effects of Law Forms

Secondary Effects of Structural Options

Law Forms of the Veto	Expedited Procedures		Amendability		Longer Time Period		Submission by or through President	
	Leverage	Time	Leverage	Time	Leverage	Time	Leverage	Time
Joint Resolution: Approval	+	−	+	+	+	+	+	−
Joint Resolution: Negation	+	−	+	+	+	+	−	−
Waiting Period	o	o	o	o	+	+	−	−

Congressional Leverage ←

Time Costs ←

Key: ↑   = increase in primary effect
       +   = augments primary effect
       −   = depresses primary effect
       o   = no variation in structural option

Source: Author's analysis.

more than made up for limitations on amendability. The point is rather that the possibilities for variation in law forms are much broader than may first appear and thus that opportunities for fine tuning and experiments in design exist.

The use of law forms to compensate for the loss of congressional forms might not be a viable strategy if this were not the case. It is a delusion to look for one standard law form to replace the scores of veto provisions that were outlawed by the *Chadha* decision. Those vetoes were not of one form. They included a variety of one-House, two-House, and committee vetoes and even mixtures of these forms.[86] Nor did the range of options that existed in 1980 exist in 1940. They developed over time. And, if the profusion of forms was excessive, it nonetheless testifies to the power of congressional ingenuity to shape structure to the needs of varying and particular circumstances.

The use of law forms must be similarly eclectic, inventive, and adaptive. Even at this early stage, however, some broad guidelines can be suggested on the basis of the primary effects of basic forms and the secondary effects of subsidiary structural options.

Congress should design and apply law forms of the veto by balancing time pressures against the degree of control that would be desirable in an absolute sense.

The joint resolution of approval form is thus best suited to areas of substantial political importance where relatively limited numbers of proposed actions or decisions need to be considered. Arms sales or war powers provide a good example. Given the press of other business and the variety of special calendars that already exist, wholesale or widespread use of this form would be a mistake. The range or scope of the approval form can be extended, however, by including provisions for limited debate and nonamendability, so that matters can be voted up or down quickly. Such provisions involve costs for congressional leverage, but they make approval forms viable for the control of matters such as appropriations recisions.

Waiting period forms are at the other end of the scale. They are most appropriate for areas of limited importance that involve large numbers of proposed actions or decisions. Control over various types of projects and contracts provide good examples. The power of the waiting period form can be extended by lengthening the time period required for veto review beyond the normal 60 or 90 days, but allowing the committees to waive it whenever they see fit. This increases the power of the form and its suitability for use in important areas of policy. Possible uses include disposals of government properties or private use of the public lands. Increases in time also intensify problems of delay in executive action, however, and this cost must also be borne in mind.

Joint resolutions of negation are appropriate for the broad middle range in which the matters to be controlled are too important to be left to waiting period control and too numerous to be subjected to individual approval. In terms of encompassing large numbers of issues, the range of this form can be extended by requiring nonamendability. Appropriation deferrals thus might be appropriate for negation by joint resolution, as would various trade policy items and rule making, insofar as it is not controlled by the appropriations form of the veto recommended in the next section.

In applying law forms of the veto, Congress must rely heavily upon negative rather than approval forms of the device. A rifle rather than a shotgun approach is preferable for approval forms. The sting of relying primarily on negative law forms may be attenuated, however, by several expedients: changing House rules to make it easier to amend appropriations bills on the floor in cases where waiting period forms of the veto are in place, blending the use of joint resolutions of approval and negation so that the most critical items are subject to tighter control, and inventing different types of expedited procedures for negative joint resolution forms that vary in their effectiveness.[87]

Preserving Congressional Forms

Reliance on law forms of the veto should not be Congress's only response to the *Chadha* decision. Substantial grounds exist for disagreeing with this decision. The points at issue are not merely academic. In fact, negative one and two-House congressional forms combine the power or leverage advantages of affirmative law forms with the efficiency or flexibility advantages of negative law forms. It is not surprising that these forms were the most heavily used congressional forms before the *Chadha* decision.[88] Although law forms have some advantages that congressional forms lack, they do not provide an adequate substitute for one and two-House vetoes. Congress thus ought not simply give up what are the most effective and desirable forms of the veto overall because of an opinion as weak and as flawed as the *Chadha* decision. The rub, of course, is how to contest the Court while observing legal proprieties and staying safely within constitutional boundaries.

Two possibilities may be suggested. First, Congress should seek to mobilize and apply support that exists for congressional forms of the veto in the academic and legal communities. The veto did not lack defenders in the legal community before *Chadha*, and since the decision a number of respected legal scholars have found fault with the Court's opinion.[89] Congress should keep the issue alive through hearings, committee-sponsored studies in particular areas, Congressional Research

Service (CRS) reports, and special conferences involving members, academics, lawyers, and respected columnists.

Second, Congress should test the *Chadha* decision in the Courts. The issue needs to be brought forward again; the Court should be required to rethink it in a context less narrow and prejudicial to the veto than private immigration bills. Perhaps the best way to accomplish this end is carefully to construct a usage in which the veto is tied to the appropriations process and applied to rule making. As noted earlier, the procedural or sequential approach to legislative power, adopted in the *Chadha* case, is particularly vulnerable to a veto usage tied to the appropriations process. If legislative power is equivalent to decision making within legislative processes and procedures, and executive power commences when legislative decision making is completed, then it is exceedingly difficult to object constitutionally to the manner in which Congress structures its processes for making appropriations. Indeed, when the issue arose in the Eisenhower administration, President Dwight D. Eisenhower on the advice of his attorney general conceded the constitutionality of vetoes tied to the appropriations process, though he objected to other forms of the veto.[90] Similarly, using vetoes with respect to rule making is desirable because it highlights the highly discretionary nature of the subject matter being controlled. It also limits the possibility for critics of the veto to fall back on an inherent function approach, even though such an approach clashes with other positions they take and is not compatible with the rationale used in the *Chadha* decision.

The precise manner in which an appropriations veto over rule making should be constructed remains open to discussion. One way that appears promising is as follows. First, pass a waiting period requirement for a specified category of administrative rules. Second, change House and Senate rules so as to permit agency rules subject to the waiting period requirement to be disapproved as contrary to congressional intent by simple resolution. Third, include, as a feature of the above change in House and Senate rules, instructions to the Appropriations Committees to add provisos, barring the expenditure of funds for implementing rules so disapproved, in any and all future funding measures. Fourth, permit any member to raise a point of order against a funding bill that is not in accord with this new rule.

Conclusion

Earlier I noted that pristine notions of a legislature that "legislates" and an executive that "executes" were not fully descriptive or functional in the nineteenth century and are even less so today. The veto's critics understand and accept this reality as far as executive decision making is concerned. They well understand and approve of the fact that the executive "legislates." They refuse to acknowledge or accept, however, the propriety of legislative participation or intervention in executive decision making.

They therefore object to congressional forms of the veto and rest their case on two grounds that are emotionally, if not substantively, interrelated. On the one hand, critics of the veto argue that congressional forms of the veto are unconstitutional because they violate Article I provisions for bicameral agreement and presentment to the president and thereby injure separation of power principles and goals. Upon examination, however, their argument turns out to be circular and based on presumption. The ability of the veto's critics to straddle the inconsistencies involved in accepting the constitutional legitimacy of a modern administrative state and yet in denying Congress the ability to protect its policy prerogatives through the veto thus turns out to be an illusion.

On the other hand, critics of the veto question the institutional value of the mechanism. They regard congressional forms of the device as both venal and unnecessary. And their logic applies to law forms as well. Yet, in institutional as well as in legal terms, their ability to straddle the inconsistencies in their views of the proper scope of executive and legislative decision making rests on presumption. They ignore the realities of the administrative process and confuse the ideal with the real. At the same time, they take a Manichaean view of legislative decision making in which committee power is equated with sin, and they enjoin Congress to act in ways that would diminish its power and its importance.

The critics' case against the veto need not be accepted. Nor should it be. The *Chadha* decision is so willfully blind to history and context that it betrays the separation of powers principles it purports to serve. After all, limits can be put on congressional forms to protect presidential prerogatives without banning them entirely, for example, submission through the president and nonamendability. The institutional critique is no less mistaken. To deprecate the value of the veto is to fail to understand the indispensable role congressional power plays in maintaining the rigorous balance between consent and action that the U.S. constitutional order requires and intends.

The struggle to preserve the veto is thus one that Congress must not avoid. Recent events strongly suggest that there is little need for concern in this regard. In the two and one-half years since the *Chadha* decision Congress has taken a number of actions that testify both to its strongly felt need to preserve the device and to its ability to exploit the leeway the Court has left it.

First, Congress has replaced congressional forms with joint resolution of approval, joint resolution of negation, and waiting period forms in a variety of policy areas. These include executive reorganization, bans on the export of agricultural commodities, and energy plans. Such replacements have been made on an ad hoc basis and will continue.[91] Second, in response to particular circumstances, Congress has used law forms to control matters or decisions that were not previously subject to veto review. Some prime examples are the authorization and funding of MX missiles, aid to the contras in Nicaragua, and exports of technology to countries that support terrorism. Thus, despite *Chadha*, the purposes for which the veto mechanism is used continue to expand.[92]

Third, Congress has begun to develop an appropriations form of the veto that satisfies the logic of the *Chadha* decision. A recent Senate bill, now in conference, subjects Federal Trade Commission and Consumer Product Safety Commission rules to disapproval by joint resolution. In addition, this bill furnishes amendments, which bar the use of funds to implement disapproved rules, with special status when appropriations bills for these agencies are considered on the floor.[93] Finally, Congress has begun to experiment with the potential for complex variation that law forms possess. It has blended joint resolution of approval and joint resolution of negation forms in redesigning veto control of nuclear agreements. It has given committees greater bargaining leverage by authorizing them to suspend expedited procedures with respect to bills or resolutions required to implement executive proposals. It has become more lax about requiring nonamendability and on one occasion has amended an approval resolution so as further to condition the executive authority granted in the original enabling act.[94]

The story of the legislative veto is thus far from over. In general, Congress appears to have adopted the basic strategies recommended in this chapter. As a result, the *Chadha* decision does not mark the end of the mechanism, but simply a new stage in its history. It is a stage in which the executive branch as well as the legislative branch will pay a price for the outlawing of the traditional congressional forms of the device. Nonetheless, the veto's fate remains important. Congress's ability to use the device effectively and wisely will play a substantial role in determining whether long-run tendencies toward the erosion of its power will diminish or intensify as the United States enters its third century.

Notes

1. See H. Lee Watson, "Congress Steps Out: A Look at Congressional Control of the Executive," 63 *California Law Review* 983 (1975); James Sundquist, *The Decline and Resurgence of Congress* (Washington, D.C.: Brookings Institution, 1981), 344–367; Arthur Maass, *Congress and the Common Good* (New York: Basic

Books, 1983), 191–202; and Barbara Craig, *The Legislative Veto: Congressional Control of Regulation* (Boulder, Colo.: Westview Press, 1983), 15–45.

2. *Immigration and Naturalization Service v.* Chadha, 51 United States Law Week 4907 (1983).

3. The cases were both from the D.C. Circuit. *Consumer Energy Council of America v. Federal Energy Regulatory Commission (FERC)*, 673 F. 2d 425 (1982) and *Consumers Union v. Federal Trade Commission (FTC)*, 691 F. 2d 575 (1982).

4. Joseph Cooper and Patricia Hurley, "The Legislative Veto: A Policy Analysis," 10 *Congress and the Presidency* 6–9 (1983) and M. S. Cavanagh et al., *Congressional Veto Legislation: 97th Congress* (Washington, D.C.: Congressional Reference Service, 1982), Issue Brief no. IB81138.

5. Ibid. In addition, see Clark Norton, *Congressional Review, Deferral, and Disapproval of Executive Actions: A Summary and an Inventory of Statutory Authority* (Washington, D.C.: Congressional Reference Service, 1976), 1–10 (Report No. 76–78G).

6. Joseph Cooper, "The Legislative Veto: Its Promise and its Perils," 7 *Public Policy* 158–165 (1956).

7. Norton, *supra* note 5 at 4.

8. For details on usage in the 1950s see Joseph Cooper and Ann Cooper, "The Legislative Veto and the Constitution," 30 *George Washington Law Review* 468–469 (1962). For a recent, though isolated, example see Clark Norton, *Congressional Veto Legislation in the 96th Congress: Proposals and Enactments* (Washington, D.C.: Congressional Research Service, 1982), 112–113 (Report no. 82–26 GOV).

9. Norton, *supra* note 5 at 5.

10. See War Powers Resolution of 1973 (P.L. 93–148) and impoundment provisions of Budget and Impoundment Act of 1974 (P.L. 93–344).

11. Cooper and Hurley, *supra* note 4 at 5 and Cooper, *supra* note 6 at 128–129.

12. Cooper and Hurley, *supra* note 4 at 5 and Norton, *supra* note 5 at 22–50.

13. 51 *United States Law Week* 4920–4921 (1983).

14. Ibid., 4921.

15. Martin Tolchin, "Congress Digs in After Legislative Veto," *New York Times*, July 31, 1983.

16. 51 *United States Law Week* 4916 (1983).

17. Ibid.

18. 673 F. 2d 465–468 (1982).

19. 51 *United States Law Week* 4917 (1983). For a discussion of the differences between an inherent function and procedural approach to legislative power see U.S. House. Committee on Rules. *Regulatory Reform* Hearings, Testimony of Antonin Scalia, 96th Cong., 1st sess., 1979, pp. 532–535. Washington, D.C.: USGPO, 1979.

20. 673 F. 2d 468 (1982). See also 469–470.

21. Ibid.

22. 51 *United States Law Week* 4917 (1983).

23. 673 F. 2d 471 (1982).

24. 51 *United States Law Week* 4917 (1983).

25. 51 *United States Law Week* 4916–17 (1983).

26. 51 *United States Law Week* 4917–18 (1983) and 673 F. 2d 463–465 (1982).

27. 51 *United States Law Week* 4924 (1983). In addition, see *Buckley v. Valeo*, 424 U.S. 285 (1976) and *Atkins v. United States*, 556 F. 2d 1063 (Ct. Cl., 1977).

28. 51 *United States Law Week* 4917 (1983). See also hearings *supra* note 19 testimony of Benjamin Civiletti, pp. 395–400 and "The Legislative Veto," 34 *Record of the Association of the Bar of the City of New York* 214 (March 1979).

29. 51 *United States Law Week* 4926 (1983).

30. Ibid., 4925.

31. Ibid., 4925–26.

32. Ibid.

33. Nor is this surprising given reliance on a procedural approach. The premise is that once Congress has delegated a power, the power becomes executive and because Congress cannot execute the laws, it cannot meddle or interfere with performance unless it passes a new law. See *Atkins v. United States*, 556 F. 2d 1066–67 (Ct. Cl., 1977). In addition, the attention critics of the veto feel they must devote to the character of conditions that may validly be attached to delegations of legislative power also supports the point. See, for example, Robert Dixon, "The Congressional Veto and Separation of Powers: The Executive on a Leash," 56 *North Carolina Law Review* 453–457 (1978) and John B. Henry, "The Legislative Veto: In Search of Constitutional Limits," 16 *Harvard Journal of Legislation* 752–756 (1979). Indeed, one critic explicitly bases his argument regarding violation of the presentment and bicameral provisions of Article I on the veto's alleged effect of vesting congressmen with executive office with the result that in his view it cannot be accepted validly as a precedent condition. David Martin, "The Legislative Veto and the Responsible Exercise of Congressional Power," 63 *Virginia Law Review* 293–300 (1982).

34. 51 *United States Law Week* 4917 (1983) and 673 F. 2d 457–460 (1982).

35. 51 *United States Law Week* 4927 (1983). White also notes that "all of these carefully defined exceptions to the presentment and bicameralism strictures do not involve actions of Congress pursuant to a duly-enacted statute," Ibid, 4926. See also *Atkins v. United States*, 556 F. 2d 1068 (Ct.Cl., 1977).

36. Hearings, *Supra* note 19, testimony of Eugene Gressman, 464–478.

37. *Atkins v. United States*, 556 F. 2d 1069 (Ct.Cl., 1977).

38. 51 *United States Law Week* 4925 (1983).

39. Ibid., 4928.

40. Ibid., 4920–23 and 4929–30.

41. Cooper and Cooper, *supra* note 8 at 468.

42. In *Sibbach v. Wilson*, 312 U.S. 1 (1941) the Supreme Court upheld a waiting period form of the veto over federal rules of civil procedure on grounds that determining such rules was a function of Congress over which it could reserve power. If the Court had taken a more procedural approach, however, it would have been difficult to argue that setting an effectuation date is separable from the act of legislating or lawmaking. In *Chadha* Chief Justice Burger

distinguished *Sibbach* because the statute only gave Congress power to review the rules before they became effective and required congressional action to take the form of regular legislation. 51 *United States Law Week* 4912 (1983).

43. Cooper and Cooper, *supra* note 8 at 469.

44. Congress's discretionary right of appropriations was established in the 1790s. George Galloway, *History of the House of Representatives* (New York: Thomas Y. Crowell, 1961), 193–194.

45. See 673 F. 2d 470–477 (1982). See also, for example, Civiletti, *supra* note 28 at 407–412; Dixon, *supra* note 33 at 440; 69 *American Bar Association Journal* 1259 (1983); and Carl McGowan, "Congress, Court, and Control of Delegated Power," 77 *Columbia Law Review* 1152 (1977).

46. Some opponents of the veto read recent decisions of the Court regarding Richard Nixon to mean that the test of whether executive functions have been infringed is whether congressional action "prevents the executive branch from accomplishing its constitutionally assigned functions." *Nixon v. Administration of General Services*, 433 U.S. 425, 433 (1977). They then argue that because congressional forms of the veto involve delay, undermine notice and comment procedures, etc., they disrupt executive functions and violate Article II. See 69 *American Bar Association Journal* 1258–59 (1983). This, however, is simply to read implied executive power into the Constitution despite the steel seizure case. *Youngstown Sheet and Tube v. Sawyer*, 343 U.S. 579 (1952). The executive branch, apart from express powers granted to the president, has no constitutionally assigned functions other than to execute the laws Congress has written within the terms specified. 51 *United States Law Week* 4929 (1983). Indeed, because all forms of oversight "interfere" with execution, the argument that equates "disruption" with infringement provides a rationale for undermining congressional review in general. See Cooper and Cooper, *supra* note 8 at 488–489.

47. See Judge Wilkey's opinion in *FERC*, 673 F. 2d 476 (1982).

48. In addition to arguing that congressional forms of the veto infringe executive prerogatives under Article II, critics also argue that the veto allows congressmen to assume executive office in violation of Section 6 of Article I. See Dixon, *supra* note 33 at 441 and Martin, *supra* note 33 at 299. This argument takes many forms, but in all its forms boils down to the claim that to allow congressmen to make binding decisions regarding the implementation of delegated authority outside the lawmaking process transforms them into "administrators." Once again this is to assume what needs to be shown, however: that decisions necessarily become executive once delegated and thus that Congress cannot impose the veto as a condition in the original enabling act. See also Cooper and Cooper, *supra* note 8 at 499–501.

49. Some critics also contend that congressional forms of the veto infringe on judicial duties and prerogatives under Article III. The premises are procedural: that Congress through the veto interprets the law and that this usurps judicial functions. See Civiletti, *supra* note 28 at 412; *Brief of American Bar Association as Amicus Curiae in Immigration and Naturalization Service v. Chadha*, Supreme Court of the United States, October Term, 1981, p. 12; and *Consumer Energy Council of America v. Federal Energy Regulatory Commission*, 673 F. 2d 477 (1982).

Once again, however, the argument rests on the presumption that the veto cannot validly be stipulated as a precedent condition. In addition, it may be asked how the same veto decision can simultaneously invade executive and judicial functions. In *Chadha* Justice Powell rules against the veto on grounds that in deciding on the deportation of specific individuals Congress assumed a judicial function. Justice White's answer is powerful, but in any event this type of objection does not apply to any other instance of veto usage. 51 *United States Law Week* 4918–20 and 4930 (1983).

50. See Geoffrey Stewart, "Constitutionality of the Legislative Veto," 13 *Harvard Journal on Legislation* 613–615 (1976).

51. See, for example, Arthur Miller and George Knapp, "The Congressional Veto: Preserving the Constitutional Framework," 52 *Indiana Law Journal* 367 (1977) and Charles Black, "Some Thoughts on the Veto," 40 *Law and Contemporary Problems* 87 (1977).

52. See, for example, Joseph Harris, *Congressional Control of Administration* (Washington, D.C.: The Brookings Institution, 1964), 204–248.

53. See *Bar Association Journal, supra* note 46 at 1258–1259.

54. See Dixon, *supra* note 33 at 445.

55. See, for example, Harold Bruff and Ernest Gellhorn, "Congressional Control of Administrative Regulation: A Study of Legislative Vetoes," 90 *Harvard Law Review* 1369 (1977); John Bolton, *The Legislative Veto: Unseparating the Powers* (Washington, D.C.: American Enterprise Institute, 1977); Robert Gilmour, "The Congressional Veto: Shifting the Balance of Administrative Control," 2 *Journal of Policy Analysis and Management* 13 (1982); and Craig, *supra* note 1 at 123–138.

56. See *Bar Association Brief, supra* note 49 at 9–15 and *Bar Association Journal, supra* note 46 at 1258–1259.

57. Bruff and Gellhorn, *supra* note 55 and Craig, *supra* note 1.

58. See *Bar Association Journal, supra* note 46 at 1261, Bruff and Gellhorn, *supra* note 55 at 1420–1423; and Robert Gilmour, "Administrative Consequences of the Congressional Veto," Unpublished Paper, University of Connecticut, 1981.

59. See Craig, *supra* note 1 at 45–62. In addition, see Bolton, *supra* note 55 at 42.

60. See Arthur Maass, *supra* note 1 at 201–202. In addition, see Glen Robinson, "The FCC: An Essay on Regulatory Watchdogs," 69 *Virginia Law Review* 189–193 and 197–203 (1978) and "The Federal Communications Commission," in Glen Robinson, ed., *Communications for Tomorrow: Policy Perspectives for the 1980s* (New York: Praeger Publishers, 1978), 356–358 and 374–377.

61. See William West and Joseph Cooper, "The Congressional Veto and Administrative Rulemaking," 98 *Political Science Quarterly* 291–298 (1983). In addition, see Robinson cites, *supra* note 60; U.S. Senate. Committee on Governmental Affairs. "Public Participation in Regulatory Agency Proceedings," *Study on Federal Regulation* (Sen. Doc. 95–71, vol. III). Washington, D.C.: USGPO, 1977; U.S. House. Committee on the Judiciary. Subcommittee on Administrative Law. *Public Participation in Agency Proceedings* Hearings, 95 Cong., 1st sess. Washington, D.C.: USGPO, 1977.

62. West and Cooper, *supra* note 61 at 294.

63. Ibid., 294–298.

64. Cooper and Hurley, *supra* note 4 at 14–23.

65. See, for example, Michael Kirst, *Government Without Passing Laws* (Chapel Hill, N.C.: University of North Carolina, 1969) and Louis Fisher, "Congress and the President in the Administrative Process," in Hugh Heclo and Lester Salaman, eds., *The Illusion of Presidential Government* (Boulder, Colo.: Westview Press, 1981), 21–41. In addition, see Bruff and Gellhorn, *supra* note 55 at 1389 and Ernest Gellhorn, "The Role of Congress," in Robinson, *Communications, supra* note 60 at 445–460.

66. See, for example, Craig, *supra* note 1 at 146 and cites in notes 67–70 *infra*.

67. See, for example, Glen Robinson, Ernest Gellhorn, and Harold Bruff, *The Administrative Process* (St. Paul, Minn.: West Publishing Co., 1980), 80 and Bolton, *supra* note 55 at 15–24.

68. *Bar Association Journal, supra* note 46 at 1261–1262 and Bruff and Gellhorn, *supra* note 55 at 1437–1440.

69. Gellhorn, *supra* note 65.

70. Antonin Scalia, "The Legislative Veto: A False Remedy for System Overload," 3 *Regulation* 19 (1979).

71. See Gellhorn, *supra* note 65; Scalia, *supra* note 70; and Harold Bruff, "Presidential Power and Administrative Rulemaking," 88 *Yale Law Journal* 456–459 (1979).

72. See Maass, *supra* note 1 at 119–216. In addition, see Allen Schick, "Congress and the 'Details' of Administration," 36 *Public Administrative Review* 516 (1976) and "Politics through Law: Congressional Limitations on Executive Discretion," in Anthony King, ed., *Both Ends of the Avenue: The Presidency, the Executive Branch, and Congress in the 1980s* (Washington, D.C.: American Enterprise Institute, 1983), 170–184.

73. See Cooper and Hurley, *supra* note 4 at 14–18. In addition, see Schick cites, *supra* note 72 and Cooper and Cooper, *supra* note 8 at 508–512.

74. Craig, *supra* note 1 at 22–25.

75. See Norman Ornstein et al., *Vital Statistics on Congress, 1982* (Washington, D.C.: American Enterprise Institute, 1982), 137 (Statute pages) and U.S. Senate. Committee on the Judiciary. Subcommittee on Administrative Practice and Procedure. *Administrative Procedure Act Amendment of 1978* Hearings, 95th Cong. 2d sess. p. 1033 (register pages). Washington, D.C.: USGPO, 19.

76. Ronald J. Penoyer, *Directory of Federal Regulatory Agencies* (St. Louis, Mo.: Center for the Study of American Business, 1981), 13 and 93–121.

77. See cites in note 71 *supra*.

78. See Ornstein, *supra* note 75 at 137 and 139.

79. See Joseph Cooper, "Schauffler and the Veto," 8 *Public Policy* 328 (1958). In addition, see Schick, *supra* note 72.

80. For comments on all three constraints and examples see Sundquist, *supra* note 1 and Maass, *supra* note 1.

81. See I. M. Destler, "Dateline Washington: Life After the Veto," 52 *Foreign Policy* 181 (1983) and James Sundquist, "The Legislative Veto: A Bounced Check," 2 *The Brookings Review* no. 1 (Fall 1983) 13–16.

82. See, for example, Scalia, *supra* note 70 at 25.

83. Gellhorn, *supra* note 65 at 459.

84. Ibid., 445–459. In addition, see Scalia, *supra* note 70. John Stuart Mill's famous comment on the proper mode of operation of a legislature can be found in John S. Mill, *On Representative Government* (New York: Macmillan, 1947), Ch. 5. It may also be noted that Woodrow Wilson's critique shares the same presumptions. The irony is that the book has become a classic for its insightful description of operations that Wilson himself so vehemently disapproved on the basis of his preference for the English model. See Woodrow Wilson, *Congressional Government* (Boston: Houghton-Mifflin, 1884).

85. This, indeed, was one of the prime reasons for the invention of the negative two-House form of the veto mechanism. See John Millett and Lindsay Rogers, "The Legislative Veto and the Reorganization Act of 1939," 1 *Public Administration Review* 176 (1941).

86. See cites in note 4 *supra*.

87. Blends of affirmative and negative joint resolutions have been proposed to control arms sales and rulemaking. See H.R.3939 and S.1050, 98th Cong. In addition, a provision blending these forms has been enacted with respect to nuclear agreements. 99 *Stat.* 160.

88. Cooper and Hurley, *supra* note 4 at 9.

89. See, for example, Peter L. Strauss, "Is there A Baby In The Bathwater? A Comment On The Supreme Court's Legislative Veto Decision," 1983 *Duke Law Journal* 789–819 (1983) and Lawrence H. Trike, "The Legislative Veto Decision: A Law By Any Other Name?", 21 *Harvard Journal On Legislation* 1–27 (1984).

90. Cooper and Cooper, *supra* note 8 at 469.

91. See 98 *Stat.* 3192, 99 *Stat.* 102, and 99 *Stat.* 140. In addition, though the issue of severability is complex, in some areas at least the Department of Justice has held that the advance notification features of congressional forms remain in effect. In these instances the effect of the *Chadha* decision is to transform congressional forms into waiting period forms, and Congress has used such leverage with respect to arms sales to block major weapons deals with Arab nations in 1984, 1985, and 1986. See *Congressional Quarterly Weekly Report*, March 17, 1984, p. 612, November 16, 1985, p. 2387, and February 1, 1986, p. 186.

92. See 98 *Stat.* 1916, 98 *Stat.* 1935–37, and 99 *Stat.* 135.

93. See S.1078, 99th Congress. In addition, in several dozen instances since the *Chadha* decision Congress has subjected certain, specified uses of appropriated funds to the approval of the Appropriations Committees. Such vetoes are highly suspect in terms of the logic of *Chadha* because the control is post hoc and vested in committees. Congress, however, may feel that executive officials will not challenge the Appropriations Committees on spending issues these committees have traditionally controlled. See Louis Fisher, *Legislative Vetoes Enacted*

After Chadha (Washington, D.C.: Congressional Research Service, March 25, 1985).

94. For the first two examples cited in this paragraph see 98 *Stat.* 3014 and 99 *Stat.* 160. For the last see S.J. Res. 238, 99th Congress.

Commentary: On the Congressional Veto

Paul Findley

The 1983 *Chadha* decision of the Supreme Court is widely accepted as striking down hundreds of congressional veto provisions in public law. In my view, it is a setback to the orderly functioning of government. From the standpoint of the broad public interest, the veto tradition made sense. It facilitated a comfortable and productive relationship between Congress and the president and simplified the handling of issues between the two branches. Rarely invoked, the veto was not an encumbrance on the president. Nor did it add new burdens to the legislative process. It permitted the president to proceed with decisions but provided him with a strong incentive to keep closely in mind the sentiments of the legislature. Although the wisdom—or unwisdom—of the veto tradition may be debated, few dispute the effect of the Court's ruling. The decision is accepted as invalidating the veto in all domestic and most foreign policy matters. The notable exception relates, or should relate, to war powers.

The congressional veto is a product of modern times. Since the Great Depression, the authority of the federal government has been expanded enormously. It has gained new power to tax and spend. It has established an intrusion into many realms that previously had been regarded as private. Most of the new authority, of course, resides in the president, the nation's chief magistrate. With each new session of Congress, the presidency becomes an instrument of new power. During this same period, almost nothing was done to balance the new power with brakes— new devices of restraint. The only notable examples were the ratification of the constitutional amendment that prohibits the election of a person to more than two consecutive terms in the presidency and the introduction of the legislative veto. An engineer, impressed with the sound principle of braking power, would be appalled to note that so little is done to establish new braking power as the presidential engine gains new horsepower.

Asked to convey broad authority to the president in a bewildering array of governmental activities, Congress reserved the right to rescind

Paul Findley represented the twentieth district of Illinois for the Republican Party in the U.S. House of Representatives from 1961 to 1982. During his congressional career, he focused on agricultural legislation, especially its international aspects, and on opening dialogue internationally as a means of resolving disputes. He has written *They Dare to Speak Out: People and Institutions Confront Israel's Lobby* (Westport, Conn.: Lawrence Hill, 1985) on the impact of the Arab-Israeli dispute on U.S. institutions.

bits and pieces of this authority through the veto process. This reservation took various forms. The Legislation Reorganization Act let the president undertake sweeping changes in bureaucratic structure without the tedious and contentious process of legislation. Congress went along because the veto provision let the Congress pass judgment on each presidential recommendation.

With an eye to home-district interests, Congress let the president establish certain projects, like those relating to water conservation, subject to the possible veto by a congressional committee. Usually the veto option was reserved not just to a committee or combination of committees or to a single chamber, but to the entire Congress. Both Houses would have to agree before a presidential decision could be rejected. For example, Congress gave the president the authority to sell military equipment to foreign countries but reserved the right of veto within a stated period after it received notification of the proposed sale. Sometimes, public law provided that a negative resolution of either the House or the Senate would suffice to veto a scheduled presidential decision.

The veto was invoked hardly at all. Of the hundreds of statutory provisions that established authority for congressional veto and the thousands of instances in which presidents have exercised authority subject to such veto, I can recall only two occasions on which the veto was actually used—one involving the regulation of funeral directors and the other, the sale of used cars. In fact, a legislative veto was rarely even attempted. This inactivity suggests that the veto provisions have inspired the president and his staff to consult closely with congressional leaders as statutory authority was carried out. Resolutions to exercise a veto seldom reached the floor of either the House or the Senate. When they did, a storm sometimes occurred but the president usually weathered it. The president was never rebuffed by a congressional veto relating to foreign policy. The two most notable attempts were the resolutions to stop the proposed sale to Saudi Arabia of fighter aircraft in 1978 and of airborne warning and control systems (AWACS) in 1981. On both occasions, the president prevailed when the Senate rejected the veto motion by small margins.

The most fundamental congressional veto provision is included in the War Powers Resolution, which was a product of the Vietnam War experience. It differs from other veto provisions in several important respects. First, it deals with the most awesome of governmental powers, the power to authorize war. Second, it stands on its own. It is not a provision of a statute conveying certain new authority to the president. Rather, it fills a void in the statutory foundation of war powers. Until the War Powers Resolution became law, Congress had not attempted to define its relationship to undeclared wars.

The War Powers Resolution arose from the frustrations felt by those who served in Congress during that agonizing period, who recognized the tragedy of the enormous human and material investment being made by the United States in the Vietnam struggle, and who sought a mechanism that might reduce the likelihood of such undeclared military involvement in the future.

The resolution established for the first time a statutory relationship between the president and Congress in the conduct of war powers. Of course, it did not alter the constitutional relationship between the two branches of government—indeed it specifically denied such intent—but rather established procedures through which the two branches would work together in meeting security challenges in future years.

The congressional veto over war powers is worthless in the absence of vigilance and courage on the part of congressional leaders. If they fail to exhibit vigilance and courage, the War Powers Resolution may even be viewed by the president as a 90-day blank check for adventurism. On the other hand, the resolution provides congressional leaders with an explicit procedure through which they can examine the bases for presidential decisions in a timely fashion, and, if deemed advisable, demand that certain military operations cease.

I use the word demand, because a willful president can continue military operations notwithstanding a congressional decision to the contrary. As commander in chief of the armed forces, the president can, as a practical matter, continue a military operation after the expiration of the 90-day period specified in the resolution or, in defiance of a concurrent resolution demanding that he withdraw forces. In those circumstances, a president could use the vast resources of the executive branch to mobilize public opinion to his side. Given the usual lethargy of Congress, the tendency of representatives to shun prickly nettles, and the normal impulse of the nation to rally behind the commander in chief of forces under hostile fire, a strong-willed president could readily nullify the resolution. He could proceed to defy Congress and the requirements of the resolution, confident that the Supreme Court would be unlikely to intervene, as historically it has had little to say when Congress and the president have been at odds over war powers. The limp manner in which Congress reacted to the question of U.S. Marines in Lebanon in 1983 gives no encouragement that future Congresses will use the resolution with wisdom.

Nevertheless, the War Powers Resolution is a valuable instrument of public policy, and, in my view, its most important provision is the section that authorizes Congress, by concurrent resolution, to order the withdrawal of military forces from hostile action. Some may argue that this is invalidated by the *Chadha* case. Others may argue, as they did during the debate of the War Powers Resolution, that it is an unconstitutional interference in the exercise of presidential power. But, in my view, the Supreme Court *Chadha* decision did not reach the question of congressional veto in the War Powers Resolution. The Court made no mention of war powers, and, if history is a guide, it will remain silent if a future Congress should get up enough spirit to enact a concurrent resolution demanding that the president pull back forces from foreign hostilities.

Meanwhile, it would be helpful if Congress, by concurrent resolution or the simple statement of bicameral leadership, would declare the War Powers Resolution unaffected by the *Chadha* decision. Otherwise, an aggressive president might choose to ignore the congressional veto by concurrent resolution in the war powers legislation, a provision of immense importance in restraining the presidency.

3

The Many Faces
of Congressional Budgeting

Allen Schick

Budgeting has been a demanding business on Capitol Hill and in the White House in recent years.[1] Approximately 70 percent of the Senate's roll call votes in 1981 and 50 percent of the House's pertained to the federal budget.[2] In 1982, Congress adopted only one budget resolution (rather than the two called for in the Congressional Budget Act), and it failed to act on a number of the regular appropriation bills. Hence, budgetary business dropped to 60 percent of the Senate's and 40 percent of the House's roll calls. Nevertheless, budgeting was the largest component of congressional activity.

The budget also claims a great deal of presidential attention. In addition to the budget submitted early in each congressional session, the president is required to issue updated estimates in the spring and summer. He also must attend to budget issues when economic conditions shift and when congressional action varies from his recommended course. In 1981, for example, shortly after celebrating congressional approval of his tax and spending proposals, President Reagan was compelled by fresh economic and budget estimates to reopen budget issues that had been recently settled.

Allen Schick is a professor of public policy in the School of Public Affairs at the University of Maryland. He also serves as an adjunct scholar at the American Enterprise Institute and as a consultant to the Congressional Research Service. He is currently directing a study, under the auspices of the Organization for Economic Cooperation and Development, on the capacity of industrialized democracies to adapt their budget practices to economic and political stress. Schick is the author of various books and articles on budgeting and government, including *Congress and Money: Budgeting, Spending, and Taxing* (Washington, D.C.: The Urban Institute, 1980).

One reason for the heavy workload is that the budget requires repeated legislative attention. The defense budget is a case in point. In 1982, Congress allotted $254 billion in new budget authority to national defense in its fiscal 1983 budget resolution. It then approved a $178 billion defense authorization bill for the fiscal year. Finally, it enacted—as a part of a continuing resolution—a $232 billion defense appropriation for fiscal year 1983. The differences in the various figures were almost entirely due to differences in the scope of the three measures.[3] In acting on these measures, Congress repeatedly had to consider the same issues: the amount of real growth, the extent to which it should cut the president's defense budget, and the cost and value of controversial weapons, among others. The MX missile, for example, was a prominent concern in the debate on the budget resolution. It also was subject to floor amendments to delete or curtail expenditures when the House and Senate acted on the appropriation and authorization bills.[4]

The White House and executive agencies must monitor each stage of legislative budgeting. They cannot withdraw from the legislative process once the budget resolution is adopted, nor can they assume that the decisions made in authorizing legislation will be upheld when the appropriation bill is considered. Not only do executive officials have to appear at numerous hearings by the various committees involved in congressional budgeting, they also must operate behind the scenes to influence legislative outcomes.

Hardly anyone in government is satisfied with an arrangement that requires triple consideration of the same issues. Ronald Reagan has attacked Congress's "Mickey Mouse" budget procedures, and Caspar Weinberger has complained about the effects on the Pentagon of continuing resolutions and duplicative legislative processes.[5] Members of Congress also feel frustrated by the current state of affairs. Congress seems to be working harder but accomplishing less as its machinery is overloaded by a multiplicity of budget processes.[6] As the fiscal 1983 defense budget shows, issues do not get settled once and for all. The same defense issues that disturbed Congress in 1982 and 1981 were debated and voted on in 1981 and in previous years. Nowadays, a budget decision, whether in the executive or the legislative arena, often is regarded as just one phase in a seemingly endless round of budget battles. A participant who loses at one stage can reopen the issue at the next, as MX opponents did in 1981 and 1983. A participant who wins cannot be sure of what has been won, as Ronald Reagan has learned during his White House years. Some of the domestic budget cuts he obtained in 1981 were rolled back in subsequent years when Congress acted on authorizations and appropriations.

The recurring budget battles take a tremendous toll in political trust and good will. There have been repeated confrontations between the Reagan White House and Congress on budget matters and frequent presidential appeals for public support. Budget issues have set the Budget Committees against the authorizing and appropriating committees—and sometimes the latter sets of committees against one another as well—and there have been numerous flareups concerning committee jurisdictions, legislative procedure, spending policy, and the estimates and assumptions used for costing out legislation. The multiplicity of budget actions has spurred many members to behave inconsistently, voting to lower taxes and the deficit when considering budget resolutions, but to raise expenditures when particular programs are being decided.[7]

Budget considerations have become so prominent that, in many instances, they have crowded out other legislative interests and impelled Congress to define issues solely in financial terms. In defense, there has been more legislative debate about the rate of real growth than about the state of readiness; in food stamps, more has been heard about limiting expenditures than about the nutritional needs of the poor; in social security, the argument has raged more over the dollar savings needed to maintain solvency than about the economic condition of retired workers; and in education and many other grant programs, Congress has fought over the flow of dollars to states and communities, not over program merits.

Arguably, the budget's inflated status has been due more to economic and political conditions than to the manner in which budget decisions have been made. Because of protracted recession in the early 1980s, there was pressure to consider legislation in terms of its cost and budgetary effects. If vigorous economic growth were to persist, Congress would probably give greater emphasis to program issues than it has in recent years. The "fiscalization" of legislative debate also has been spurred by President Reagan's determination to curtail the size of the national government and to revamp budget priorities. If the president's budget objectives were incremental, both the executive and legislative branches could lessen their attention to the budget.[8]

It cannot be denied, however, that budget procedures have contributed to the problem. Congress has three distinct processes for making program and financial decisions, each with its own way of measuring and reporting the financial aspects of legislative actions.[9] Members of Congress are deluged by budgetary data from executive agencies and their own staffs, but many feel frustrated by the inadequacy of the information at hand.

This chapter begins with a brief survey of how the various congressional budget processes have evolved over the years. It then examines how the authorization, appropriation, and budget processes relate to one another. The chapter concludes with an assessment of the implications of congressional practice for both the legislative and executive branches and a discussion of proposals for improving congressional budget processes.

Historical Development
of the Congressional Budget Process

The triplication of congressional budget processes offers a tempting target for reformers who seek to simplify budgeting. After all, why should Congress require three separate processes when the executive branch can make do with one? But before reformers excise one or more of Congress's processes they should be aware of why the legislative branch has felt a need for separate authorizations, appropriations, and budget procedures. The distinction between legislation—the term used during most of U.S. history for what is now commonly referred to as authorization—and appropriations is as old as the U.S. Congress. Budgeting, however, is of recent origin; it was introduced by the Congressional Budget Act of 1974.

The First Congress that met in 1789 clearly understood that matters included in legislation were not suited for appropriations. Thus, it first enacted legislation establishing the Department of War and specifying its principal offices and duties; it then passed a separate measure making an initial appropriation to the department.[10] Legislation dealt with substantive matters such as determining, or limiting, the uses of public funds and authorizing government officials and agencies to conduct certain activities. Appropriations supplied the funds to carry out these activities; they did not contain any substantive provisions, nor did they finance activities that were not previously authorized in legislation. When Congress wanted to limit the authority of agencies or officials, it did so in legislation; when it wanted to provide funds, it did so in appropriations. Appropriations did not make policy, and legislation did not mention money. Legislation usually was permanent; appropriations usually were for a single fiscal year.

There is reason to believe that the separation between legislation and appropriations predated the establishment of Congress and was so well recognized in the first years of U.S. history that there were few breaches of it.[11] Members of Congress understood that disputes over substantive matters included in appropriations might delay the supply of funds needed for the continuation of government. Moreover, the inclusion of substantive provisions in appropriations might force the enactment of matters that would not be enacted into law if they were considered in separate legislation. Over time, the distinction between legislation and appropriations acquired an additional purpose: the distinction dispersed congressional power broadly among committees and members and inhibited those who controlled the purse strings from extending their control to legislation as well.

There were, and continue to be, two major exceptions to the division between legislation and appropriations. First, Congress could legislate in a special appropriation bill—a bill in which the appropriation was for a single object, in contrast to a general appropriation bill for one or more government agencies. The reason for this exception was that delay in the enactment of special appropriations would not impede the flow of funds to federal agencies. The second exception was for limitations—provisions in appropriations bills barring the use of funds for particular purposes. The concept of limitations was based on the principle that when it makes appropriations, Congress could deny funds for certain purposes or place conditions on the grant of money.

Although riders—legislative provisions in appropriation bills—were infrequent during the early Congresses, they became more common and troublesome in the 1820s and 1830s. As a result, the House and Senate no longer could rely on the unwritten understandings concerning the two measures. In 1837 the House adopted a rule that has been its basic policy on the subject for almost 150 years; "No appropriation shall be reported in such general appropriation bill, or be in order as an amendment thereto, for an expenditure not previously authorized by law."[12] This rule against unauthorized appropriations did not break new ground in House procedure; it merely reflected the prevailing understanding that, despite numerous violations, legislation should be separate from appropriations. The basic Senate rule was adopted in 1850 and has been amended a number of times since then: "No amendment proposing an additional appropriation shall be received to any general appropriation bill. . . ."[13]

The adoption of these rules by the House and Senate did not end unauthorized appropriations or legislation in appropriation bills. As masters of their own rules, the House and Senate could ignore the distinction when it suited them. But the rules were powerfully reinforced during the first century of congressional operation by assigning the two types of measures to different sets of congressional committees. Legislation was in the jurisdiction of the various legislative committees; the general appropriation bills were handled by the House Ways and Means Committee and the Senate Finance Committee before the Civil War and by newly established House and Senate Appropriations Committees after the war.

The two types of committees perceived the activities and expenditures of the government differently. The main interest of the legislative committees was the work of federal agencies; the main concern of the Appropriations Committees was the financial condition of the government. The legislative committees tended to favor the expansion of government activities; the Appropriations Committees favored expenditure reductions. For more than 100 years, these sets of committees have competed for congressional power. When Congress has been in an expansionary mood, it has strengthened its legislative committees; when it has sought contraction, it has tilted in favor of the Appropriations Committees.

The first such tilt occurred in the 1870s, when an economy-minded House adopted the Holman Rule that permitted the Appropriations Committee to report legislation to "retrench expenditures."[14] In the 1880s, however, the pendulum swung in the other direction, and the House, followed by the Senate in the next decade, assigned jurisdiction over half of the appropriation bills to legislative committees, including those for the army and navy. This jurisdictional shift weakened the division between legislation and appropriations and led to the increased insertion of substantive provisions into the latter. Congressional sentiment shifted again after World War I in response to the steep rise in federal spending and deficits during wartime, and Congress returned jurisdiction over all appropriation bills to the Appropriations Committees.

The rules adopted by the House in 1920 and the Senate in 1922 have not been changed significantly during the past 60 years.[15] Yet as the national government was enlarged, the structure and content of legislation and appropriations was altered. Virtually unused before the 1920s, the phrase "authorized to be appropriated" appeared in legislation. This language led to the use of the term authorization for what was previously termed legislation.[16] Another development that can be traced to the enlargement of government was the formulation of broad, programmatic legislation that grouped related activities or concerns into a single measure. There was a parallel shift from line item to lump sum appropriations. As the federal government expanded, the number of appropriation accounts declined.[17]

The most far-reaching development was the increased use of annual and multiyear authorizations, which under the rules of the House and Senate have to be renewed by Congress for the affected program to be eligible for continued funding.[18] Prior to the 1950s, the entire federal government operated under permanent authorizations, which meant that most agencies had to go through only the annual appropriations process. Since then, however, Congress has converted some major programs and agencies and intelligence activities—such as the Justice and State Departments—to temporary authorizations, and Congress has authorized most new programs on a temporary basis, especially grants to state and local governments. The trend to temporary authorization of defense programs began in 1959 when Congress—reacting to Sputnik and the missile gap—mandated annual authorization for the procurement of aircraft, missiles, and naval vessels. Annual authorizations were extended 10 times during the next two decades, so that virtually the entire Defense Department budget, except for military retirement pay, now is subject to annual authorization.[19]

Temporary, and especially annual, authorizations significantly affect the relationship between legislation and appropriations. Unlike permanent authorizations, which are indefinite as to amount and authorize "such sums as may be necessary," temporary authorizations specify an amount for each fiscal year covered by the legislation. In the case of annual authorizations, Congress first authorizes an amount for the next fiscal year, and, in the same session, also appropriates funds for the next fiscal year. Before the appropriation is considered, Congress has gone on record concerning the program's financial needs. Often the appropriation is close to the authorized amount.[20]

Annual authorizations, such as for defense, tend to be fiscal rather than programmatic legislation. Congressional debate is oriented to financial considerations—the amount to be spent, how much should the president's budget request be increased or decreased, the items to be funded, and so on. The marginal changes made in the subsequent appropriation can have important implications, but the overall financial plan set forth in the authorizing legislation usually survives intact.

The Working of the Congressional Budget Process

Appropriations and authorizations are fragmented into numerous measures. Each year there are 13 regular appropriation bills, a number of supplemental appropriations, and dozens of authorizations. In addition, close to half of the federal budget is funded in permanent appropriations that do not occasion any periodic action by Congress. In the early 1970s, this fragmentation was alleged to have a number of serious defects:

- Congress did not act on the budget as a whole or vote on total revenues, expenditures and deficit or surplus;
- It did not set fiscal priorities by weighing the various claims on the budget against one another or by assessing the impact of its budget actions on the economy;
- It had weak control over federal spending.[21]

Congress responded to these perceived shortcomings by establishing its own budget process. As spelled out in the Congressional Budget Act of 1974, Congress is supposed to adopt two concurrent resolutions on the budget each year.[22] These budget resolutions set forth various fiscal aggregates—total revenues, new budget authority, outlays, surplus or deficit, and public debt—and allocate the outlays and budget authority among 21 budget functions—national defense, agriculture, income security, among others.[23] Over the past decade, Congress has expanded the budget process by adding three-year budget targets and a credit budget and by adopting a reconciliation procedure that instructs committees to report legislation, thus conforming existing law to its budget decisions.

Congress did not discard or significantly alter its existing appropriations and authorizations processes in establishing its budget process. Because the budget resolutions do not have legal effect, Congress cannot authorize programs or provide funds in them. The budget process coexists with the two older processes and is intended to provide the framework within which particular program and spending decisions continue to be made. The aggregates and functions in budget resolutions are linked to specific appropriations and authorizations through various forms of information, principally crosswalks, cost estimates, five-year projections, and scorekeeping reports.[24] When it considers an authorization or appropriation bill, Congress is informed of the estimated budgetary impacts of the measure. Congress is then free to act in a manner it deems appropriate and often has no difficulty providing more funds than were intended when the budget resolution was adopted.[25]

The Ways and Means
of Budgetary Triplication

Authorizations, appropriations, and budget resolutions have distinct niches on Capitol Hill and are cordoned off from one another by the rules of the House and Senate. According to the rules, Congress would formulate substantive legislation in authorizations; it would not finance programs in them. It would finance authorized programs in appropriations that would not contain any legislation. Congress would set fiscal policy and broad budgetary priorities in budget resolutions that would not deal with specific programs.

If the rules meant what they say, there should be unbridgeable differences among these processes: what Congress does in one, it would not be able to do in the others. This tripartite division of congressional labor has not operated as intended, however. As noted at the outset, the boundaries separating the three processes are not so clearly marked as to prevent the same issues from arising again and again. As a result, the processes often are redundant rather than differentiated. At the root of the problem is the inability or unwillingness of Congress to distinguish clearly the processes from one another. Congress makes the rules but it also makes exceptions to, or ignores, the rules. It is not uncommon for Congress to legislate in appropriation bills, appropriate in authorizing legislation, and decide particular program issues when formulating budget resolutions.

There have been times in Congress's history when the boundaries between the various processes have been more strictly enforced than they have been in recent years. The contemporary fragmentation of Congress, about which much has been written in recent years, has encouraged some committees to stretch their jurisdictional reach and has made it easier for members to offer floor amendments to any vehicle available for their purposes.[26] Congress cannot maintain discipline in its budgetary processes when it is permissive about so many other key facets of its operations.

Program Assumptions in Budget Resolutions

The budget resolutions adopted by Congress do not earmark funds to particular programs. They distribute the budget authority and outlays among a small number of functions and leave program decisions to the authorizing and appropriating processes. The $268.6 billion in new budget authority for national defense in the 1983 resolution was allocated in a single line that did not mention the forces to be financed by that level of expenditure.

In fact, however, a budget resolution often influences and sometimes makes program decisions. A resolution is just the tip of the budgetary iceberg. Subsumed beneath the published aggregates and functional allocations is a mass of program and financial detail. This detail sometimes surfaces in the form of assumptions, but often it is stored in the data banks of the Congressional Budget Office (CBO) or in private understandings among the various participants in the budget process.

To make, interpret, or enforce a budget resolution requires that there be an understanding as to how the figures in it were derived, the program and spending policies in it anticipated, and some sense of how major issues and conflicts over money are to be resolved. When the president submits his budget, members and committees of Congress focus on how much has been recommended for the programs in which they are interested. When the Budget Committees formulate a budget resolution, much of the legislative debate relates to its implications for particular programs and activities. Members and committees, as well as the legions of "outsiders" who monitor congressional actions, want to know whether the amount allocated for a function would allow particular programs to grow or compel cutbacks in operations. They want to know how the amounts assumed for particular programs compare to the previous year's spending, to the president's request, and to the workload and inflation projections for the next fiscal year.

These concerns lead inexorably to a consideration of the amounts assumed for the many programs that comprise the federal budget. A veteran congressional budget expert explained why those who put together budget resolutions must be knowledgeable about funding for particular programs:

> . . . there may be no way that you can ensure that a budget process can be at the macro level . . . one of the prices you pay for a budget process may be the fact that you have to focus on line items, basically on the theory that a budget is made up of parts and the parts have to be identified. . . . It doesn't make sense to have a budget unless you understand what the parts are.[27]

The Budget Committees are in a quandary in dealing with program assumptions. If they limit their decisions to the aggregates and functions, they might have difficulty defending or enforcing their resolutions; if they reveal their program assumptions, they might offend the committees of jurisdiction. Since 1975, the Budget Committees have published only a small portion of the assumptions that comprise the budget. Nevertheless, the budget process impels participants to be explicit about many of the programs assumed in the resolutions. This tendency can be illustrated by tracing the various steps in the formulation and enforcement of a budget resolution.

The Baseline. The federal budget consists of more than 1,000 accounts and thousands of programs. At the start of the annual congressional budget cycle, the CBO projects the spending trend for each account and for major programs over a five-year period. This baseline assumes that existing policies will continue, but it adjusts spending levels for expected price and workload changes.

The baseline provides a common set of program assumptions and spending computations for the various participants in the congressional budget process. Spending reductions and increases proposed by the Budget Committees are calculated in terms of the baseline, which for budget accounts and programs are maintained in the CBO data banks. Some of the data also appears in such documents as the "views and estimates" reports and the markup documents used by the Budget Committees.[28]

It is not possible to interpret the figures in budget resolutions and reconciliation instructions without using the current policy baseline.

Inevitably, however, the baselines sensitize participants to the program implications of congressional budget decisions. As a consequence, a budget resolution effectively decides many program issues facing Congress, although it does not earmark funds to any programs.

The "Views and Estimates." Attention to program issues begins several months before adoption of the budget resolution, when House and Senate committees formulate their "views and estimates" reports. These reports are submitted to the Budget Committees by March 15 of each year. When the Congressional Budget Act of 1974 was framed, it was assumed that because the budget resolutions "would deal only with macroeconomic issues and broad functional priorities, the various committees would not find it necessary to undertake any detailed consideration of budget matters in preparing their views and recommendations."[29] In practice, however, many committees use these reports to go on record concerning the programs in their jurisdictions. They want to ensure that the budget resolution can accommodate their programs at preferred funding levels. Accordingly, they discuss program details in these reports. The views and estimates of House committees on the fiscal 1983 budget were so detailed that they filled two volumes totaling more than 1,400 pages.[30]

Committees differ greatly in their propensity to recommend specific funding levels for particular programs. The House Energy and Commerce Committee's report for fiscal 1983 contained more than 450 pages and provided baseline data for 163 programs. The House Armed Services Committee filed a three-page report that briefly addressed the overall national defense needs of the United States but refrained from making recommendations on specific programs. The House Appropriations Committee hedged its report with the warning that "much information remains to be developed before any recommendations can be made. Thus, it is not possible at this time to make specific recommendations. . . . The Committee on Appropriations, of course, will make its own specific recommendations to the House when it reports the various appropriations bills."[31] The Senate Appropriations Committee also reserved judgment on specific programs, noting that to make appropriation decisions, it "must examine the budget on an exacting, line-by-line basis, not merely in terms of functional aggregates."[32]

The process of preparing their views and estimates has made authorizing committees more aware than in the past of the budgetary status of their programs. Before the Congressional Budget Act of 1974, many of these committees did not know how much was appropriated or spent for their programs. Now, most have detailed comparisons of the authorized and appropriated amounts. This information has spurred some legislative committees to try to influence the amounts provided for their programs by putting "appropriations forcing" language into authorizing legislation.

Markup. The CBO baseline and the views and estimates reports give the Budget Committees a great deal of program detail that they aggregate into the functions that comprise the budget resolution. Budget Committee members usually know how the programs they are interested in are likely to be affected by the functional allocations, though (as noted earlier) the program assumptions are published only in piecemeal fashion. The House Budget Committee marks up its resolution on the basis of published *Recommendations*—by the chairman in some years and by the Democratic majority in others.

The recommendations are explicit about the assumed levels of funding for many major programs. For example, the fiscal 1984 recommendations for the Commerce and Housing Credit function assumed enactment of $760 billion in mortgage foreclosure relief, $179 million for the Small Business Administration guaranteed loan defaults, termination of the tandem mortgage purchase program of the Government National Mortgage Association, a $200 million increase for small business loans, $668 million for housing for the elderly and handicapped, and so on. Interestingly, no specific recommendations were made for the defense function; instead, the budget focused on the amount of growth to be allowed for national defense. The Senate Budget Committee uses the unpublished "Markup Book," which discusses program and spending options in the various functions and provides historical data on the major program categories in each function. It sometimes also uses a "Background Book" that provides additional details on individual budget proposals.

The detailed markup documents ensure that Budget Committee members do not engage in a pig-in-a-poke exercise when making highly aggregated decisions on the budget resolutions. They know how likely the programs they are concerned about are to be advanced or impeded by the functional allocations adopted in markup, and they make these allocations with particular programs in mind. In its markup of the fiscal 1983 resolution, the House Budget Committee added funds for the Coast Guard, AMTRAK, interstate highways, unemployment benefits, veterans pensions, and the space shuttle program. The Senate Budget Committee tries to avoid explicit line-item decisions in markup, but even as it votes on "big picture" functional allocations, members check the assumptions to ensure that their program interests are protected.

Many of the program decisions made during markup are identified in the reports accompanying the budget resolutions. The Senate Budget Committee's report of the fiscal 1984 resolution, for example, added $30 million in Medicaid money for Puerto Rico, assumed the termination of the Appalachian Regional Commission and the economic development program, and assumed that mass transit would be funded at levels authorized by recently enacted legislation and that a new conservation corps program would be launched. These were but a few of the programs for which assumptions made in markup were published in the committee report.

These program assumptions influence subsequent authorization and appropriation decisions. In 1980 Rep. James Jones (D-Okla.) supported a floor amendment to add $50 million to the appropriation for the Internal Revenue Service (IRS) on the ground that "this amendment simply carries out the mandate of the first budget resolution for fiscal year 1981." This argument provoked Appropriations Committee Chair Jamie Whitten to protest: "It is my understanding that the budget resolution merely sets targets by function and does not deal with line items. One reason we are in trouble with budget resolutions now is the effort on the part of some to provide for specificline items."[33] Despite protests from Whitten and others, the trend has been toward greater reliance on the assumptions to justify program decision. In 1983, the House Education and Labor Committee reported legislation that authorized funds for nine specific programs at "such funding levels as are assumed under the first budget resolution . . . for fiscal year 1984." This explicit citation of the budget resolution's assumptions appeared in the text of a bill reported by the Education and Labor Committee; it was not hidden in a committee report.[34]

Baseline computations, assumptions, and other line-item details surface whenever committees or members find it convenient to release these data. Participants who complain when the line items are used against them do not hesitate to go public with assumptions when it suits their purposes to do so. As a result, it has been impossible for Congress to confine discussion of the budget resolutions to aggregates and functions.

The Reconciliation Process. The assumptions underlying budget resolutions have been given augmented attention in recent years because of the manner in which Congress has used its reconciliation procedures. The designers of the Congressional Budget Act of 1974 contemplated that reconciliation would be used pursuant to adoption of the second budget resolution in the fall, if at all, after program and spending decisions for the next fiscal year already had been made by Congress. But when Congress started to apply the provisions of the act, it realized that the second resolution comes too late in the legislative session to influence budget outcomes. So instead, the Budget Committees began to enforce the decisions made in, and the assumptions underlying, the first resolution that is adopted prior to congressional action on appropriations and other spending legislation.

This development led, in 1980, to the attachment of reconciliation instructions to the first resolution. As used since then, reconciliation has been a process to conform existing laws—principally entitlements—to the levels set in the spring resolution. Committees recommend and Congress adopts omnibus reconciliation legislation that implements the instructions contained in this resolution.[35] The reconciliation instructions specify the dollar reductions that designated committees have to make, but they do not mention which programs are to be reduced or how the savings are to be realized. Nevertheless, the Budget Committees that formulate the instructions and the legislative committees that carry them out share understandings as to what the dollar amounts mean and the program changes that have to be made. In 1981, a year in which reconciliation was put to extraordinarily broad use, the Senate Budget Committee listed dozens of program changes that it assumed in the instructions, but it also noted that ". . . each committee that receives a reconciliation instruction is free to make the required savings in any manner it sees fit. The itemization considered by the Budget Committee does not have to be observed so long as each committee reports savings in an amount equal to the reconciliation instruction."[36]

The manner in which reconciliation was applied in 1981 generated a great amount of controversy on Capitol Hill. Of special concern was its application to conventional authorizations funded in annual appropriations. Since 1981, reconciliation generally has been limited to entitlement and revenue legislation, considerably narrowing its scope.[37]

Section 302 Crosswalks. Each budget resolution divides total budget authority and outlays among the various functional categories. Congress does not operate according to a functional structure, however; rather legislative jurisdiction is parceled out among House and Senate committees. Accordingly, section 302 of the budget act provides for the budget authority and outlays in each resolution to be allocated among House and Senate committees and for each committee to subdivide its share of the budget among its programs or subcommittees. To make these crosswalks, the Budget Committees must rely on the detailed assumptions and program data discussed earlier. The two Budget Committees differ in the detail in which their crosswalks are published. The Senate committee makes a single allocation to each committee, but distinguishes between "direct spending" and "appropriated entitlements." It provides no functional or program detail, although this is readily available to each committee receiving an allocation. The House committee distinguishes between "current level" and "discretionary action" and itemizes the amount allocated to each function.

Enforcing the Resolutions. The section 302 allocations and the program assumptions underlying them have become the principal means of

ensuring that legislation reported by congressional committees conforms
to the expectations of the budget resolution. Both Budget Committees
become involved in program and financial details by policing legislative
actions that affect the budget.

In the early years of the budget process, the Senate committee was
more vigorous than the House committee in enforcing the assumptions
of budget resolutions. In the 1980s, however, the House Budget Committee
has been the more active enforcer. Its main enforcement instruments
are "early warning reports" on appropriations, entitlements (legislation
establishing a legal right to payment from the government), and certain
authorizations scheduled for floor action. These reports, prepared by the
committee staff, are keyed to the amounts allocated in the section 302
crosswalks. In analyzing a measure's budget impact, the early warning
report "pays particular attention to programs over which a committee
has spending discretion."[38]

It should be clear that the Budget Committees are interested in more
than "big picture" aggregates and functions. They are interested in the
same program and financial details that concern the authorizing and
appropriating committees, which is the reason these committees feel
their jurisdictions are violated by the budget process. But it is important
to keep in mind that the Budget Committees encroach more by assuming
than by deciding. The powers to appropriate and to legislate still reside
in the committees that report these types of measures, but these powers
are exercised in the context of budget decisions. Congress is awash in
budgetary data, and debate on Capitol Hill often is so dominated by
budget matters that members of Congress conclude that there is more
to the budget process than the few pages of a budget resolution.

Legislating in Appropriations Bills

Although appropriations measures are not supposed to contain legislative provisions, there have been few periods in U.S. history during
which this congressional norm has been adhered to fully. The creators
of the House and Senate rules that bar legislation in appropriations
recognize that actual practice is otherwise. Clause 3 of House Rule XXI
requires reports on appropriation bills to "contain a concise statement
describing fully the effect of any provision . . . which directly or indirectly
changes the application of existing law."[39] Senate Rule XVI requires the
Appropriations Committee to identify each recommended appropriation
that does not "carry out the provisions of an existing law, a treaty
stipulation, or an act or resolution previously passed by the Senate
during that session."

Despite the rules, legislation can be included in appropriations if no
point of order is raised against it or if the matter is deemed to be a

limitation. The distinction between legislation and limitations has been the subject of countless parliamentary disputes; slight variations in wording can greatly affect the decision of an issue. As a rule, a provision is likely to be deemed legislation if it requires either an action or a determination by a government official; it is likely to be regarded as a limitation if its sole effect is to withhold funds from a particular object. Thus, an antiabortion rider that was contingent on a determination regarding the health of the mother was ruled to be legislation; an absolute ban on the use of funds for abortions was ruled to be a limitation.

The House often waives its bar against legislation in appropriation bills by adopting a special rule that sets the terms under which the measure to which it pertains is to be considered on the floor. The Senate permits unauthorized appropriations recommended by a Senate committee for legislation passed during the session but not yet enacted into law and for matters requested in the president's budget. The Senate often disposes of points of order by deciding whether the challenged provision is germane to the appropriation. If the Senate votes that the provision is germane, the point of order automatically falls.[40]

Members complain frequently about legislation in appropriations bills, but they continue to insert these provisions when they gain from the practice. According to data compiled by the Democratic Study Group and the Congressional Research Service, the number of limiting amendments offered and agreed to by the House has increased substantially during the past two decades. An average of 15 such floor amendments were offered during the 1963–1970 period, but the annual average soared to 39 between 1970 and 1982.[41] During the years prior to 1970, only 28 percent of the proposed limitations were approved by the House; during the next dozen years, more than half of these amendments were adopted.

The increased use of general provisions in appropriations bills is another measure of the comingling of legislation and appropriations. Approximately 115 such provisions were incorporated into the regular appropriations bills for the 1953 fiscal year; the fiscal 1965 appropriations had 160 general provisions; the regular appropriations bills for fiscal 1982 had more than 250. The number of general provisions in the defense appropriations bills escalated from 38 in fiscal 1956 to 99 in the 1983 fiscal year. Many of these provisions are substantive matters that might otherwise be placed into authorizing legislation. Many have become boilerplate and are continued from year to year without change. A number of new legislative provisions, or changes in existing ones, are inserted into the annual appropriations bills, however. Thus, the House Appropriations Committee recommended 37 changes in existing law in the general provisions attached to the fiscal 1983 defense appropriations bill.

The enactment of legislation in appropriations has been spurred recently by reliance on continuing resolutions to fund federal agencies that have not received their regular appropriation by the start of the fiscal year. Under House precedents, continuing resolutions are not general appropriation bills; hence, the bar against the inclusion of legislation does not apply to them. In recent years some continuing resolutions have been vehicles for the enactment of provisions that otherwise might not make it into law. The first continuing resolution for the 1983 fiscal year (P.L. 97-276) covered more than 20 pages in the *Statutes* and included restrictions on the procurement of imported goods by the Defense Department, rules for the disposal of federal lands and for the exploration of wilderness areas, restrictions on legal assistance to aliens, and rules for the importation of steel products. The first continuing resolution for fiscal 1984 was a lean measure virtually devoid of extraneous legislative provisions, however. This experience demonstrates that Congress can, if it chooses to do so, enforce the distinction between legislation and appropriations.

Line Items in Appropriations Reports. Despite the vast increase in its size and expenditures, the federal government now has fewer appropriation accounts than it had 50 or 100 years ago. Although there are more than 1,000 accounts, virtually all federal spending is channeled through fewer than 300 appropriations. Funds for the entire Defense Department are appropriated in approximately 50 accounts, half the number the department had when it was created after World War II.

Shrinkage in the number of accounts has not meant a loss of congressional interest in the details of expenditure. Although Congress no longer makes line-item appropriations, its appropriations reports are directives and prohibitions that do not have the status of law, but to which federal agencies carefully adhere.[42] The reports often allocate funds among the elements that comprise the various appropriation accounts. Expenditures for particular districts and states, such as river and harbor projects, usually are itemized in committee reports. So, too, are the appropriations for the Defense Department. The four operation and maintenance accounts for the military services are subdivided among more than 130 elements. The procurement funds are distributed to more than 400 weapon systems and projects enumerated in Appropriation Committee reports, while the research, development, training, and evaluation (R,D,T&E) funds are divided among more than 700 listed projects.

Although they are not included in the appropriation bills, the line items often govern agency expenditures. Agencies that wish to reprogram funds from one item to another within the same appropriation must follow the rules and procedures set for that particular appropriation. These rules vary among appropriations subcommittees, but over the past decade they have become increasingly formalized and restrictive.[43]

Spending Decisions in Authorizing Legislation

Congress has been making spending decisions in legislation since its first session. Prior to the 1920s, it usually did so in special appropriations that, as allowed by the rules, often contained legislative provisions; afterward, it often enacted "backdoor spending" that bypassed the appropriations process. New backdoor legislation was curtailed, not eliminated, by the budget act, but entitlements have become the fastest growing component of federal expenditure.

Appropriations are not supposed to be made in legislation, yet many entitlement laws contain permanent appropriations making funds available each year without new action by Congress. Even when an entitlement is funded in annual appropriations, the effective expenditure decision is made in substantive legislation, not in the appropriation bill. Although they do not mandate expenditures, discretionary authorizations can influence the level of appropriations. Annual authorizations usually exert a strong influence; multiyear authorizations usually have less effect on annual appropriations. Authorizing legislation is supposed to set the terms and conditions under which appropriations are to be spent. The comptroller general has held that "appropriations to carry out enabling or authorizing laws must be expended in strict accord with the original authorization both as to the amount of funds to be expended and the nature of the work authorized."[44] If an authorization is silent as to how the funds are to be used, however, then the terms set in the appropriations measure govern. An appropriation can override expressly the conditions set in authorizing legislation but cannot do so implicitly. In assessing the relationship between authorizations and appropriations, it is necessary to examine carefully the actual wording of each statute. Seemingly slight changes in terminology can decisively change the balance of power between these two congressional measures.

The trend in recent years is for authorizing legislation to be increasingly specific as to how the funds are to be spent. A number of methods devised by authorizing committees to "force" appropriations are discussed below.

Earmarking. Authorizing legislation can specify an amount of an entire program or earmark amounts for various elements within the program. The earmarks do not force Congress to appropriate funds for the designated elements, but they strongly influence the appropriations.

Earmarking is used extensively in the defense authorization bill. The fiscal 1984 defense authorization earmarked funds for 17 research and development projects. The earmarking language provided that, of the authorized amounts, a certain sum "is available only for" each of the designated projects. Because appropriations, such as those for the Defense Department, are lump sums, they usually do not specify amounts for individual projects or activities. As a result, the earmark in the authorizing legislation often determines how much of the total appropriation shall be available for each designated project.

It was noted earlier that the reports accompanying appropriations bills often specify how the funds are to be spent. This practice increases the possibility of conflict between earmarks in authorizing bills and report language for appropriation bills.

Mandating the Availability of Funds. Earmarks are permissive because they do not compel that funds be spent for the designated purpose. The authorizing legislation has a stronger effect when it stipulates that a certain amount "shall be available" for a particular activity. This mandates the affected agency to spend the designated amount on the stated purpose unless the appropriation itself, and not simply report language, expressly provides otherwise.

The "shall be available" mandate has been inserted into authorizing legislation for a number of federal agencies, including the Immigration and Naturalization Service, the Nuclear Regulatory Commission, and the International Communication Agency.[45] As can be expected, the Appropriations Committees are opposed to mandates and have deleted them from a few authorizing bills. In 1980, for example, the Senate Foreign Relations Committee inserted "shall be available" language into authorizations for the Board of International Broadcasting and the International Communication Agency, but this phrase was deleted on the floor.[46]

Reprogramming. Authorizations normally precede appropriations. Because it has the last word, the appropriation usually is decisive. But there are occasions when the authorization for the next fiscal year is considered while the appropriation for the current year is in effect. This legislative sequence provides an opportunity for the authorizing legislation to reprogram appropriated funds from one use to another. This can lead to conflict between the authorizing and appropriating committees. Thus, on August 11, 1982, the House gave final approval to a two-year authorization for the State Department that reprogrammed funds from a previously enacted appropriation. On the same day, however, Senator Lowell Weicker (R-Conn.) secured Senate approval of a floor amendment to a supplemental appropriations bill that barred use of the funds for the purpose specified in the State Department authorization, "unless reprogrammed in accordance with the procedures established by the Committees on Appropriations of the House and Senate."[47]

During the past decade, a number of authorizing committees have become active in the reprogramming process. The Armed Services Committees, as well as the defense appropriations subcommittees, review reprogrammings submitted by the Defense Department. In 1983, the House Foreign Affairs and the Senate Foreign Relations Committees took an active interest in the reprogramming of funds by the State Department for El Salvador. The trend toward greater participation in reprogramming decisions by authorizing committees means that, increasingly, two sets of committees contribute to the process.

Proportionality in Expenditures. Paradoxically, as authorizations have become more detailed and specific, they have generated increased uncertainty and conflict regarding the intention of Congress. When authorizations are cast in broad program categories, agencies can spend the funds as prescribed in appropriations or in the reports of the Appropriations Committees. When the authorization is distributed among a number of designated items, however, the affected agency may not know how to allocate the appropriated funds. This occurs when the appropriation is less than the total authorized for the various activities. In this situation, the agency cannot spend the full amount authorized for each activity; to do so would exceed the total appropriation. It could spend according to the instructions provided in Appropriation Committee reports, but to do so would accord report language a higher status than authorization statutes.

The National Science Foundation (NSF) has been one of the agencies caught in this dilemma. The solution devised for it and subsequently applied to other agencies establishes a modus operandi between the rival authorizations and appropriations committees. The NSF authorization specifies amounts for more than 20 listed activities, but it also provides that if the subsequent appropriation is below the total authorized, the amount available for each of these activities shall be proportional to its share of the authorization. An activity that constitutes 10 percent of the authorization would receive 10 percent of the appropriation. The proportionality rule is recognized by a provision in the NSF appropriation that if "the amount appropriated is less than the total amount authorized . . . all amounts, including floors and ceilings, specified in the authorizing act for those program activities or their subactivities shall be reduced proportionally."

Under this bilateral arrangement, the two sets of committees maintain their basic functions: the authorization sets program priorities and the appropriation establishes spending levels.

Triggers. The proportionality rule enables authorizing committees to determine the relative priority to be accorded particular activities. It does not, however, determine the amount of money available for these activities. The smaller the appropriation, the less that is available for the authorizing committee's priorities. To strengthen their role in determining actual expenditures, some authorizing committees have devised "thresholds" that preclude funds for a designated program unless the appropriation for another program is above the threshold level. The purpose of this tactic is to obtain more funds for the threshold program. This tactic can be effective when the authorizing and appropriating committees have different priorities or when a program favored by the authorizing committee has weak political support and its financial prospects can be improved by linking it to a program that has broad political appeal. For example, the Middle Income Student Assistance Act of 1978 barred any spending for Basic Educational Opportunity Grants if appropriations were less than $370 million for supplemental grants, $500 million for work-study programs, or $286 million for direct student loans.[48]

One cannot generalize about the impact of authorizing committees on spending outcomes. But as they become more involved in financial matters, they are likely to seek stronger influence over appropriations decisions. Authorizing committees are likely to devise additional mechanisms and to expand the use of those discussed above. These efforts will lead over time to increased conflict between the authorizing and appropriating committees.

Implications for the Legislative
and Executive Branches

The picture that emerges from the preceding sections is of three processes that have become increasingly detailed and similar to one another. On the surface, the three types of measures are easily distinguishable—one would never mistake an appropriations bill for an authorization or a budget resolution—but all three deal with the same program and financial issues. The three processes continue to have distinct purposes and perspectives, but the lines separating them have become less clear.

The triplication of legislative activity would be of little concern were it cost-free. Congress would have the advantage of diversity and competition and still benefit from the strengths of each process. But triplication does burden the legislative and executive branches: it makes the two branches work harder, shortens their budgeting and programming perspectives, and generates conflict within and between the two branches.

This formidable bill of particulars is based on the recent performance of Congress.

Legislative Workload

The statistics show an enormous increase in congressional workload during the 1970s, a decade in which the budget process was introduced, annual reauthorizations become more common, and the insertion of legislation and limitations into appropriations measures more frequent. The workload grew in both the House and the Senate, in committees and on the floor. During the 1971–1980 period, Senate committees and subcommittees held 5,000 more meetings—almost a 40 percent increase—than during the previous decade. The House held about 9,000 more meetings during the same 10-year period—a 50 percent increase.[49] The number of recorded votes doubled in the Senate, from 2,734 to 5,562 while the House had a threefold increase, from 1,787 to 5,816 during the 1970s, compared with the previous decade.

It would be erroneous to attribute the upsurge in legislative workload solely to the budget, appropriations, and authorizations processes. Congress underwent many changes during the decade that made it more open to outside pressure and easier for rank and file members to demand roll calls and to convene committee meetings. But the triplication of legislative processes also contributed to the increased demands upon Congress. As appropriations, budget resolutions, and authorizations became more detailed, they occasioned more legislative activity. It takes more time and more votes to clear a budget resolution whose program assumptions are debated than one in which interest is confined to fiscal aggregates and functions. Similarly, an appropriations bill loaded with legislation and limitations will generate more controversy and consume more floor time than a bill that deals only with spending levels.

Agency Workload

The effects of congressional budget activity on the executive branch vary among federal agencies. An agency subject to annual authorizations will likely face heavier demands than one whose programs are permanently authorized. Although it is not possible to generalize about all federal agencies, there can be no doubt that demands on the executive branch have increased enormously over the past 10–15 years. Agencies have to be more responsive to more committees and members than they were in the past. The triplication of legislative budget work means that agencies cannot be sure of where a particular issue will be decided, or whether a decision made in one process will be reviewed in another. Agencies have had to staff themselves with more legislative liaison and public affairs people to keep on top of what is happening on Capitol Hill.

The demands on executive agencies have increased not only because of recurring and repetitive legislative action but also because Congress has required agencies to submit more reports and to respond to more requests for data and analysis.[50] The burden of monitoring and influencing legislative action tends to escalate the higher one goes in executive agencies. Top officials give much time to following congressional hearings, maintaining contact with individual members, and keeping informed of legislative developments.

Data provided by a senior official of the Department of Defense (DoD) reflects the extent to which congressional demands have escalated:

> In 1983 DoD has testified before 96 committees and subcommittees. This compares with only 21 committees in 1970, a growth of 357 percent in thirteen years. 1,306 witnesses provided 2,160 hours of testimony. In addition, there were approximately 85,000 written inquiries and nearly 600,000 phone calls from Congress. In 1983, DoD provided Congress with 21,753 pages of justification documents in support of the FY 1984 request; this is a threefold increase over 1970. . . . In addition, Congress directed 483 specific actions and called for 300 reports in 1983 legislation.[51]

A Short Time Perspective

Three separate processes might be justified if they were differentiated in terms of time. In fact, from the first meeting of Congress in 1789 until the 1950s, appropriations and authorizations were oriented to different periods. Regular appropriations were, and with few exceptions still are, for a single fiscal year; authorizations were permanent, without a time limit. Although appropriations focused on expenditures for the next fiscal year, authorizing legislation often dealt with long-term program and organizational matters.

The trend to temporary, frequently annual, authorizations and the establishment of the congressional budget process mean that Congress now makes three sets of decisions for many programs and agencies each year. Inevitably, these decisions address the same concerns: spending and activity levels for the next fiscal year. When a budget resolution, authorization bill, and appropriation all are handled within the space of a few months, it is unlikely that they will be riveted to different time periods. In the legislative environment within which Congress works, the budget, authorizing, and appropriating committees all want to influence what happens in the near term. To look ahead three to five years means that these committees would be forgoing the opportunity to make the decisions that count. Thus, the committees compete with sameness, by looking over each other's shoulders to ensure that their immediate interests are not prejudiced by other congressional participants. In this competition over near-term policy, the future is given short shrift.

One consequence of this truncated time perspective is the "dollarization" of national policy. With all eyes focused on spending for the current and upcoming fiscal years, there is a tendency to examine legislation in terms of the dollars that would be added to or subtracted from expenditure. The various scorekeeping activities discussed earlier reinforce this tendency. Many authorizations today are evaluated principally in terms of their budgetary impact, as if they were budget resolutions or appropriations. When it legislates one year at a time, Congress is not in a position to think about long-term policy matters.

Congress considers medium-term financial issues when it formulates budget resolutions. Each resolution sets aggregate and functional targets for the next three fiscal years. These multiyear targets, however, do not lengthen significantly Congress's time horizon, nor do they encourage it to look at long-term issues rather than immediate spending questions. Most of the debate on the budget resolutions revolves around spending for the next fiscal year. The outyear figures are targets that members expect to revise before the start of the fiscal year to which they apply. The targets really are three sets of annual spending levels. Each set has assumptions with respect to authorizations and appropriations for a particular fiscal year. In implementing the multiyear resolutions, Congress focuses on the amount of money, if any, available for program expansion and the amount of cutback necessary to keep spending within target. It seeks quick fixes that will trim spending to stay within the budget or that will make use of the margin available for expansion. The reconciliation bills approved by Congress in 1981 and 1982 pursuant to multiyear budget instructions exemplify this behavior. In the tense and deadline-sensitive atmosphere in which the reconciliation measure was developed, Congress could not consider far-reaching program changes. Instead, it was content to enact legislation that met the dollar targets of the reconciliation instructions.

The work demands of the three processes crowd out the future and force participants to attend to more immediate concerns. There simply is not time to think ahead, beyond the current issue or the next deadline. This problem is probably most critical at the highest echelons of executive agencies where senior officials must attend multiple sets of hearings in both the House and Senate and be prepared to make quick decision on matters pending before Congress.

The Institutionalization
of Budgetary Conflict

The budget is a breeding ground for conflict. Too much is at stake for the budget to be settled without fights among claimants or participants. Conflict intensifies when the budget is oriented to cutbacks rather than to incremental growth, but the budget process has means of moderating tensions and bringing issues to closure. Protracted strife would threaten the continuation of government programs and agencies and disrupt the lives of those dependent upon the government for financial assistance. The exclusion of legislation from appropriations bills is one means of containing budgetary conflict and facilitating the uninterrupted flow of funds to federal agencies.

The existence of three parallel processes in Congress fuels budgetary conflict and complicates the task of reaching agreement on federal programs and expenditures. Conflict flourishes because jurisdictional lines are blurred and contested, because three sets of committees with divergent perspectives and interests are involved in the process, and because participants have multiple opportunities to raise issues previously thought to have been settled. During the decade that the congressional budget process has been in operation, there has been continuing tension between the Budget Committees on the one hand and the authorizing and appropriating committees on the other. The Appropriations Committees regard line-item assumptions in budget resolutions as a trespass on their jurisdiction; the authorizing committees chafe under the dictates of reconciliation instructions emanating from the Budget Committees. Neither the appropriations nor the authorizing committees like the fact that their actions are monitored by the Budget Committees, nor do they agree always with the cost estimates used by the Budget Committees to assess the budgetary impact of legislation.

Budgetary warfare also rages between the authorizing and appropriating committees. The former are perennially upset by the enactment of unauthorized appropriations; the latter by the extensive recourse to backdoor-spending schemes, which evade the regular appropriations process, and by the progressive enlargement in the portion of the budget spent on mandatory entitlements. Flareups frequently occur over the inclusion of limitations and legislation in appropriation bills as well.

The multiplicity of budget processes have spawned conflict and misunderstanding between the legislative and executive branches. Agencies have become skilled in playing one set of committees against another and in shopping around for the most favorable forum for consideration of their programs. In 1981, President Reagan skillfully exploited the budget reconciliation process to obtain sweeping changes in national priorities; in 1983 and 1984, he sought to undermine the process because he felt that more favorable results could be obtained from the appropriations and authorizations committees.

The three sets of budget-making committees do not see eye-to-eye on many of the matters in their shared jurisdictions. Not surprisingly, they differ on the value of particular programs to which funds are to be put and the discretion of government agencies in managing their programs. Often agencies are trapped in a no-win situation in which satisfying the wishes of one committee compels them to ignore the dictates of another. If the Appropriations Committees want more multi-source procurement and the Armed Services Committees mandate sole source procurement, the Defense Department cannot meet both sets of demands simultaneously. When the Appropriations Committees differ with the Science and Technology Committee on the NSF's spending priorities, the agency cannot satisfy both masters. The problem often is most intractable when legislative expectations are etched in committee reports rather than in law or when they are transmitted orally by members or staff. Legal conflicts can be worked out according to rules of interpretation; informal conflicts can be resolved only by forging understandings among the contesting parties.

Conflict leads to legislation by exhaustion. It produces a grinding, frustrating legislative process in which legislation is held hostage not because of opposition to it, but to advance or impede some other cause. Rather than crafting legislation carefully, committees and members seek to outmaneuver one another by loading their ideas onto "veto-proof" measures. "In this environment," Representatives David Obey (D-Wis.) and Richard Gephardt (D-Mo.) have argued, "those who are more adept (or gutsy) at holding up legislation until they get their way are the winners in the legislative process."[52]

Bickering and brinksmanship thwart the determination of Congress to complete its required budget actions in a timely manner. Recourse to continuing appropriations that provide stopgap funding until the regular appropriation bills have been enacted has become commonplace. During the fiscal years 1980–1983 more than 90 percent of the regular appropriation bills were not enacted by the start of the fiscal year.[53] In-fighting among the committees on the budget, appropriations, and authorizations is the leading cause of delay in the enactment of these spending bills.

Legislative Irresponsibility

The Congressional Budget Act of 1974 was predicated on the notion that Congress should take responsibility for its budgetary actions. Responsible budget action would be manifested in a number of ways. Congress would have to vote on the deficit and on total spending; it would have to adopt arithmetically consistent budget resolutions; and it would be informed of the budgetary consequences of pending legislation and of the status of the budget.

But the multiplicity of budget processes breeds a new type of irresponsibility: Congress can vote for budget resolutions without knowing what it is voting for or against and without committing itself to uphold its budget decisions when it votes on authorizations and appropriations. It can assume anything it wants about the numbers in a resolution—in fact, members voting for the same numbers can hold conflicting assumptions about what they are doing—but then abandon these assumptions when it acts on authorizations or appropriations. Congressional behavior is characterized by what Obey and Gephardt have called escapist budgeting and taking cheap-shots:

> Because budget resolutions do not really decide anything but do confront members with difficult choices, the easy way out is to make believe that the numbers in the resolution can be achieved by voting for them. If the political climate calls for a balanced budget, vote for one regardless of whether economic conditions permit such an outcome or legislative process are prepared to produce one. . . . So much worse for the economy if it fails to deliver on congressional pipe dreams. . . .
>
> If the budget doesn't mean what it says, neither do members have to vote the way they really believe. To do so would jeopardize their standing back home. Instead, they take cheap shots at the budget. They vote more money for favorite programs but against higher total outlays or a bigger deficit. When a budget resolution is on the floor, they can support amendments allocating more funds for defense, veterans benefits, or anything else, and then vote against final passage because the deficit is too high.[54]

Toward More Manageable
Congressional Budget Processes

What, if anything, should be done to ameliorate the workload problems arising out of the triplication of congressional budget activities? One approach would be to do nothing and to let the future take care of itself. This position rests on the twin expectations that economic recovery will ease pressure on Congress and executive agencies and that Congress will make piecemeal adjustments, as it often has in the past, to alleviate its problems. The first expectation assumes that economic turbulence is the root cause of congressional dysfunction. Because the economy was unstable and weak in the decade after the first oil shock, Congress was forced to remake the budget again and again. It engaged in repetitive budgeting, much in the manner practiced by poor countries.[55]

When the budget promised growth and the economy delivered stagnation, budgetary conflict between the two branches increased, along with heightened tension among the authorizing, appropriating, and budget committees. Discrepancies between expected and actual economic performance led to inconsistent budgetary behavior as legislative decisions made in one process were challenged in another. According to this view, Congress recovers when the economy recovers. Evidence in support of this position can be gleaned from the 1983 session of Congress, which completed its budget work more expeditiously than in the four preceding sessions, loaded less extraneous provisions onto continuing resolutions, and took fewer budget-related votes. Congress performed in a more effective manner while retaining its three budget processes.

The second expectation is anchored in the view that Congress is a self-correcting institution that periodically repairs its own malfunctions. If Congress is overloaded by a multiplicity of budget processes, or, if the boundaries of these processes are inadequately defined, Congress can remedy the problem through small adjustments without a "big bang" overhaul that might be difficult to implement and cause unforeseen problems. Congress benefits from having three processes, each with its distinctive niche and perspective. The congressional budget process enables it to make economic policy in a consistent and coordinated manner; its authorization machinery enables Congress to shape organizations and programs according to its will, and the appropriations process gives it the capacity to control federal expenditures.[56]

Congress recently has made adjustments to simplify these processes. A few annual authorizations, such as for the State Department, have been shifted to a biennial cycle. Since 1982, Congress managed with only one budget resolution rather than with the two prescribed by the budget act; in 1983, the House revised its rules making it more difficult to insert riders into appropriations bills; and, as noted, the continuing appropriations enacted in 1983 had few legislative provisions.

Yet self-correction might not suffice. Congress has not come to grips fully with the impact of the budget and reconciliation processes on its authorizations and appropriations machinery. The current arrangement invites confusion, conflict, overlapping jurisdictions, duplication of effort, and legislative overload.

Structural Realignment

Congress can eliminate one or more of its processes by consolidating or by discarding certain functions. Obviously, Congress cannot get rid of the appropriations function that was assigned to it by the Constitution, nor can it abandon its basic legislative function. For most of its history, however, Congress has operated without budget and reconciliation processes, and prior to the 1920s, it did not have a well-defined authorizations process.

Structural realignment would be the most far-reaching and dramatic. It would signal that Congress intends to put an end to confusing and overlapping processes. Nevertheless, structural change might be a less promising and more uncertain path to improvement than would boundary or procedural adjustments.

If Congress were to abandon reconciliation, it would have a clearer demarcation between authorizations and appropriations on the one hand and budget decisions on the other.The incentive to line-item budget resolutions would be diminished, and use of the reconciliation bill as a vehicle for substantive legislation would be ended. Conflict between the Budget Committees and other legislative participants would abate.

But without reconciliation, Congress might find it difficult to enforce its budgetary decisions. Budget resolutions might be little more than statements of intent or accommodations to the financial preferences of legislative committees. Congress might lose its capacity to force changes in entitlements, and uncontrollable spending might consume an increasing share of the federal budget. The issue for Congress should not be whether to have or not have reconciliation, but how to maintain a proper jurisdictional balance between this and other congressional processes.

Congress could simplify its workload by terminating the budget process and relying on annual appropriations and other legislative decisions for establishing financial priorities. The budget's "macro" functions might be handled by means of a coordinating mechanism that links revenue and spending decisions. Congress no longer would make symbolic budget decisions that are as contentious as they are ineffective.[57]

One structural change that was proposed before the congressional budget process was established would be to merge authorizations and appropriations into program committees that would perform both functions. Inasmuch as authorizations now are used for making financial decisions, they have an affinity to the appropriations process. The placement of both processes in the same committees might diminish the incentive for back-door spending. The merger might strengthen legislative oversight by encouraging committees to seek more efficient and effective programs.

Despite these potential advantages, there is the possibility of an upsurge in the attachment of riders and legislation to appropriation bills. This happened a century ago when half of the appropriations bills were assigned to legislative committees. Moreover, the combination might strengthen the advocacy role of committees at the expense of Congress's guarding of the treasury. In a legislature that balances both roles, careful consideration should be given to the basic reasons for separating legislative decisions from appropriations.

Representative Obey has proposed that Congress combine spending, revenue, and entitlement decisions to an omnibus budget bill that would include budget targets. Prior to the consideration of the omnibus bills, the Budget Committees would formulate a budget resolution, but this measure would not be voted on until the appropriations, revenue, and entitlement committees had submitted their proposals. Then, there would be an opportunity on the floor to adopt revenue and spending legislation consistent with the budget resolution.[58]

The omnibus approach has a number of promising features. It might put an end to delays in the consideration of appropriations bills when Congress fails to adopt the first budget resolution on time, and it might bring about greater consistency in budget-related decisions. But omnibus legislation would introduce fresh risks into congressional budgeting. Enactment of the omnibus bill might be delayed by conflict over its components, and deals might be longer and more costly than under the current arrangement. One can envision situations in which virtually the entire session's legislative output would center around a single bill. Substantive legislation would be tucked safely into the omnibus bill, with little opportunity for careful review by the House and Senate. The procedures for considering the omnibus bill would be more complex than those currently applied to the budget process. Also, it would impair the president's veto power and thereby redistribute power from the executive to the legislative branch.

A more modest change would be to establish a two-year cycle for appropriations, authorizations, and budget resolutions. It has been argued that a biennial process might relieve workload pressures, curtail unauthorized appropriations, and enable legislative committees to devote more time to their oversight responsibilities. But it is also possible that budget issues would sprawl over a two-year period much as they now do and that there would be a plethora of supplemental authorizations, appropriations, and budget resolutions. Having completed their legislative business in one year of the cycle, authorizing committees would have little incentive for oversight.

A biennial cycle would affect differently each of the processes covered in this report. The budget process would be least affected because Congress now adopts three-year resolutions. The figures for the second and third years are targets, and this status is not likely to change even if Congress were to stretch the annual routines into a two-year cycle.

Even if they were labeled as binding decisions, the out-year levels are certain to be modified before the start of the fiscal years to which they apply.

Appropriations would be the most affected of the processes. It has operated on an annual basis since 1789, and the Appropriations Committees appear to be wedded firmly to the notion that control of the purse depends on annual review. The size and importance of supplemental appropriations would be magnified by a two-year cycle. A biennial appropriations process would not be workable unless all authorizations were for two years or longer. To inch toward a biennial cycle by establishing a two-year minimum duration for authorizations would be sensible. If Congress were to demonstrate its willingness to authorize for no less than two years, it then might extend the biennial concept to some appropriations, such as those for the continuing operations, salaries, expenses, and government agencies or for grants to state and local governments.

A Cautionary Conclusion

Congress is an institution with multiple roles, a diversified membership, a fragmented structure, and a long history. It is not the most disciplined or consistent of institutions, nor can it be. In the current legislative environment, it is tempting to seek simpler procedures by merging or eliminating some of the existing processes. Yet each process has its own niche and history; if one were terminated, there would be ripple effects throughout Capitol Hill.And not all the effects would have been intended. What might seem to be simply a matter of improved efficiency can redistribute power within Congress or between the legislative and executive branches. The competing drives for legislation and appropriations might become unbalanced, with unpredictable consequences.

Congress is an institution in which process and substance are intertwined. Can one be certain that the current attention to budgetary matters is because of procedural complications rather than political conditions? If the economy were to recover and political conflict were to abate, Congress might return to a more stable and less budget-oriented life. Yet the changes made in response to short-term problems are likely to have long-term consequences and so should be undertaken with caution.

Notes

1. Except when referring expressly to the congressional budget process, throughout this paper, budgeting (or the budget process) refers to the appropriations, authorizations, and budget processes of Congress.

2. These computations are based on the author's classification of all the roll call votes reported in the *Congressional Quarterly Almanac* for 1981 and 1982 (Washington, D.C.: Congressional Quarterly, 1982 and 1983). Budget-related votes include all roll call votes on budget resolutions, reconciliation measures, appropriation bills, and tax legislation, and those votes on authorizations that pertain directly to the budget.

3. The national defense function in the budget resolution covers all of the Defense Department (other than its "civil" functions) and certain activities conducted by other agencies. The authorization bill deals only with those components of the Defense Department budget that are authorized annually; it therefore excludes the pay of active and retired personnel. The appropriation covers virtually all defense spending (although there is a separate appropriation for military construction), including active and retired pay.

4. On May 13, 1982, the Senate tabled an amendment to the defense authorization bill that would have deleted research and development funds for the MX missile. It also tabled on September 29, an amendment to a continuing appropriation that would have prohibited the use of MX procurement funds until Congress had approved a basing mode for the missile. But then on December 16, it adopted an amendment to another continuing appropriation barring procurement funds until Congress had approved a basing mode. A similar string of votes occurred in the House.

5. U.S. Senate. Committee on Armed Services. *Organization, Structure, and Decisionmaking Procedures of the Department of Defense Hearings*, July 28, 1983. Washington D.C.: USGPO, 1983.

6. In recent years, there have been significant increases in congressional staff resources and workload, but a sharp decline in the enactment of public laws. In fact, the 97th Congress (1981–1982) enacted fewer public laws than any Congress in the previous 60 years. For data on congressional workload and output, see Norman J. Ornstein and others, *Vital Statistics on Congress, 1982* (Washington, D.C.: The American Enterprise Institute, 1982), especially chapter 6.

7. For a discussion of this behavior, see the "Statement of Reps." David R. Obey and Richard P. Gephardt in U.S. House. Committee on the Budget. *Report on the First Concurrent Resolution on the Budget, Fiscal Year 1982*. (H. Rept. 97–23) April 16, 1981, pp. 327–332). Washington, D.C.: USGPO, 1981.

8. The effects of stagnation and cutbacks on budgetary behavior are discussed in Allen Schick, "Incremental Budgeting in a Decremental Age," *Policy Sciences* 16 (1983): 1–25.

9. Of the three processes, only the appropriations process expressly is mentioned in the Constitution. Though authorizations clearly are subsumed under the legislative powers of Congress, the requirement of authorization prior to appropriation is found in the rules of the House and Senate. The budget process owes its existence to the Congressional Budget Act of 1974.

10. The very first appropriation act passed by Congress in 1789 provided for the entire federal government but consisted of barely 100 words. A lump sum of $137 thousand was appropriated for the Department of War. See 1 *Stat.* 95.

11. The British Parliament and some colonial legislatures barred or discouraged the attachment of substantive provisions to "supply" bills. The Maryland Constitution of 1776 provided that "the House of Delegates shall not, on any occasion, or under any pretense annex to, or blend with a money bill, any matter, clause, or thing, not immediately relating to . . . the taxes or supplies to be raised for the support of government, or the current expenses of the State."

12. The current rule (Rule XXI, Clause 2) reads as follows: "No appropriation shall be reported in any general appropriation bill, or be in order as an amendment thereto, for any expenditure not previously authorized by law, unless in continuation of appropriations for such public works and objects as are already in progress. Nor shall any provision in any such bill or amendment thereto changing existing law be in order, except such as being germane to the subject matter of the bill shall retrench expenditures. . . ."

13. The current Senate rule (Rule XVI, Clause 1) reads: "On a point of order made by any Senator, no amendment shall be received to any general appropriation bill the effect of which will be to increase an appropriation already contained in the bill, or to add a new item of appropriation, unless it be made to carry out the provisions of some existing law, or treaty stipulation. . . ." Clause 2 bars the inclusion of legislation in appropriation bills.

14. Because of the relative ease of attaching limitations to appropriation bills, the Holman Rule has not been used much in recent years. To qualify under the Holman Rule, a provision must on its face show a retrenchment.

15. Among the changes made in 1920 was adoption by the House of a rule (now Rule XXI, Clause 5) barring legislative committees from reporting appropriations: "No bill or joint resolution carrying appropriations shall be reported by any committee not having jurisdiction to report appropriations, nor shall an amendment proposing an appropriation be in order during the consideration of a bill or joint resolution reported by a committee not having that jurisdiction." There is no comparable prohibition in the Senate rules.

16. Similarly authorizing committees once were known as legislative committees. It should be noted, however, that an authorization is but one aspect of legislation. If an "authorized to be appropriated" clause expires, the permanent legislation to which it pertains would continue in effect.

17. Harris reports that between 1941 and 1959, the number of appropriation items for the Department of Agriculture declined from 137 to 43 and for the Treasury Department from 61 to 16. See Joseph P. Harris, *Congressional Control of Administration* (Washington: The Brookings Institution, 1964), 91.

18. Congress often makes appropriation for expiring authorizations that have not yet been renewed. It does so by waiving or ignoring the rules against unauthorized appropriations or by making the appropriation in a continuing resolution.

19. See Louis Fisher, "Annual Authorizations: Durable Roadblocks to Biennial Budgeting," *Public Budgeting and Finance* (Spring 1983): 23–40.

20. While annual authorizations come close to being fully funded, multiyear authorizations often are much higher than the appropriations. Many multiyear

authorizations have "escalator clauses" with successively higher amounts authorized for each year covered by the legislation. In subsequent years, however, when the appropriations are considered, the amounts provided usually are only slightly higher than the levels appropriated for the prior year.

21. For a discussion of the factors leading to the Congressional Budget Act of 1974, see Allen Schick, *Congress and Money: Budgeting, Spending, and Taxing* (Washington, D.C.: The Urban Institute, 1980).

22. Since 1982, however, Congress has not adopted the "second" resolution, but has provided instead that the "first" resolution would become a ceiling on budget authority and outlays and a floor on expenditures on October 1, when the fiscal year starts.

23. From time to time, Congress has increased the number of functions by splitting off some categories of expenditure from existing functions. Thus, in 1983, Congress added two functions by splitting social security from income security and medical insurance from health.

24. "Crosswalking" is a procedure prescribed by section 302 of the Congressional Budget Act. A crosswalk involves (1) the allocation of budget authority in each budget resolution to House and Senate committees and (2) the division by each committee of its budget authority among its programs or subcommittees. Cost estimates are prepared by the Congressional Budget Office for legislation reported by House and Senate committees. The Congressional Budget Office also prepares five-year budget projections and "scorekeeping" reports that show the status of congressional budgetary actions.

25. The Budget Act bars Congress from considering any appropriation (or other measure) that would cause total budget authority or outlays to exceed the level set forth in the second budget resolution. In recent years, however, Congress has waived or ignored this provision on a number of occasions.

26. On the fragmentation of Congress, see Thomas E. Mann and Norman J. Ornstein (eds.), *The New Congress* (Washington, D.C.: The American Enterprise Institute, 1981).

27. U.S. House. Committee on Rules. Sante Esposito, "The Authorization Process," unpublished transcript of briefing for the Task Force on the Budget Process. June 24, 1982, p. 26.

28. As part of its evaluation of the president's budget, however, the Congressional Budget Office publishes, usually in February of each year, baseline budget projections for the next five fiscal years. These projections are highly aggregated and with a few exceptions do not provide baseline data for specific programs.

29. See U.S. House (H. Rpt. 93–658) November 20, 1973, p. 37. Washington, D.C.: USGPO, 1973.

30. The House Budget Committee compiles the views and estimates reports of all House committees in a single document, but the reports of Senate committees are not published together.

31. U.S. House. Committee on the Budget. *Views and Estimates of Committees of the House on the Congressional Budget for Fiscal Year 1983*, H. Print, 97th Cong., 2d sess., 1982. Washington D.C.: USGPO, 1982.

32. U.S. Senate. Committee on Appropriations. *Views on the First Concurrent Resolution on the Budget, Fiscal Year 1983,* March 18, 1982, p. 1. Washington, D.C.: USGPO, 1982.

33. *Congressional Record* 126. (August 19, 1980) Daily ed. H7193.

34. Sec. 401 (a) of H. R. 3520 (98th Cong., 1st sess.) "authorized to be appropriated for fiscal year 1984 for programs under the jurisdiction of the Committee on Education and Labor such funding levels as are assumed under the first budget resolution . . . for fiscal year 1984."

35. See Allen Schick, *Reconciliation and the Congressional Budget Process,* (Washington, D.C.: The American Enterprise Institute, 1981).   '

36. See U.S. Senate. (S. Rpt. 97–28) March 23, 1981. Washington, D.C.: USGPO, 1981. This language was used for every committee receiving a reconciliation instruction.

37. The future of reconciliation is uncertain. In 1983, Congress failed to consider legislation called for in reconciliation instructions. This failure may be a temporary problem or it may harbinger a decline (and perhaps discontinuation) of the process. In any case, it is unlikely that reconciliation will be used as extensively in the near future as it was in 1981.

38. This language was used in the early warning reports on the fiscal 1983 appropriation bills. Virtually each year, the House Budget Committee changes the structure or content of these reports.

39. This clause, inserted in the House rules in 1974, generally is interpreted to require the Appropriations Committee to identify new changes in law, but not legislative provisions re-enacted each year.

40. For an explanation of this procedure, see Floyd M. Riddick, *Senate Procedure,* (Document 97–2) 1981, pp. 129–134.

41. See Democratic Study Group, *The Appropriations Rider Controversy,* (Special Report no. 95–12) February 14, 1978; and Richard S. Beth, Daniel P. Strickland, and Stanley Bach, "Limitation and Other House Amendments to General Appropriations Bills: Fiscal years 1979–83" (Washington, D.C.: Congressional Research Service, December 28, 1982).

42. In the 19th century "line items" referred to lengthy lists of the objects (such as supplies and equipment) to be purchased; at the present time, it usually refers to any detailed breakdown of broad categories into more specific items. In the context of a budget resolution, line itemization means the identification of the programs comprising a function; in the context of an appropriation bill, it means identification of the activities within an account.

43. For a brief discussion of some of these rules, see Bernard T. Pitsvada, "Flexibility in Federal Budget Execution," *Public Budgeting and Finance* 3, no. 2 (Summer 1983): 96–99.

44. U.S. General Accounting Office, *Principles of Federal Appropriations Law,* (Washington, D.C.: USGPO, 1982), 2–38.

45. For a discussion of "appropriations-forcing" language, see Louis Fisher, "The Authorization-Appropriation Process in Congress: Formal Rules and Informal Practices," *Catholic University Law Review* 29 (1979): 65–67.

46. See *Congresional Record* 126. (June 16, 1980) Daily ed. S7051.

47. *Congressional Record* 128. (August 11, 1982) Daily ed. S10240.

48. P.L. 95–566, 92 *Stat.* 2402.

49. These data are drawn from Norman J. Ornstein and others, *Vital Statistics on Congress, 1982,* (Washington, D.C.: The American Enterprise Institute, 1982), tables 6–1 and 6–2.

50. The General Accounting Office publishes an extensive listing of the reports required by Congress. For the latest such listing, see U.S. General Accounting Office, *Requirements for Recurring Reports to the Congress,* PAD 82–28, 1982.

51. See paper presented by Assistant Secretary of Defense (Comptroller) Vincent Puritano on "The Budget Process in DOD," at the Patterson School, December 2–3, 1983.

52. See "Supplemental Views of Representatives David Obey and Richard Gephardt" in U.S. House. (H. Rpt. 97–23) April 16, 1981, p. 329.

53. For recent data on the use of continuing resolutions, see Daniel P. Strickland, Ilona B. Nichels, and Stanley Bach, "The Duration and Scope of Continuing Appropriations Acts: Fiscal Years 1968–1983" (Congressional Research Service, July 5, 1983).

54. U.S. House. (H. Rpt. 97–23), p. 328.

55. See Naomi Caiden and Aaron Wildavsky, *Planning and Budgeting in Poor Countries* (New York: John Wiley, 1974).

56. When it recently established a "credit budget process" to deal with direct and guaranteed loans, Congress utilized its authorization, budget, and appropriations machinery. This indicates the extent to which it is accustomed to three separate processes.

57. Congress experimented with ad hoc coordination to produce a legislative budget after World War II, but abandoned the attempt after two years.

58. The Obey proposal is being considered currently by the House Task Force on the Budget Process chaired by Rep. Anthony Beilenson.

Commentary: On Congressional Budgeting

R. James Woolsey

Periodic changes have indeed occurred in congressional budget procedures. Budget process reforms have tended to take place following major wars. The Appropriations Committees were created at the close of the Civil War and strengthened after World War I. Following World War II, authorizations were made annual and not permanent. The Vietnam War begat the Congressional Budget Act of 1974. The pattern is clear: every time there has been an enhancement of executive control, as inevitably happens in war, Congress responds by adding another budget control while leaving extant controls in place, resulting in budgetary triplication. Not surprisingly, therefore, the budget processes have multiplied to consume excess congressional time and effort.

The current procedure is derived from the Congressional Budget Act of 1974, which created the third process involving the Budget Committees. The budget act was implemented not only because Congress intended to strengthen its influence over fiscal policy in dealing with the White House, but also because of the specific observation of the effect of the Vietnam War on fiscal policy. Experience had demonstrated that neither the executive nor Congress was capable of matching revenues and expenditures in a rational way. One of the primary virtues that it was hoped would be derived from the budget act was the greater responsibility that would devolve on the members of Congress, who would be required to vote yes or no on a budget resolution that would include not only expenditures and revenues, but also deficits. It was assumed that members of Congress would recoil at the prospect of voting for huge deficits and that they would force the process to come up with a budget resolution with either a minor deficit or none. The years since 1975, and particularly those since 1982, have proved this assumption wrong. Congress nonetheless needed some sort of coordinating device to examine and balance expenditure and revenue aggregates, and, despite the seeming lack of success of the 1974 budget act in this area, any modification of the present process will have to face the same issue.

The inadequacies of the current budget process have become readily apparent with congressional and executive circumvention of the budget act's procedures. The second budget resolution called for in the fall has

R. James Woolsey is a partner in Shea & Gardner and counsel to CSIS. He has served as under secretary of the navy and as general counsel to the Senate Armed Services Committee.

been dropped, and reconciliation procedures originally intended to be implemented in conjunction with the second resolution have been attached to the first resolution since 1980. But these have been practical changes instituted to make the process more realistic. A more serious indication of substantive problems with the budget process was the perceived need to conduct negotiations on the FY 1985 budget outside of the processes provided for by the budget act. In his January 1984 State of the Union address, President Reagan called for an ad hoc negotiating team composed of Democratic and Republican leaders of Congress and White House staffers who would negotiate a "down payment" on the deficit. The deficit-reduction panel's task was essentially to come up with a compromise on the 1985 budget. The bipartisan, executive-legislative negotiations collapsed at the end of February, and the immediate result was to delay further the budget process in a year already truncated in work days because of the conventions and primaries.

This type of negotiation, nonetheless, could still serve as a method for facilitating the budget process in the future. Such negotiations predate the Reagan administration and actually began in the last year of the Carter administration. Similar patterns of negotiation are found within other Western democracies, within cabinets, rather than between the uniquely U.S. mechanisms of president and Congress. It may be that the industrial democracies are undergoing a transformation of the machinery of political decision making, and a form of negotiation—a new vehicle—is needed for making difficult decisions that are derived largely from economic factors rather than budget line-item issues. If the deficit-reduction negotiations had succeeded, the effect would have been to expedite the budget process. Only when the negotiating vehicle broke down was the delay compounded. Had the agents of the two legislative branches been able to reach an agreement with each other and the executive, the budget process for FY 1985 might have been greatly eased and simplified.

The perceived necessity for bipartisan, executive-legislative, deficit-reduction negotiations also reveals the extent to which politics is a driving force in the budget process. Politics made these negotiations necessary. The problems dealt with in these negotiations were political problems quite apart from the question of budget procedures. The Reagan administration has concentrated on the larger problem of slowing the growth rate of government spending and, in the last several years, reducing the deficit by cutting domestic spending and (reluctantly) enhancing revenues. These are political issues that would have to be handled, whatever the budget procedure. The deficit-reduction negotiations were initiated because the administration had no confidence that the system set down by the 1974 budget act could deal adequately with the political problems.

The executive branch has had its doubts about the budget procedure's efficacy in facilitating decisions on difficult political questions, but it also has had its aggravations with the budget procedure itself. The uncertainties involved with continuing resolutions have created frustrations for executive agencies. Executive branch bureaucrats are forced to make numerous appearances before duplicate committees, and the higher up one is in the excecutive hierarchy the more time one has to spend on the Hill on budget matters. Both the executive and legislative branches are required to invest inordinate time in making the cumbersome budget process work. The result is little time for other important tasks such as long-range planning. Concentration ends up focused on the immediate problem of the day.

A major issue for the executive branch has been one of control. It has chafed at the vast and increasing number of controls that have been established by Congress. The Department of Defense Authorization Act for 1984, for example, was approximately 100 pages in length, but of these some 80–90 pages consisted of "dos and mostly don'ts." Congress tends toward micromanagement. Committees and Congress as a whole have had an increasing penchant for instituting line-item changes when considering legislation, especially with regard to reprogramming. Yet micromanagement in itself is less a problem than the investments of time and effort required by the budget process.

Of all of the executive departments and agencies, the Department of Defense (DoD) imposes particular problems on the budget process. Defense makes up the major portion of the discretionary budget, and the attempt by Congress to manage its size and complexity has had two unfortunate results. First, Congress has required an interminable flow of reports that places a significant bureaucratic burden on the Defense Department. This, coupled with innumerable committee and subcommittee hearings, threatens to incapacitate top-level management at the DoD. Second, the proliferation of committees and subcommittees that influence defense, in part because of the triplication of function in the budget process, has given added opportunity for special pleading and special interests to incorporate themselves into the process.

The budget process, however, has reached a point beyond mere inefficiency; it now verges on the unmanageable. It consumes so much time and effort that the entire legislative process has become congested and overloaded. Productivity has declined. Determining the winners and losers has become difficult. The 97th Congress in 1981 produced fewer pieces of legislation than any other Congress since the early 1930s.

Much of the executive branch's difficulties with the budget process could be resolved through more adept and perceptive management of the process. For example, executive branch appointees need to take a broader view of the extended time involved with the budget process. While executive branch departments and agencies are immersed in the battle over the current year's budget, the rough-cut budget figures for the following year's budget already have been done at the Office of Management and Budget (OMB). Power in the budget process rests wherever aggregation occurs, and the policy people in each executive department or agency are usually one, if not two, years behind the aggregates already formed by the OMB. The majority of executive appointees tend to concentrate on the current budget, while decisions are being made elsewhere—usually at a lower level—about what is going to happen in the coming years. These decisions rarely reach the top level until they are already largely a fait accompli.

Top-level executive branch appointees need to involve themselves throughout the entire period that a budget is considered. Not only will this enable greater control at critical points in the decision-making process, but also it will further assist executive appointees when they appear at hearings on the Hill. When appointees articulate the executive branch's position before congressional committees, they are confronted by congressional staff people with a strong institutional knowledge and an institutional memory that often exceeds their own. If superior knowledge wins, as is usually the case, the executive budget can and does emerge from committee with 50 percent or more of the line items changed.

The executive branch and Congress each has its part, but the executive branch cannot be successful in fulfilling its role unless it can enter the bargaining process on at least an equal basis with Congress, which at present time it does not do.

The position of the executive branch could be strengthened by the procedural change of implementing a presidential line-item veto. Although the line-item veto certainly would not solve the major problems inherent within the budget process, it would be of some assistance in granting the executive additional leverage with which to negotiate. Some of Congress's favorite add-ons, such as those in the area of defense, could be handled successfully by using the line-item veto. For example, the executive would be able to thwart efforts to maintain such things as aircraft production lines even after the aircraft is obsolete.

Budget process changes focused on the executive branch—enhanced executive management of the process and the implementation of the line-item veto—will not, in themselves, alter significantly the budget process. Only through reform of the congressional budget procedures can the overall budget process be streamlined and made more effective. Schick's recommendations for moving toward a more manageable budget process are a step in the right direction, although his instincts for reform are perhaps too stifled. At the head of needed reforms is a scaled-back budget process with one suggestion being to make appropriations on a biennial, instead of an annual, basis. Authorizations, as well, need not be made annually but at key points. In the area of defense, an example of key-point authorization would be the development of weapon systems. Authorization would be given first to start development and a second time, however many years down the road, to initiate full production.

Any reform of the budget process also must take into consideration the fragmentation of power that has occurred in Congress in general, and with the budget process in particular. More people are now working on the Hill, including the General Accounting Office, Congressional Research Service, and others, than at the Pentagon. The opportunities for these people to become participants in the budget process are numerous, and the more people that become involved in the process, even when they are in general agreement in concept, the more difficult it is to limit the number of proposed modifications. The result for the budget process is that the outcome can become contradictory to the original intentions. The problem then, from an overall perspective, is not simply that successive administrations implement alternating policies, but rather that once a policy is set by the executive branch, almost assuredly the final version will be quite different from the initial proposal—in a myriad of ways. The antidote for the confusion caused by this fragmentation of power within Congress is greater centralization. Caution needs to be exercised in this, of course, but fewer participants are needed in the review process.

There are several ways in which the fragmentation of congressional power might be reversed. One procedural change could be to adjust the subcommittee bill of rights in the House. Twenty-five years ago there were perhaps a dozen really powerful members in the House. The president or the Senate could bring about a solution to a problem by working with just those few people. As a result of the subcommittee bill of rights, however, there are now some 150 individual power centers in the House. Executive branch and Senate dealings with the House thus have become immeasurably more complicated. A step in the direction of simplification and centralization would be some modification in the subcommittee bill of rights so that subcommittee chairs do not have total freedom in deciding what their subcommittees are doing and who their staff members are.

A second procedural change toward the centralization of power within Congress and the simplification of the budget process would be to amend the system instituted by the 1974 budget act. A major step toward undoing the triplication wrought by the budget act would be to have the macro functions of the Budget Committees turned over to the Appropriations Committees. This is not necessarily as major a change as it might seem because many people handle micro and macro budget functions simultaneously. In the Senate, for example, a senator is on one of the four major committees other than the Budget Committee. The membership of the Budget Committee rotates, and senators serving on the main four standing committees also serve on Budget. Thus there are senators who are on both Appropriations and Budget at the same time. A senator is not exclusively a line-item person simply because he or she serves on the Appropriations Committee; when the same senator takes a seat the next day on the Budget Committee, he or she does not become a different human being.

There are nevertheless serious difficulties with any proposal to shift the Budget Committee's function to Appropriations. Although significant cross-fertilization occurs between Appropriations and Budget on the Senate side, there is nothing similar in the House. Representatives do not serve on both committees simultaneously. Serving on the Appropriations Committee, while it does not exclude one from wider horizons, focuses attention on line items and does not sensitize committee members to larger economic considerations. The Appropriations Committee, on these larger issues, has a history of being incapacitated. During the Vietnam period, which preceded the budget act, for example, Appropriations had no interest in the macro budget issue. The Appropriations Committees, in short, might find making economic policy very difficult. Appropriations is a process of supplying money to agencies, and, unless their behavior and orientation were modified, their committees could not fulfill the macro function. Transferring the Budget Committee's functions to Appropriations would be no more difficult than setting up the Budget Committee in the first place, but as long as the Appropriations Committees themselves do not press for such a change, it is of course not going to take place.

In reality, it is unlikely that any consolidations of power in the budget process, whatever their scope, will be implemented within the foreseeable future. The executive branch's proposal for a presidential line-item veto lies dead in the water. The procedures established by the 1974 budget act, aside from a few minor adjustments and unique annual variations, are entrenched firmly. A significant procedural overhaul, barring the inevitable changes that a major military conflict would entail, will not take place in the absence of a major change in the composition of the Congress, and this is not probable in the near future.

Given, therefore, that the current budget process is so complex and time consuming, it tends not only to preclude other congressional activity but also itself to break down and become inoperable. And given that Congress has little inclination to institute serious procedural reforms at the moment, then what are the possibilities for the amelioration of difficulties of the budget process? Schick's do-nothing approach might give time for an economic recovery to ease pressure on both Congress and the executive branch. In any case, if Congress is not interested in even piecemeal adjustments, what other alternative is there?

A laissez-faire approach to the difficulties of the budget process, however, will not resolve the problem. Action can be taken, even if the road to major procedural reform cannot be traveled.The procedural and the substantive are both important sides to the budget process crisis. Political decisions about substantive economic issues are a part of the process, and political decisions, as much as economic recovery, can ease the budget process difficulties. The preeminent political problem with regard to the budget process is, at the moment, the question of revenues. The ultimate problem is matching revenues with expenditures to produce a rational overall fiscal policy. The process has become bogged down because of the imbalance of revenues and outlays. Eight to ten years ago when there was money available, there was not such a problem with the budget process. Now, something has to be done. Either substantial additional revenues must be raised or substantial additional spending cuts must be made or a combination of the two must be instituted. What happens will be a political decision, but it must be made if the budget process is to operate more smoothly and with greater efficacy.

The predominance of revenues in the political equation points out the significance of the congressional tax committees for the budget process. Certainly Senator Robert Dole, chairman of the Senate Finance Committee, thinks his committee is an integral part of the budget process, and the major role that he has played in recent budget negotiations confirms this.This chapter has given us an excellent historical review and a superb static description of the budget process.We must realize, however, that the discussion was limited to a small portion of the budget, dealing with its controllable parts such as defense, and mentioning little of the entitlements process and its relationship to overall federal expenditures.To consider fully whether or not Congress can adequately deal with the budget, we need to add an assessment of how both the revenue side and the nondiscretionary part of the budget work their influence.

4

The War Powers Resolution: A Continuing Constitutional Struggle

Frederick S. Tipson

The War Powers Resolution of 1973 marks an area of continuing turmoil in executive-legislative relations. The atmosphere surrounding the resolution's passage and its subsequent invocations has been contentious and confused. Continuation of this state of affairs indefinitely would be divisive domestically and possibly dangerous internationally. Responsibility for this situation rests on all three branches of the federal government, and the prospects for significant improvement will depend upon the restrained realism and determined collaboration of both Congress and the executive branch, as well as the cooperation—or at least the indulgence—of the federal courts.

This chapter is a short study of the War Powers Resolution in the broader context of executive-legislative relations. It is written from the perspective of a former congressional staff member, who was not "present at the creation" but who was directly involved in congressional-executive deliberations on the subject between 1978 and 1984—nearly half the life of the resolution. Its premise is that the War Powers Resolution was a necessary and important initiative but that the current state of constitutional contention should not be allowed to continue.

The first section provides a chronological summary of the record of executive-legislative relations during the resolution's passage and sub-

Frederick S. Tipson is currently serving as counsel for AT&T. He was chief counsel on the Senate Foreign Relations Majority Staff from 1981 to 1984, and prior to this he was minority counsel on the Senate Foreign Relations Committee. Tipson has also worked in the Department of State as a legal assistant in the Office of Assistant Legal Adviser for European Affairs.

sequent implementation, followed by an issue-by-issue discussion of the provisions subject to continuing disagreement. It draws upon two indispensable studies of these issues—John Sullivan's careful summary issued in 1982 by the House Foreign Affairs Committee and Taylor Reveley's excellent *War Powers of the President and Congress*.[1] As both of these studies make clear, the War Powers Resolution is but one aspect of a larger and still unfinished saga. (The entire text of the resolution is printed in an appendix directly following this chapter.)

Passionate Passage, 1970–1973

The War Powers Resolution and the pressure for its enactment are best understood not simply as the consequence of a "runaway" presidency—as some people described the situation at the time—but also, in a different sense, of a "runaway" Congress. For years Congress had tended to run away from the recognition and acceptance of its constitutional responsibilities regarding the commitment of U.S. forces to hostilities. Events leading up to final passage of the resolution over President Nixon's veto in November 1973 reflected widespread uncertainty and disagreement among the legislators as to what those responsibilities were. But the veto override also marked a turning point in the views of most members of Congress that, whatever the defects of the final version might be, Congress had a duty to assure itself a central role in decisions by the United States to use armed force. In short, the War Powers Resolution offered an opportunity that should not be lost. The significance of the resolution is as much in the message it sent to future Congresses as in the framework it prescribed for future presidents.

The executive branch, in contrast, tended to approach the issue as an illegitimate effort to rewrite the Constitution. In the defensive, confrontational atmosphere created by the Vietnam War and Watergate in 1972–1973, the White House found it difficult to cooperate with the architects and engineers of the war powers effort in the Senate, despite overtures from key senators in that direction.[2] By late 1973, the president had also succeeded in alienating certain key members of the House, including the late Clement Zablocki (D-Wis.), who had originally opposed any resolution not acceptable to the administration.

Relations between Congress and the White House at the time of passage and override were not simply confrontational, but openly hostile. The veto message was considered shortly after the resignation of Vice President Spiro Agnew, the president's dismissal of the Special Watergate Prosecutor Leon Jaworski (the "Saturday Night Massacre") and the serious Soviet-U.S. confrontation in the Middle East during the Yom

Kippur War—in short, at a time when the atmosphere of crisis and the taint of White House corruption and megalomania were at a high point. The siege mentality and low credibility of the president removed any prospect for a last-minute compromise that might have made the law more palatable to future presidents, and they undoubtedly accounted for the margin necessary to override the veto in the House.

Nonetheless, to view the War Powers Resolution as merely an anti-Nixon aberration lacking broad, long-term support in Congress would be a serious mistake. Nor was it a hastily drafted, undebated piece of legislation peculiar to the circumstances at the time. The three-year development of the resolution itself was part of a broader effort by important members of Congress to rethink the role of Congress in foreign affairs. Any serious effort to adjust the provisions and procedures of the law will likewise have to address the issue not as a raw power struggle, but as a problem of institutional and constitutional definition.

Yet it bears remembering, in any discussion of the War Powers Resolution and its history, that the law was born in an atmosphere of unusual strain and suspicion, and that the original objective of its authors—to establish a consensus in the Congress and a compact with future presidents on a national issue of the utmost gravity—was thwarted by the circumstances of its birth.

Cambodian Invasion

Congressional initiatives on the war powers issue began in earnest in 1970, following the invasion of Cambodia in April. That operation began a day after Secretary of State William P. Rogers testified before the Senate Foreign Relations Committee in closed session on U.S. policy in Indochina without any indication that such an action was planned. Key members of Congress took this as an unnecessary insult and an unacceptable provocation.[3] The public outcry that followed the invasion reinforced their determination to insist upon a stronger congressional role in decisions regarding the use of force.

In the Senate, proposals initially centered on the use of funding restrictions—the "power of the purse"—to confine (the Cooper-Church amendment) and even prohibit (the McGovern-Hatfield amendment) further conduct of the war. A parallel effort, led by Senators Charles Mathias (R-Md.), Mike Mansfield (D-Mont.), and Robert Dole (R-Kans.), involved repeal of the Tonkin Gulf Resolution, although at the time this step was viewed by many as having more symbolic than constitutional effect.[4]

Many members of the Senate, including some strong critics of the war, were not comfortable, however, with resorting to funding limitations during an ongoing conflict. In their view this approach was not only poor policy and poor politics, but also implied that Congress had no direct, determinative role in major decisions about war and peace. Senators Jacob Javits (R-N.Y.), John Stennis (D-Miss.), and Thomas Eagleton (D-Mo.), in particular, set about the task of framing more comprehensive and generic legislation to assure meaningful congressional involvement in future decisions to go to war.[5]

Senate Version

The Senate's approach, under Javits's leadership, proceeded from an interpretation of the original intent of the authors of the Constitution. Drawing largely upon James Madison's notes of the Philadelphia Convention, Javits interpreted the Constitution as retaining in Congress the basic authority to decide whether to introduce U.S. forces into combat, except for such emergency authority as the president might need to "repel sudden attacks" upon the territory, forces, or citizens of the United States. His drafts of the legislation—which essentially prevailed in the Senate—enumerated the circumstances in which the president was deemed to have authority to commit the armed forces to hostilities or to introduce them into "situations where imminent involvement in hostilities is clearly indicated by the circumstances." Javits also sought to establish a time limit for the president's exercise of emergency authority and—drawing upon a bill passed by the very first Congress with respect to the president's authority to respond to Indian attacks—set that limit at 30 days.

House Version

The House proceeded in a much different manner. Except for the early proposals of Representatives Paul Findley (R-Ill.) and Dante Fascell (D-Fla.), whose initial drafts for a war powers bill were closer to the Senate approach, few members of the House supported the idea of explicitly enumerating the president's authority.[6] Furthermore, the most influential member of the House on this issue, Clement Zablocki, seemed determined until the late stages of consideration to reject any approach not supported by the president himself. As the bill evolved in the House, it embodied a different framework from the Senate drafts. The House approach relied heavily upon advance consultation, detailed reporting requirements, and, eventually, a legislative veto mechanism—all of which grew out of provisions developed by Representative Findley. The final House version also provided a far more generous period of emergency authority, 120 days.

House-Senate Conference

The key process in producing the final version was, therefore, the House-Senate conference in the fall of 1973. The eventual compromise version was closer to the House approach than to the Senate bill. Although Javits tried to retain the Senate's definition of presidential authority, the final compromise relegated that provision to a nonbinding "purpose and policy" section of the legislation and left out one of its central features—the authority of the president to rescue U.S. citizens abroad.[7] The remainder of the bill approximated the provisions for consultation, reporting, and congressional veto contained in the House bill, with a compromise on the emergency time period of 60 days.

Presidential Veto

President Nixon's veto message outlined the practical and constitutional objections to the resolution that his successors have generally shared.[8] It centered on the 60-day time limitation on presidential authority—Section 5(b)—and the procedure for terminating unauthorized involvement in hostilities by concurrent resolution—Section 5(c). Notwithstanding the override of his veto, the president's position remained that such legislation is inconsistent with the Constitution itself and therefore without effect on the authority of the presidency.

Sporadic Sparring, 1973–1983

Nearly 10 years passed without a test of the War Powers Resolution's provisions relating to extended hostilities. During this period the central differences reflected in President Nixon's veto message remained largely dormant. In particular, the 60-day limitation and the concurrent resolution veto did not come into play because the country confronted no situations involving serious, prolonged hostilities.Disputes did arise from time to time, however, with respect to various matters of interpretation and application and revealed a continuing reluctance on the part of executive branch officials to concede the constitutionality—much less the desirability—of the resolution.

The Ford Administration

President Ford first confronted the questions of consultation and reporting in a series of rescue operations in Indochina during the spring of 1975—at Danang, Phnom Penh, and Saigon, and of the U.S. merchant ship *Mayaguez* . Ford had led the fight against passage of the resolution while minority leader in the House; he was convinced of its unconstitutionality and unworkability.[9] At the same time, he did not wish to be seen as violating the provisions on consultation and reporting or to complicate his larger problems by unnecessarily provoking constitutional confrontations with Congress. Furthermore, as a product of the congressional leadership, Ford undoubtedly had little difficulty with the idea that the president should consult key members of Congress whenever possible on such matters, and he made sincere efforts to do so.[10]

He also wanted to preserve the argument that such cooperation could not be compelled by statute, however, and therefore established the pattern of pro forma reports "taking note" of the resolution, but refusing to acknowledge its legitimacy. Instead, he rested his authority on the Constitution's commander in chief clause. Because all four emergency rescue operations were concluded in a matter of days, the broader constitutional issues between the president and Congress simply were not joined.

The Carter Administration

President Carter took a considerably different tack at the outset of his term. Responding to a question in one of his first radio "phone-ins," Carter indicated that he regarded the resolution as providing for an "appropriate reduction" in the powers of the presidency.[11] Statements by other key members of his administration also implied that they were prepared to live with the statute even though there might be provisions they did not endorse.[12]

Until the ill-fated hostage rescue attempt in Iran in April 1980, the Carter administration was also spared a situation in which "imminent involvement in hostilities was clearly indicated by the circumstances." A few, mainly definitional, questions arose at the time of the U.S.-assisted airlift of Belgian troops into the Shaba province of the Congo in 1978, but this episode was not widely viewed as a war powers dispute.[13]

The hostage rescue mission provoked a brief flurry of congressional comments relating to the War Powers Resolution and the lack of prior consultation. Administration officials argued in response that the requirement for advance consultation "in every possible instance" did not apply to situations of such paramount secrecy and sensitivity as the Iran rescue plan. During this discussion, Presidential Counsel Lloyd Cutler produced a brief memorandum on the subject, suggesting that the failure of the resolution to recognize the inherent authority of the president to rescue U.S. citizens raised serious questions about its constitutionality.[14]

The Reagan Administration

President Reagan came to office with a record of professed hostility toward the War Powers Resolution. Nevertheless, his designated spokesperson on foreign policy, Secretary of State Alexander Haig, made clear in his confirmation hearings that "despite some honest differences on certain aspects of the application of the act," he intended to "live by the letter of the law and the spirit of the War Powers Act" and foresaw "no difficulty in doing so."[15] Haig's successor, George Shultz, made similar comments during his own confirmation hearings 18 months later.[16] Until 1983, there was little reason to doubt such professions of acceptance, despite several occasions on which the applicability of the resolution was an issue.

El Salvador provided the first opportunity. The dispatch of 55 military advisers to that country in early 1981 resulted in extensive hearings and discussions about the role and limits of U.S. involvement.[17] Administration officials gave firm assurances that these personnel would neither be "equipped for combat," as the resolution provides, nor sent into areas of likely hostilities. Furthermore, they would not be permitted to direct the ongoing combat operations of Salvadoran troops even from a distance—a function that would have come under the resolution's definition of "introduction" into hostile situations. From time to time legislators questioned whether such restrictions were being observed fully, but the greater congressional concern was that President Reagan might consider the possibility of larger, more direct military involvement in the area.

A second occasion was the highly publicized skirmish in the Gulf of Sidra in August 1981, during which U.S. fighters downed two Libyan attackers without further involvement.[18] Although the incident became better known because the president was not awakened in the middle of the night to be told of it, questions were raised as to whether the reporting requirements of the resolution should apply to situations in which U.S. forces in international waters were fired upon without warning. The point was not pressed, however, and no formal report was submitted.

During the Falkland Islands conflict in March 1982, Congress itself considered whether the passage of concurrent resolutions in support of the British effort might somehow be construed as providing authority for direct U.S. involvement. The final Senate resolution was carefully drafted to avoid such an implication.[19] Later that year, the effort by Senator Steve Symms (R-Ida.) to reenact the exact language of the 1962 joint resolution on Cuba also prompted debate regarding the implications of such a step for the War Powers Resolution. The version that finally passed as an amendment to a continuing appropriations bill contained language preserving the full requirements of the resolution.[20]

Finally, in August 1982, and again in September, the dispatch of U.S. Marines to Beirut generated a number of congressional calls for presidential reports triggering the authorization procedures of the resolution.[21] For nearly a year, however, the level of danger seemed sufficiently manageable to most members of Congress that the issue was not pressed to the point of confrontation. At the end of the congressional session in December, 14 of the 16 members of the Senate Foreign Relations Committee sent a letter to the president urging him to consult carefully with Congress before substantially changing or enlarging the U.S. role in Lebanon.[22] In the spring of 1983, that restriction was formally written into the Lebanon Emergency Assistance Act.[23]

Sudden Shocks, 1983

The latent tensions of the first 10 years of the War Powers Resolution became prominent public disputes during the second half of 1983. On June 23, the Supreme Court announced its landmark decision on the legislative veto issue, *Immigration and Naturalization Service v. Chadha*, which seemed to nullify completely Section 5(c), one of the key provisions of the resolution. Two months later, an outbreak of hostilities in Lebanon resulted in the death of four marines and led to congressional action under the other major provision of the resolution, the specific authorization procedure of Section 5(b). Finally, on October 25, 1983, the United States led an invasion of the island of Grenada to protect Americans and restore order; Congress responded not with endorsement or condemnation, but by passing language invoking the applicability of the War Powers Resolution. Each of these developments had critical significance for the future of the resolution and dwarfed all earlier skirmishes regarding its application.

The Chadha Decision

The Supreme Court delivered its constitutional rejection of the legislative veto in a sweeping and categorical opinion.[24] At first it seemed to leave no question about its impact on the War Powers Resolution, except perhaps as to whether the effected section was "severable" from the remainder of the statute. Administration spokespersons followed up the decision with carefully modulated statements reinforcing the view that Section 5(c) had been surgically removed from the law.[25]

On October 20, the Senate took steps to salvage what little seemed left of the veto procedure by amending the War Powers Resolution to substitute a joint resolution in place of the concurrent resolution for termination of unauthorized combat involvement.[26] Because of strong resistance from the House, however, this provision was changed in conference to create a free-standing, expedited procedure for joint resolutions mandating troop withdrawals, without reference to the War Powers Resolution itself.[27]

On closer analysis of the Supreme Court's decison, such sweeping conclusions are difficult to reconcile with other long-established lines of argument used by the Court. Beginning with the landmark *Curtiss-Wright Export Corporation* opinion in 1936, the Supreme Court repeatedly has distinguished the standards governing congressional authority in foreign and domestic affairs.[28] Most recently, in the 1981 *Dames & Moore* decision upholding the hostage-release agreements with Iran, the Court found that congressional silence was "acquiescence" and equivalent to the necessary congressional authorization, because Congress had the opportunity to express its opposition by means of a concurrent resolution and did not do so.[29]

By this reasoning, if the president can derive authority from congressional silence, Congress should at least be able to employ the concurrent resolution procedure to register its dissent and lack of support for presidential actions. In circumstances in which its authorization is required for presidential action, such opposition should be sufficient to disallow such actions. In other cases, it could be used as an effective political restraint, even if it were not available as a legally controlling procedure.[30] Nevertheless, it is clear that the *Chadha* decision dealt a blow to the perceived legitimacy of the War Powers Resolution and thereby made all the more significant the subsequent experience with procedures under its other principal provision—Section 5(b).

Lebanon Resolution

The rapid deterioration of the Lebanese situation in August 1983 not only resulted in U.S. Marine fatalities on August 29, but also began a series of hostile exchanges of fire that left little doubt that the resolution's threshold definition of hostilities had been crossed. Despite White House reluctance to concede the obvious, the president did report to Congress as required by Section 4 of the resolution within 48 hours.[31] But he did not specify that he was reporting under Section 4(a) (1), the provision relating to hostile situations, which automatically would have triggered the further requirement for specific authorization within 60 days.

When Congress returned from its Labor Day recess, therefore, the ball was in its court. Senator Mathias was the first to take the next logical step; he introduced a joint resolution of specific authorization as contemplated under the resolution, which included a finding that hostilities had commenced on August 29 and provided for an authorization extending six months from that date.[32] Under the "priority procedures" of the resolution, this gave Congress 60 days to consider the matter and come to a decision regarding further authorization.

The following week, after intense negotiations with the White House, a coalition of congressional leaders led by House Speaker Thomas O'Neill, Jr. (D-Mass.) and Senate Majority Leader Howard Baker (R-Tenn.) introduced a compromise version of an authorizing resolution entitled the "Multinational Force in Lebanon Resolution." It keyed the authorization to the limited mandate of the Multinational Force (MNF) and placed an 18-month time restriction on it. [33] After intense debate the joint resolution was passed by both Houses, essentially as introduced, and signed by the president. The vote in the Senate was almost completely along party lines.[34] In his statement at the signing, President Reagan made it clear that he did not believe an authorization was required to enable him to maintain U.S. troops in Lebanon, and he reiterated his constitutional objections to the War Powers Resolution itself.[35]

Despite efforts to reduce and even repeal the authorization and the tragic loss of 264 U.S. Marines in a terrorist bombing on October 19, the law remained in place through the withdrawal of the marines in February 1984.[36] But the process of passage and implementation revealed once again the intense feelings surrounding the war powers issue. For many members of Congress, it was the first occasion on which they had confronted the constitutional questions involved, at least in the context of having to vote for a specific authorization when U.S. lives were immediately at stake. For all members, it was the first experience in considering such an authorization under Section 5(b) and the expedited procedures of the War Powers Resolution—a process that was completed within 30 days of the original outbreak of hostilities, despite the Labor Day recess.

Apart from the Lebanon context, therefore, this experience revived some of the openly contentious atmosphere that prevailed between the branches during the period of original enactment. The Lebanon episode accentuated once again the resistance and objections that presidents have maintained against the authorization requirements of the resolution and also revealed the strong determination of most members of Congress to maintain a legislative role in such decisions. Constitutional abstractions were once again made concrete—as during the Vietnam War—by the commitment and sacrifice of U.S. lives in a foreign country.

Grenada Operation

The U.S.-led invasion of Grenada marked a further important chapter in the war powers experience of 1983. Undertaken without even token efforts at consultation, the operation quickly gained widespread bipartisan support in the Congress as the circumstances and apparent success of the effort became known.[37] Once again, the key congressional role was played by House Speaker O'Neill, whose initial skepticism was overcome by the report of a House delegation dispatched to the island.

From a constitutional standpoint, the president's initiative seemed well founded on the need to protect a thousand or more U.S. citizens in a situation of apparent anarchy. On international legal grounds, the United States also had a strong case for intervention, based on the collective request of the Organization of Eastern Caribbean States (OECS) following an urgent appeal from the governor general of Grenada.[38]

Without challenging the constitutional or other grounds for the operation, Congress moved to make clear that the War Powers Resolution applied to the situation. The Senate passed an amendment to the debt-ceiling bill introduced by Senator Gary Hart (D-Colo.) that was identical to language reported by the House Foreign Affairs Committee in a free-standing joint resolution passed later by the full House.[39] Neither vehicle was approved by both Houses.

It is not clear, however, what such an invocation of the War Powers Resolution was intended to accomplish in this situation. Presumably, the purpose was to accelerate the process of U.S. extrication from Grenada by implying the need for a further authorization to maintain combat troops on the island beyond the 60-day period contained in the War Powers Resolution. Apparently, the action did have its intended result, as the Reagan administration was careful to remove all U.S. combat forces within the 60-day time frame.

Nevertheless, it is by no means certain that congressional authorization would have been required by the War Powers Resolution under the circumstances of the Grenada operation. In particular, the question has never been resolved whether the "60-day clock" begun by the introduction or outbreak of hostilities can be said to "stop ticking" if those hostilities cease, as they did in Grenada within a couple of weeks. Because the War Powers Resolution is premised on the theory that the president requires specific authorization to maintain combat forces in actual or imminent hostilities beyond an emergency period—but not simply to maintain such forces abroad in a peaceful environment—arguably he would not require congressional action once hostilities end. The administration's decision to withdraw the forces within the deadline avoided this potential dispute.[40]

Continuing Contention, 1984–?

Despite the intense attention paid to the War Powers Resolution in 1983, little was resolved or revised by the year's events—with the possible exception of the legislative veto issue. Yet even with respect to that issue, questions remain unanswered as to how its loss can be reconciled with other established constitutional lines of argument. The issues that arose during the Lebanon and Grenada operations continue, adding to a decade of other, less prominent disputes that underlie executive-legislative relations in this area. These issues can be summarized in six broad categories.

Constitutional Theory

The basic dispute about the Constitution remains unresolved. The theoretical basis of the resolution—that the authority of the president to engage in hostilities is of a temporary, emergency nature requiring eventual congressional sanction and subject to congressional termination—has not been accepted in practice by any of the four presidents who confronted it. The theory itself has not been helped by the presence of Section 2(c) of the resolution defining the limits of presidential authority, which, even in the view of some of the resolution's authors, is too narrowly drawn to be viable.

On the other hand, the contrary view that the commander in chief clause grants virtually unrestricted authority to the president to deploy the armed forces whenever and wherever he sees fit, subject only to the availability of appropriations and the prospect of electoral defeat or impeachment, finds scant support in the Constitution or the record of its ratification. Such an interpretation would effectively read out of the Constitution the powers reserved to the Congress to declare war and to make rules for the armed forces. It would thereby nullify one of the fundamental objectives of the Constitution's authors in mitigating the dangers of unchecked presidential adventurism.

The argument that the president has authority to conduct defensive military operations and requires congressional approval only before launching offensive actions also begs the question of how and by whom such distinctions are to be drawn.[41] Given the ease with which it generally is possible to justify any operation as defensive in nature, this distinction appears more like an assertion that the president has independent authority to do what is lawful under the UN Charter and requires congressional approval only to do what is unlawful.

There are also related questions. Can Congress limit or prohibit peacetime deployments in other countries? Congressional leaders clearly thought so in the early 1950s regarding the dispatch of additional forces to Europe, notwithstanding the existence of the NATO treaty.[42] Regarding the NATO and other defense treaties, can the Senate delegate to the president the authority to commit forces in defense of other countries without further congressional action? Most U.S. defense treaties refer to action by the United States "in accordance with" U.S. "constitutional processes." During Senate consideration of the NATO treaty, Secretary of State Dean Acheson agreed that the treaty did not obviate the need for congressional action in the event of war.[43] Yet undoubtedly most Americans assume that mutual defense treaties amount to advance authorizations. Could they? And should they?

Finally, how far could Congress go, even by means of a statute passed over a presidential veto, in directing or confining a means of a statute passed over a presidential veto, in directing or confining a planned or ongoing military action? This issue arose in the Lebanon context, even though it was defused to some degree by the compromise resolution achieved with the White House. Is any statutory time limit, for example, constitutional?

None of these questions is purely theoretical. Each relates to concrete problems that surround any consideration of the war powers issue and may, sooner or later, be the cause of serious disagreements between the branches in the midst of future crises.

Thresholds

Assuming that such broader constitutional issues can be managed or resolved in principle, what are the appropriate triggering points and definitions that should apply to such matters? Is war, for example, the same thing as hostilities? Or, is it something greater in scope or duration? Are "peacekeeping" operations such as that undertaken in Lebanon something different still?

Does "introduction" of forces refer only to the deliberate initiation of an action? Or, does it also apply to situations in which U.S. forces already located abroad are attacked or unintentionally drawn into combat situations? Are "United States Armed Forces" only those uniformed services personnel on active duty, or should the War Powers Resolution be extended—as Senator Eagleton originally sought to do—to include all personnel under the control of the U.S. government, including covert operatives?[44] Finally, what does "equipped for combat" mean? Are sidearms sufficient or does one need an M–16, or even something more? All of these issues have arisen in the Central American context.[45]

Consultation

Few issues are greater cause for acrimony between the branches than whether or not genuine consultation has taken place. Yet there is seldom agreement on any dimension of the matter: the who, what, how, when, or why.

Which committees or leadership groups should be consulted and in what priority?[46] What should be discussed with them? Should they be presented with the principal options and facts and asked for their recommendations, or is the point simply to elicit reactions to a course already decided upon? How and where should it be done—by convening a designated congressional crisis group or simply by a series of individual phone calls?

At what stage should such consultation take place? Can members of Congress and their staffs be trusted to keep a secret and to maintain the proper security precautions? Or, is it in fact expected that they will consult both their staffs and their colleagues to provide more effective responses?

Finally, what is the purpose of such consultations? Is it to obtain advance approval or blessing for the operations, or is it simply to test and prepare for the probable congressional and public reaction? Is there a value simply in using consultation to combat the kind of inbred "group-think" mentality that sometimes governs secret decision making among a restricted group of presidential advisers?

Reporting

Another point of contention is the reporting requirement of Section 4(a) of the resolution. Formal reports are required from the president in any one of three contingencies: the introduction of combat forces into a hostile situation, the commitment of such forces into a foreign country regardless of the danger, and the enlargement of an existing combat presence abroad. Only in the first situation does the report itself trigger the requirement for congressional authorization within 60 days.

As President Reagan demonstrated in the late summer of 1983, however, there is great reluctance in the White House to set in motion the authorization requirements of the law. Even when favorable action by the Congress can be expected, presidents no doubt will be loath to initiate a procedure that implies that they lack the constitutional authority to proceed without it. Furthermore, the law does not explicitly require that the president specify in his report which section of the law—the triggering provision, Section 4(a)(1), or one of the other grounds for a report—under which he is reporting. Although President Reagan did report within the time frame required in the Lebanon case, he took advantage of this loophole. Recognizing this possibility, the statute was drafted to allow Congress to proceed even without receipt of the report.[47] Nevertheless, the resistance of the president on this point generated friction and resentment in Congress, which can and did erode the mutual respect and trust that should otherwise characterize relations on such important questions.

The noncombat reporting requirements of course seldom come into play, largely because of the exclusion from the law of supply and training operations.[48] Even large joint military maneuvers, such as those conducted in recent years with Egypt and Honduras, are not covered.

Sixty-Day Limit

The theoretical objection to this provision from the beginning emphasized the danger that Congress, by its inaction, could pull the rug out from under the commander in chief, leaving him without authority even though no vote had been taken on the matter. In practice, however, that circumstance is unlikely; the priority procedures of the law make it almost a certainty that the House or the Senate will consider a specific authorization for military operations expected to last longer than two months.

The greater danger, as nearly illustrated by the Lebanon operation, is that Congress and the president might be unable to agree upon the terms of such an authorization, thereby producing a constitutional confrontation in the midst of an ongoing military crisis. The apparent demise of the legislative veto procedure actually makes such a prospect more likely.

Legislative Veto

Removing the veto may do little to reduce—and may actually increase—the potential for friction between the branches on this issue. Without the congressional veto framework, Congress must become more active and aggressive if it is to retain a role in the war powers area. The veto provided the flexibility for a case-by-case, wait-and-see approach. In its absence, the tendency probably will grow toward more narrowly drafted authorizations on shorter time frames.

Reasonable Resolution

The elements of a reasonable, workable, and constitutional accommodation between the branches are contained within the War Powers Resolution itself. Whether or not the resolution is amended formally to clarify this framework, the law could be interpreted and applied so as to preserve the prerogatives of both branches, while providing a basis for national security to be protected and democratic checks and balances to be maintained. No single formula can guarantee good government by wise leaders. But the essential elements of a much-needed consensus are essentially within the bounds of the current statute if both branches were determined to apply them:

- A presidential initiative to respond to emergencies with mobilization, positioning, and the threat or use of force as the president deems necessary.
- A congressional responsibility to advise, review, and judge the president's actions as soon as possible, but in any case, within the 60 days specified in the resolution. The failure of Congress to act by majority vote would constitute acquiescence to the president's behavior and policy.
- A presidential obligation to accept the majority position of Congress as expressed either by a positive authorization or resolution of support or by a negative concurrent resolution.

In such a framework, the courts would play no role in second-guessing the president in the event of congressional silence or in ruling on the constitutionality of congressional resolutions. This general accommodation could be reached in negotiations between the White House and congressional leadership at the beginning of a Congress and eventually might be embodied in a concurrent resolution or even in an amendment to the War Powers Resolution.

This approach would satisfy neither the "presidential imperialists," who concede no meaningful role for Congress, nor the "congressional overreachers," who demand nothing less than prior approval of presidential actions. But it would be a more constitutional and more appropriate condition than either have proposed and should relieve much of the dangerous disagreement, confusion, and procedural pettiness that will otherwise continue to surround this critical issue.

Both branches must also recognize that control of the military option is also exercised through policies affecting the development, deployment, and capabilities of U.S. armed forces, including such issues as research and development, foreign military assistance and collaboration, and arms control. In general, Congress may more effectively and constructively influence decisions on the use of military force in the nuclear age by careful execution of the authorization and appropriations processes than by its participation in discrete commitments of U.S. forces to hostile situations abroad.

Postscript

On March 2, 1984, Secretary of State George Shultz was quoted as expressing strong criticism of the War Powers Resolution and suggesting that congressional behavior may have been responsible for the failure of the Multinational Force in Lebanon: "I'm not saying I'm sitting here with the answer, but I think the experience shows that the War Powers

Act and the way it works ought to be reviewed carefully." He went on to say that "[i]t's hard to conduct a policy in which you're on-again-off-again in terms of what you might be authorized to do. . . . I think we could have probably been more flexible with our forces than we were because you get involved in a process of consultation, which in the situation we were in is difficult to do privately."[49]

Without disputing or accepting the criticism expressed by Secretary Shultz, his comments demonstrate the importance of recognizing a critical distinction in all discussions of the war powers issue, namely, the difference between constitutional authority and wise behavior. Whether or not Congress effectively and responsibly discharges the authority granted to it in the Constitution—whatever that authority may be—is a very different question than whether the opportunity to exercise that authority should be assured.

Notes

1. U.S. House. Committee on Foreign Affairs. *The War Powers Resolution*, Special Study (H. Rpt. 98). Washington, D.C.: USGPO, 1982. [Hereafter cited as Sullivan Study]; W. Taylor Reveley III, *War Powers of the President and Congress: Who Holds the Arrows and Olive Branch* ? (Charlotteville, Va.: University Press of Virginia, 1981). For a highly critical study, see Robert F. Turner, *The War Powers Resolution: Its Implementation in Theory and Practice* (Philadelphia, Pa.: Foreign Policy Research Institute, 1983).

2. Senator Jacob Javits (R-N.Y.), in particular, had hoped initially that the outcome of congressional consideration would be a sort of "compact" with the executive branch. See his study *Who Makes War?* (New York: William Morrow, 1983) and his autobiography with Rafael Steinberg, *Javits: The Autobiography of a Public Man* (Boston: Houghton Mifflin, 1981). During the 1971 Senate Foreign Relations Committee hearings, Chairman William Fulbright expressed great disappointment "at the negative response to what I thought and believed to be a good faith offer . . . to try to make progress in a reconciliation . . . between the Congress and the executive in this area." (Quoted in Sullivan Study, 75.) Rep. Clement Zablocki also expressed regrets about the apparent inability of key administration officials to pursue a possible compromise. (Quoted in Sullivan Study, 61, note 45.)

One of those in the executive branch who apparently did seek a cooperative approach during this period was David M. Abshire, former President of Georgetown University's Center for Strategic and International Studies and at the time the assistant secretary of state for congressional relations. Sullivan Study, 99.

3. Conversations with former Javits staff aide and key war powers architect Peter Lakeland.

4. The Tonkin Gulf Resolution provided for its own repeal by concurrent resolution. Such a resolution (S. Con. Res. 64) was passed on July 10, 1970. The resolution was also repealed in legislation approved on January 12, 1971,

which provided retroactively for termination on January 2, 1971. This provision was passed and signed after the administration made clear that it did not regard the resolution as providing its authority to continue the war.

5. Conversations with former Javits aide Peter Lakeland.

6. Sullivan Study, 47–52.

7. In his memoirs, Javits recounts his efforts to preserve what he regarded as the essence of his approach. *Javits: The Autobiography, supra* note 2.

8. Reprinted in Reveley, *War Powers, supra* note 1 at 293–297.

9. The former president expressed some of his concerns in a speech soon after leaving office. Ford, "The War Powers Resolution: Striking a Balance between the Executive and Legislative Branches," April 11, 1977, reprinted in U.S. Senate. Committee on Foreign Relations. *War Powers Resolution* Hearings, 95th Cong., 1st sess., 1977. Washington, D.C.: USGPO, 1977.

10. These are recounted in Turner, *The War Powers Resolution, supra* noted 1 at 48–65. See also U.S. House. Committee on International Relations. Subcommittee on International Security and Scientific Affairs. *War Powers: A Test of Compliance Relative to the Danang Sealift , and the Evacuation of Phnom Penh, the Evacuation of Saigon, and the Mayaguez Incident* Hearings, 94th Cong., 1st sess., May 7 and June 4, 1975. Washington, D.C.: USGPO, 1975.

11. Quoted in Pat M. Holt, *The War Powers Resolution: The Role of Congress in U.S. Armed Intervention* (Washington, D.C. American Enterprise Institute, 1978), 2.

12. With respect to the key provisions of the War Powers Resolution, Sections 5(b) and 5(c), State Department Legal Adviser Herbert Hansell testified before the Senate Foreign Relations Committee on July 15, 1977, that "[t]his administration as a matter of policy intends to follow the letter and spirit of section 5." In his confirmation testimony, Secretary of State Vance gave no indication that he had serious problems with the consultation provisions of the resolution. U.S. Senate. Committee on Foreign Relations. provisions of the resolution. U.S. Senate. Committee on Foreign Relations. *Vance Nomination* Hearings, 95th Cong., 1st sess. January 11, 1977, p. 38. Washington, D.C.: USGPO, 1977.

13. Hearings were conducted on this question by the U.S. House. Committee on Foreign Affairs. Subcommittee on International Security and Scientific Affairs. *Congressional Oversight of War Powers Compliance: Zaire Airlift* Hearings, 95th Cong. 2d sess., August 10, 1978. Washington, D.C.: USGPO, 1978.

14. The text of this memorandum is reprinted in U.S. House. Committee on Foreign Affairs. Subcommittee on International Security and Scientific Affairs. *The War Powers Resolution: Relevant Documents, Correspondence, Reports,* 98th Cong., 1st sess., December 1983. Washington, D.C.: USGPO, 1983.

15. U.S. Senate. Committee on Foreign Relations. *Nomination of Alexander M. Haig, Jr.* Hearings, 97th Cong. 1st sess., January 9, 1981, p. 34. Washington, D.C.: USGPO, 1981.

16. Secretary Shultz was actually more careful than his predecessor in his responses to committee members on this issue, but his written responses avoided any suggestion that there might be constitutional problems with the resolution. See U.S. Senate. Committee of Foreign Relations. *Nomination of George P. Shultz* Hearings, 97th Cong., 2d sess., July 13, 1982. Washington, D.C.: USGPO, 1982.

17. See, for example, U.S. Senate. Committee on Foreign Relations. *The Situation in El Salvador* Hearings, 97th Cong., 1st sess., March 18 and April 9, 1981. Washington, D.C.: USGPO, 1981.

18. The transcript of the news conference at the Pentagon following this incident was published in the *New York Times*, August 20, 1981, p. A8.

19. S. Res. 382, initiated by Senator Biden, was passed by the full Senate on April 29, 1982 by a vote of 79–1.

20. Senate debate occurred on the Symms amendment on August 10 and 11, 1982. The Percy-Bumpers amendment on the war powers issue was passed by a vote of 97–1. *Congressional Record* (August 11, 1982). Daily ed. S10230.

21. See, for example, letter of September 24, 1982, from the Senate Foreign Relations Committee Chairman Charles Percy and the committee's Ranking Minority Member Claiborne Pell.

22. The text of this letter appears in U.S. Senate. Committee of Foreign Relations. *Lebanon Emergency Assistance Act of 1983* (S. Rpt. 98–72; to accompany S. 639), May 5, 1983, pp. 6–7. Washington, D.C.: USGPO, 1983.

23. Section 4 of the Act required the president to "obtain statutory authorization from the Congress with respect to any substantial expansion in the number or role in Lebanon of United States Armed Forces." P.L. 98–43, June 27, 1983 (97 *Stat.* 215).

24. *Immigration and Naturalization Service v. Chadha et al.*, 103 S. Ct. 2764, June 23, 1983; followed two weeks later by its rejection of a two-House veto in *Process Gas Consumers Group v. Consumers Energy Council*, 103 S. Ct. 3556.

25. U.S. Senate. Committee on Foreign Relations. *Legislative Veto: Arms Export Control Act* Hearings, testimony of Deputy Secretary of State Kenneth W. Dam, 98th Cong., 1st sess., July 28, 1983, p. 13.

26. This amendment was introduced by Senator Robert Byrd to the authorization bill for the Department of State. The Senate discussion appears in the *Congressional Record* 129, Pt. 138, pp. S14255, S14265, and S14270.

27. See Section 1013 of the Department of State Authorization Act for Fiscal Years 1984 and 1985, P.L. 98–164 (50 U.S.C. 1546A), approved on November 22, 1983.

28. *United States v. Curtiss-Wright Export Corp.*, 299 U.S. 304 (1936).

29. *Dames & Moore v. Regan*, 453 U.S. 654 (1981). See also the Court's opinion in *Haig v. Agee*, 453 U.S. 280.

30. I have made this argument elsewhere: "The War Powers Resolution . . . is constitutional and enforceable," *American Bar Association Journal* 70 (March 1984): 10–14.

31. Reprinted in 1983 compilation of documents by the House Foreign Affairs Committee, *supra* note 14 at 65.

32. *Congressional Record* 129, Pt. 116 (Sept. 12, 1983) p. S11959.

33. *Congressional Record* 129, Pt. 121 (Sept. 20, 1983) p. S12481.

34. *Congressional Record* 129, Pt. 128 (Sept. 29, 1983) p. S13167.

35. In signing the Multinational Force in Lebanon Resolution on October 12, 1983, the president stated, "I do not and cannot cede any of the authority vested in me under the Constitution as President and Commander-in-Chief of

United States Armed Forces. Nor should my signing be viewed as any ac-
knowledgement that the President's constitutional authority can be impermissibly
infringed by statute, that congressional authorization would be required if and
when the period specified in Section 5 (b) of the War Powers Resolution might
be deemed to have been triggered and the period had expired, or that Section
6 of the Multinational Force in Lebanon may be interpreted to revise the
President's constitutional authority to deploy United States Armed Forces." U.S.
Senate. Committee on Foreign Relations. *Authorization for U.S. Marines in Lebanon*
Hearings, 98th Cong., 1st sess., Nov. 10 and 15, 1983, p. 43, Washington, D.C.:
USGPO, 1983.

36. Ibid.

37. U.S. Senate. Committee on Foreign Relations. *The Situation in Grenada*
Hearings, 98th Cong. 1st sess., Oct. 27, 1983 (S. Hrg. 98–491). Washington,
D.C.: USGPO, 1983.

38. See the comments of John Norton Moore, "Grenada and the International
Double Standard," *American Journal of International Law* 78, no. 1 (January
1984): 145–168. See also the comments of Christopher Joyner, pp. 131–144 and
the letter, pp. 172–175 in the same issue.

39. *Congressional Record* 129, Pt. 144 (Oct. 28, 1983) pp. 14874, 14876–77.

40. On November 17, 1983, in response to his inquiry, the chairman of the
Senate Foreign Relations Committee received a letter signed by Acting Assistant
Secretary of State Alvin P. Drischler, addressing this issue. The Department of
State took the position that Section 5(b) of the War Powers Resolution would
"not require physical withdrawal of U.S. forces from a country where hostilities
have ceased, or where the use of U.S. forces in hostilities has otherwise
terminated." It further stated that "in the case of Grenada, the Department of
Defense determined on November 2 that the armed conflict on the island had
come to an end, and that those U.S. forces still in Grenada at the present time
are not now in a situation where hostilities are likely to occur." Letter in
Committee files.

41. See the argument in Turner, *The War Powers Resolution, supra* note 1 at
17–32.

42. See discussion of the so-called Wherry Resolution, S. Res. 8, and the
Connally-Russell alternative during a joint executive session of the Senate Foreign
Relations and Armed Services Committees on March 8, 1951, published in
"Executive Sessions of the Senate Foreign on March 8, 1951, published in
"Executive Sessions of the Senate Foreign Relations Committee (Historical Series),
Vol. III, Pt. 1, 82d Cong., 1st sess., 1951, made public August 1976, pp. 47f.

43. Acheson's answers came on questions from Senators Connally and
Vandenberg. U.S. Senate. Committee on Foreign Relations. *North Atlantic Treaty*
Hearings, 81st Cong. 1st sess. part 1, April 27, 1949, pp. 18, 25. Washington,
D.C.: USGPO, 1949.

44. See the discussion of Eagleton's amendment in Sullivan Study, 136–139.

45. See *El Salvador* Hearings, *supra* note 17.

46. See, for example, the special consultation procedures contained in the
1980 amendments to the National Security Act, Section 501 (50 U.S.C.A. 413).

47. In particular, the Resolution provides in Section 5(b) that the authorization requirement is triggered "[w]ithin sixty calendar days after a report is submitted *or is required to be submitted pursuant to section 4 (a) (1) . . ."*

48. See the language of Section 4 (a) (2) of the War Powers Resolution.

49. Secretary of State Shultz's comments to a small group of reporters on March 1 appeared in various newspapers. These quotations are taken from an Associated Press dispatch by R. Gregory Nokes on March 2, 1984.

Commentary: On War Powers

Melvin R. Laird

War powers is only one aspect—albeit a crucial one—of the foreign policy debate between Congress and the executive branch. Problems between the two branches did not begin with Secretary of State William P. Roger's failure to inform the Senate Foreign Relations Committee about the U.S. incursion into Cambodia when he was testifying before it the day prior to the action. The main problem is a growing suspicion and distrust of the executive branch by the legislative branch that began earlier. Many believe that this goes back to exaggerated reports of body counts during the Vietnam War. Perhaps it started with the 1965 Dominican crisis when the administration was accused of deliberately misleading Congress. Nevertheless, there was felt to be a great deal of misinformation during the late 1960s and early 1970s, and the mistrust that it engendered is the basis for current problems with the war powers.

Historical Considerations

The environment at the crucial point in 1973 when the law was being debated and voted upon is an important consideration. The atmospheric and attitudinal conditions existing at the time included Watergate and Vietnam as well as debate about the illegitimacy of the entire exercise. The fact that President Nixon, fighting for his own political survival, was not involved in the process culminating in the War Powers Act and ultimately vetoed the resolution precluded consensus or a compact between the two branches.

At the request of Senators Mike Mansfield (D-Mont.), Hugh Scott (R-Penn.), Representative Gerald Ford (R-Mich.), Carl Albert (D-Okla.) and other congressional friends, I served in the White House as counsellor to the president for domestic affairs from 1973–1974. At that time the war powers veto was first acted upon and overridden by both the House and Senate. The president was inactive and not in a position to exercise significant leadership. His position in vetoing the war powers legislation, however, was absolutely proper and right. Every president has to fight the encroachment of Congress; thus the veto was justified from the

Melvin R. Laird is currently senior counsellor for national and international affairs, the Readers' Digest Association. A former secretary of defense (1969–1973), counsellor to the president for domestic affairs (1973–1974), and U.S. Representative (R-Wis.) (1952–1969), Laird serves on the boards of over 50 corporations and civic organizations.

president's point of view. From a legislative standpoint, however, it was important that Congress override the veto.

Some argue that the war powers debate resulted from the misuse and misinterpretation by the executive branch of the various resolutions passed by Congress during the Vietnam period. In the white paper that the House Republican conference published in 1966, the Southeast Asia Treaty Organization (SEATO) and the Tonkin Gulf Resolution were examined. This report determined that the executive branch and the State Department had gone beyond the proper interpretation of both SEATO and the Tonkin Gulf Resolution to justify the escalation of the Vietnam conflict. As a result, in 1966 the president was called upon to formulate a declaration of war. Although this was discussed in the administration, no resolution was sent to Congress. If a resolution had come at that time, Congress would have undoubtedly supported it and avoided many subsequent problems.

It has been argued that the Vietnam buildup proceeded without any clear indication from Congress that it was supporting the conflict. In contrast, there are those who assert that war powers came about because of the misuse of executive authority. For example, Congress cut off the bombing in Cambodia in 1973, and critics argue that it could have stepped in earlier and called a halt if it had chosen to do so. Halting the bombing could not have been done without President Nixon's consent. Congress at the time could not have overridden a Nixon veto, but Nixon did not choose to veto the prohibition. Although the burden of persuasion is on the executive branch, the question seems to revolve around legislative leverage and responsibility. Whether Vietnam was in fact a "presidential war" is debatable.

The channels of effective communication were not open, which contributed to congressional mistrust of the executive. In fact, the State Department has been reluctant to keep its committees informed. During my tenure as secretary of defense, the leadership of the Appropriations and the Armed Services Committees were advised on all key policy decisions. I saw to it that there were no secrets from these four individuals in the Senate and House. The chairman and the ranking minority member must decide themselves how far they will go when informing the committee as a whole.

Because of the mistrust, resentment, and growing friction, legislative devices were formulated in the early 1970s that have served to limit the president's freedom of action. These included the Cooper-Church amendment, the Eagleton amendment, the McGovern-Hatfield amendment, the Fulbright amendment, and the War Powers Resolution itself.

There were relatively minor skirmishes both in the military sense abroad and in the political sense between Congress and the executive branch between 1973–1983, although there were important issues raised. The need still existed, however, to come to grips with the War Powers Resolution as far as what it did and did not cover.

Executive and Legislative Roles in Foreign Affairs

Because the Constitution provides ambiguous guidance in foreign policy formulation, debate continues as to who has ultimate authority to conduct foreign affairs. Necessity, history, and nationality indicate that it is the executive branch that holds the initiation and implementation responsibility.

Although there is no consensus on the issue of the proper balance between Congress and the president in the conduct of foreign affairs, strong arguments have been made for the weight of executive authority. In 1935, in the case of *United States v. Curtiss-Wright Export Corporation et al.* (299 U.S. 304), the question of "external sovereignty" was deemed to rest with the national government:

> It is quite apparent that if, in the maintenance of our international relations, embarrassment—perhaps serious embarrassment—is to be avoided and success for our aims achieved, congressional legislation which is to be made effective through negotiation and inquiry within the international field must often accord to the president a degree of discretion and freedom from statutory restriction which would not be admissible were domestic affairs alone involved.

Aside from the constitutional, judicial, and historical arguments advanced against congressional intervention in foreign affairs, a critical issue to be considered is the efficacy of such involvement. It has been maintained that the process by which domestic policy is enacted does not lend itself readily to the international arena. The influences of lobbies, shifting coalitions, regional interests, and extended debate can inhibit the need for quick, decisive, and sometimes secret response in critical situations.

The argument is made that the national mandate rests with the executive as the only representative elected by the nation as a whole. The Turkish arms embargo in 1974, the 1981 debate over the sale of airborne warning and control system (AWACS) surveillance aircraft to Saudi Arabia, and the 1973 sale of Hawk surface-to-air mobile missiles to Jordan have all been cited as examples of administration credibility and flexibility in negotiating with foreign nations being impaired by congressional involvement.

In considering the role of Congress in foreign affairs, one's feelings toward Congress or the way it performs in this area must be kept separate from the issue of whether or not Congress should have a role in the process and what that role should be. There is little doubt that a fundamental point made by the founding fathers in the Constitution is that it would be disastrous to allow a situation in which the commander in chief had relatively unfettered ability to do whatever he thought was desirable with combat forces of the United States.

Congress has a duty, therefore, to assure itself a key role in the conduct of foreign affairs. Moreover, the goals of U.S. foreign policy should be supported by a majority of Congress and the American people. Unfortunately, the War Powers Resolution was conceived in not only a confrontational but also an openly hostile environment. Arguments often were bogged down on the issues of institutional and constitutional definition rather than of substance. This intense suspicion, mistrust, and strain precluded consultation and coordination of the principal tenets of the resolution.

Nevertheless, most would agree that Congress needs a means to contribute to the foreign policy process. The concurrent resolution can provide such a mechanism. The appropriations process is also a viable way to handle the war powers issue. Congress can pass legislation terminating funds after a certain date, as it did with the action in Cambodia. Whether Congress should have a direct, determinative means for expressing disagreement with presidential policy will be debated for some time to come.

Although much was written in the late 1960s and early 1970s about the increasing powers of the presidency, less attention has been focused on the considerable increase in the powers of Congress since the early 1970s. Despite the shift of the power pendulum toward Congress, there appears to be a lack of strong leaders within Congress—the "whales" of whom President Johnson spoke. There is a continuing need for Congress to provide responsible spokespersons to communicate congressional views to the executive branch and the public. Congress will be ineffective with 545 spokespersons and too many committees sharing responsibility.

A perennial problem in the world of international affairs is that it is often difficult to get the attention of the congressional leadership until a crisis actually arises. For example, in 1982 Congress was indifferent to the initial presence of U.S. troops in Lebanon and was instead focused on whether there should be 55 or 75 U.S. advisers in El Salvador. Events forced a dramatic shift of attention. Furthermore, there is the larger question of Congress anticipating problems and being able to act on them. In this case the Persian Gulf is an example. The Carter Doctrine, a highly significant pronouncement of U.S. intentions to intervene militarily in the Middle East when U.S. interests were threatened, was promulgated in 1980, but it has never been debated in Congress. The two branches need to discuss this issue prior to the development of a crisis situation.

In addition, Congress must shorten the time it takes to react if it is to become involved more effectively. The executive branch does not have the time to wait for Congress and public opinion to catch up with the fast-paced events of the world. Possible reversal of its own decisions and jeopardizing confidentiality with open discussion of options are other congressional problem areas.

Executive-Legislative Relations

The two major branches simply do not agree what their basic roles are supposed to be. The Constitution is ambiguous in this regard. Until there is some reconciliation of views, the remaining problems are not going to be resolved. Nevertheless, the inevitable friction between the executive and legislative branches is viewed as a mechanism through which the Constitution endeavored to protect popular liberties.

The war powers controversy is viewed by some as an example of how the U.S. government is dominated by lawyers. The War Powers Resolution involves a legalistic issue, but war and war powers are ultimately political issues. War will not continue if Congress and the people do not want it to do so. Lebanon is cited as an example where the involvement of the War Powers Resolution converted a political controversy into a legal battle.

In fact, the War Powers Resolution is considered flawed because it goes into too much detail; there is simply too much minutia. Neither branch focused on why the U.S. forces were in Lebanon and what mission they were to perform. Instead, the debate centered on legal technicalities. Although legal details are necessary to decide when and under what circumstances Congress can operate, many argue that the system has failed when Congress has to stop the executive branch through legislation.

Congress does need a means of gaining executive branch attention, however. A resolution provides Congress with the leverage to make clear to the president that he can be stopped and that he should find means to avoid forcing Congress's hand. The concurrent resolution is felt by some to be unconstitutional, however, because it can deprive the president of the power to participate in legislation under Article I. In each case, the debate must distinguish between constitutional authority and the central objective of effective foreign policy. Does the war powers make for effective policy-making?

A second and more specific issue is the threshold question of what war is. This involves the interpretation of whether the concept of hostilities, or situations in which the imminent involvement in hostilities is clearly indicated by the circumstances, is what the Constitution and founding fathers had in mind in insisting that Congress play a role. What is the meaning of "equipped for combat" and "introduction of forces"? Much of the terminology causes unhealthy and unnecessary bickering.

A third unresolved issue is consultation, a constant source of unnecessary friction and continuing debate as to what it can accomplish in a military crisis situation. Although there is an obvious advantage in the president having the advice and counsel of senior members of Congress, this should not mean that the president is seeking advance approval or the conferring of congressional blessing.

Because the presidency is a "license to persuade," a close working relationship is essential between the executive and legislative branches. It is, therefore, incumbent upon Congress to provide a leadership system with which the executive may negotiate. Consultation should be designed to encourage members of Congress to express healthy skepticism. There is always a danger that momentum may build for a course of action that may have impractical long-term implications. In any event, it would be advantageous to have the majority leader or the Speaker of the House honestly reflect to the president a lack of congressional support for an executive position. Given the reluctance of junior members of the National Security Council to express disagreement with the president, this could be a useful role for congressional leadership.

Beyond providing this type of counsel and when confronted with a military situation or a set of military options, Congress cannot be expected to provide much more than a reaction to it. Often, when members of Congress go to the White House, their candor and frankness are lost. The aura of the White House tends to create the feeling that, without knowing the facts ahead of time, the member is not in a position to make substantial contributions and therefore sometimes remains silent in crucial situations.

Perhaps a more practical and useful model is to view the process as one of lobbying. Although the word consultation seems to imply that the executive branch goes to Congress to get advice, it is more accurate to say that the executive lobbies Congress with the objective of winning congressional approval. The administration must build a relationship based upon trust and information exchange—in other words, it must lobby—with the people who have the power.

The reporting provision of the resolution is the fourth continuing problem, for the president is reluctant to do anything that provides a trigger for the authorization requirements, which he then has to live with.

The last two provisions that will continue to cause problems between the branches are the legislative veto issue and the 60-day authorization limit, or the "drop dead" requirement.

It has been argued that the legislative veto was the most important part of the War Powers Resolution. Prior to its enactment, there was no statutory relationship between the president and Congress in this area. Although the efficacy of the 60 or 90-day limit is debatable, the veto provided Congress with the greatest amount of leverage. It is uncertain whether the maintenance of the legislative veto as part of the War Powers Resolution requires a constitutional amendment.

The constitutionality of the legislative veto continues to be debated. Although ruled unconstitutional by the Supreme Court, it is unclear that the *Chadha* decision necessarily affects the War Powers Resolution. Some have argued that a legislative veto procedure can be salvaged in the War Powers Resolution and that war powers is different constitutionally and tactically from what was ruled on in *Chadha*. Others have maintained, however, that the resolution works with or without the legislative veto. Congress still can have an impact on the executive branch and even without the legislative veto there are worthwhile political consequences in Congress repudiating presidential action—or at least saying, "You're on your own"—by passing a current resolution veto.

The controversy concerning the legislative veto and war powers feed on the fractionalization of the congressional leadership due to emphasis on sharing power equally in Congress rather than focusing it on recognized leaders. Although this fractionalization might be a positive factor for policy and does allow for more input, it makes it more difficult to achieve a prevailing view. Congress realizes that it cannot pass a joint resolution within the time constraints of an emergency situation, and so the leadership role falls on the executive branch. Many would argue that this is indeed desirable. The lack of congressional continuity and historical memory makes Congress always somewhat inefficient, but most citizens are willing to pay this price.

A number of unanswered questions remain, especially because the Court in the 1981 *Dames and Moore* Iranian agreement case ruled that it will infer congressional approval and authorization from congressional silence. If silence is consent, then Congress ought to have some way, short of overriding a presidential veto, of simply saying that it does not support what the president is doing.

Conclusion

The war powers controversy involves the classic debate on the use of power. Although the country seems to be out of the Vietnam syndrome, the question remains: Under what circumstances is the use of power appropriate? Neither branch has come to grips with or debated the issue of power. Although the role of leadership in both branches is integral to a successful policy, the basic power question cannot be left to the personalities of the moment, or lack thereof.

Whether Congress has authority to play a role in war powers and it exercises that authority effectively are two entirely separate matters. The issue goes beyond simple freedom of expression.

Sen. Arlen Specter (R-Pa.) proposed legislation to modify the resolution because he feels "the principal obstacle for reasserting congressional war power is the very vehicle designed to protect it." According to the Constitution, Congress has the power to commit the United States to war and must use that power. Thus Senator Specter feels that Congress must "extricate itself from the paralysis of passive policy-making and enact legislative language implementing its inherent authority to authorize armed conflict in advance." He would require Congress to withdraw troops through affirmative legislation, as opposed to policy by inaction, and the elimination of the 60-day deadline for troop commitment. He recommends that Congress, especially the Senate Foreign Relations Committee, hold hearings to explore the War Powers Resolution in terms of such situations as Central America and the Middle East while there is still "the luxury of time for reasoned analysis."

Sen. Sam Nunn (D-Ga.), member of the Armed Services Committee and the Select Committee on Intelligence and a respected Senate authority on security affairs, has stated that the War Powers Resolution is being eroded and has proved ineffective in several instances. Congress becomes bogged down debating endless technicalities such as prescribing limits in numbers of troops, length of time, or operating territory. The Constitution gives Congress the authority to decide *yes* or *no* on the declaration of war; by allowing the *maybe* and *perhaps* options under war powers, Congress tends to choose the less definitive option. Before Congress decides either for or against commitment to war, the administration should be required to present its strategy, objectives, and missions. Thus, a coherent policy would be required prior to a commitment to military action. In contrast, the current congressional role, according to Senator Nunn, is "unbecoming, and probably unmanageable."

Sen. Barry Goldwater (R-Ariz.) has proposed legislation to repeal the War Powers Resolution because he believes it denies needed flexibility to the executive, and, as such, is "impractical and dangerous." Such critics believe that the resolution has crippled U.S. diplomacy and resulted in a lack of credible deterrence, thereby greatly increasing the risk of war. Secretary of State George Shultz also has advocated the rewriting of the resolution to make it more acceptable to the executive branch.

Congress needs a process whereby it recognizes and acts on its own responsibility and authority on the issue of war powers. The Appropriations Committees could provide a focus through the power of the purse, while increased executive consultation with committee leaders, who in turn exercise more internal authority, could ease executive-legislative contention.

If Congress is to have more responsibility, it must organize itself. Under the present circumstances it can be difficult to determine its collective position on an issue. In addition, Congress needs to be consulted not only during a crisis but also on a continuing basis. Regular and continuing bipartisan consultation is needed, with regular meetings scheduled and faithful congressional attendance. Perhaps several congressional leaders could be brought in to sit with the National Security Council, although under the separation of powers the constitutionality of this recommendation has been questioned.

The War Powers Resolution, in some form, has become a permanent fixture of the system. Frequent collisions between the executive and legislative branches are inevitable. Because the basic questions are political rather than constitutional, each situation must be assessed individually. Creating a joint congressional-executive commission to study implementation and separation of powers in foreign policy, with half of the members selected by Congress and half by the president, could enhance democratic consensus and create more lasting balance between the branches in foreign policy. It would serve the broader national goal of examining the limits of appropriate congressional micromanagement of foreign policy. The commission would review the War Powers Resolution and make recommendations on alternatives, including informal guidelines for their execution.

Zbigniew Brzezinski, national security adviser in the Carter administration, feels that if a spirit of trust and cooperation exists between the executive and legislative branches, the resolution is not an impediment to effective national action. It can, however, become "a very major obstruction to effective response" if the executive-legislative relationship is polarized or contentious. The emphasis should be on the development and maintenance of a genuine consultative relationship. Describing congressional action as an intrusion or overinvolvement in the tactical or mechanical aspects of national security comes from the breakdown of trust and confidence between the two branches. Thus, according to Brzezinski, "What we lack is some mechanism for defining strategy on a continuing basis in relationships of ever-changing international situations." This mechanism should incorporate former presidents, national security advisers, secretaries of state, bipartisan congressional leaders, and respected experts in the private sector. A wealth of foreign policy expertise would therefore be utilized in a positive manner. Only through such a debate will the United States be able to come to grips with how, when, and why force should be employed.

Appendix:
The War Powers Resolution

Public Law 93–148
93rd Congress, H.J. Res. 542
November 7, 1973

Joint Resolution. Concerning the war powers of Congress and the President. *Resolved by the Senate and House of Representatives of the United States of America in Congress assembled,*

Short Title

Section 1. This joint resolution may be cited as the "War Powers Resolution."

Purpose and Policy

Sec. 2. (a) It is the purpose of this joint resolution to fulfill the intent of the framers of the Constitution of the United States and insure that the collective judgment of both the Congress and the President will apply to the introduction of United States Armed Forces into hostilities, or into situations where imminent involvement in hostilities is clearly indicated by the circumstances, and to the continued use of such forces in hostilities or in such situations.

(b) Under article I, section 8, of the Constitution, it is specifically provided that the Congress shall have the power to make all laws necessary and proper for carrying into execution, not only its own powers but also all other powers vested by the Constitution in the Government of the United States, or in any department or officer thereof.

(c) The constitutional powers of the President as Commander-in-Chief to introduce United States Armed Forces into hostilities, or into situations where imminent involvement in hostilities is clearly indicated by the circumstances, are exercised only pursuant to (1) a declaration of war, (2) specific statutory authorization, or (3) a national emergency created by attack upon the United States, its territories or possessions, or its armed forces.

Consultation

Sec. 3. The President in every possible instance shall consult with Congress before introducing United States Armed Forces into hostilities or into situations where imminent involvement in hostilities is clearly indicated by the circumstances, and after every such introduction shall consult regularly with the Congress until United States Armed Forces are no longer engaged in hostilities or have been removed from such situations.

Reporting

Sec. 4. (a) In the absence of a declaration of war, in any case in which United States Armed Forces are introduced—(1) into hostilities or into situations where imminent involvement in hostilities is clearly indicated by the circumstances; (2) into the territory, airspace or waters of a foreign nation, while equipped for combat, except for deployments which relate solely to supply, replacement, repair, or training of such forces; or (3) in numbers which substantially enlarge United States Armed Forces equipped for combat already located in a foreign nation; the President shall submit within 48 hours to the Speaker of the House of Representatives and to the President pro tempore of the Senate a report, in writing, setting forth—(A) the circumstances necessitating the introduction of United States Armed Forces; (B) the constitutional and legislative authority under which such introduction took place; and (C) the estimated scope and duration of the hostilities or involvement.

(b) The President shall provide such other information as the Congress may request in the fulfillment of its constitutional responsibilities with respect to committing the Nation to war and to the use of United States Armed Forces abroad.

(c) Whenever United States Armed Forces are introduced into hostilities or into any situation described in subsection (a) of this section, the President shall, so long as such armed forces continue to be engaged in such hostilities or situation, report to the Congress periodically on the status of such hostilities or situation as well as on the scope and duration of such hostilities or situation, but in no event shall he report to the Congress less often than once every six months.

Congressional Action

Sec. 5. (a) Each report submitted pursuant to section 4(a)(1) shall be transmitted to the Speaker of the House of Representatives and to the President pro tempore of the Senate on the same calendar day. Each report so transmitted shall be referred to the Committee on Foreign Affairs of the House of Representatives and to the Committee on Foreign Relations of the Senate for appropriate action. If, when the report is transmitted, the Congress has adjourned sine die or has adjourned for any period in excess of three calendar days, the Speaker of the House of Representatives and the President pro tempore of the Senate, if they deem it advisable (or if petitioned by at least 30 percent of the membership of their respective Houses) shall jointly request the President to convene Congress in order that it may consider the report and take appropriate action pursuant to this section.

(b) Within sixty calendar days after a report is submitted or is required to be submitted pursuant to section 4(a)(1), whichever is earlier, the President shall terminate any use of United States Armed Forces with respect to which such report was submitted (or required to be submitted), unless the Congress (1) has declared war or has enacted a specific authorization for such use of United States Armed Forces, (2) has extended by law such sixty-day period, or (3) is physically unable to meet as a result of an armed attack upon the United States. Such sixty-day period shall be extended for not more than an additional thirty days if the President determines and certifies to the Congress in writing that unavoidable military necessity respecting the safety of United States Armed Forces requires the continued use of such armed forces in the course of bringing about a prompt removal of such forces.

(c) Notwithstanding subsection (b), at any time that United States Armed Forces are engaged in hostilities outside the territory of the United States, its possessions and territories without a declaration of war or specific statutory authorization, such forces shall be removed by the President if the Congress so directs by concurrent resolution.

Congressional Priority Procedures
for Joint Resolution or Bill

Sec. 6. (a) Any joint resolution or bill introduced pursuant to section 5(b) at least thirty calendar days before the expiration of the sixty-day period specified in such section shall be referred to the Committee on Foreign Affairs of the House of Representatives or the Committee on Foreign Relations of the Senate, as the case may be, and such committee shall report one such joint resolution or bill, together with its recommendations, not later than twenty-four calendar days before the expiration of the sixty-day period specified in such section, unless such House shall otherwise determine by the yeas and nays.

(b) Any joint resolution or bill so reported shall become the pending business of the House in question (in the case of the Senate the time for debate shall be equally divided between the proponents and the opponents), and shall be voted on within three calendar days thereafter, unless such House shall otherwise determine by yeas and nays.

(c) Such a joint resolution or bill passed by one House shall be referred to the committee of the other House named in subsection (a) and shall be reported out not later than fourteen calendar days before the expiration of the sixty-day period specified in section 5(b). The joint resolution or bill so reported shall become the pending business of the House in question and shall be voted on within three calendar days after it has been reported, unless such House shall otherwise determine by yeas and nays.

(d) In the case of any disagreement between the two Houses of Congress with respect to a joint resolution or bill passed by both Houses, conferees shall be promptly appointed and the committee of conference shall make and file a report with respect to such resolution or bill not later than four calendar days before the expiration of the sixty-day period specified in section 5(b). In the event the conferees are unable to agree within 48 hours, they shall report back to their respective Houses in disagreement. Notwithstanding any rule in either House concerning the printing of conference reports in the Record or concerning any delay in the consideration of such reports, such report shall be acted on by both Houses not later than the expiration of such sixty-day period.

Congressional Priority Procedures
for Concurrent Resolution

Sec. 7. (a) Any concurrent resolution introduced pursuant to section 5(c) shall be referred to the Committee on Foreign Affairs of the House of Representatives or the Committee on Foreign Relations of the Senate, as the case may be, and one such concurrent resolution shall be reported out by such committee together with its recommendations within fifteen calendar days, unless such House shall otherwise determine by the yeas and nays.

(b) Any concurrent resolution so reported shall become the pending business of the House in question (in the case of the Senate the time for debate shall be equally divided between the proponents and the opponents) and shall be voted on within three calendar days thereafter, unless such House shall otherwise determine by yeas and nays.

(c) Such a concurrent resolution passed by one House shall be referred to the committee of the other House named in subsection (a) and shall be reported out by such committee together with its recommendations within fifteen calendar days and shall thereupon become the pending business of such House and shall be voted upon within three calendar days, unless such House shall otherwise determine by yeas and nays.

(d) In the case of any disagreement between the two Houses of Congress with respect to a concurrent resolution passed by both Houses, conferees shall be promptly appointed and the committee of conference shall make and file a report with respect to such concurrent resolution within six calendar days after the legislation is referred to the committee of conference. Notwithstanding any rule in either House concerning the printing of conference reports in the Record or concerning any delay in the consideration of such reports, such report shall be acted on by both Houses not later than six calendar days after the conference report is filed. In the event the conferees are unable to agree within 48 hours, they shall report back to their respective Houses in disagreement.

Interpretation of Joint Resolution

Sec. 8. (a) Authority to introduce United States Armed Forces into hostilities or into situations wherein involvement in hostilities is clearly indicated by the circumstances shall not be inferred—(1) from any provision of law (whether or not in effect before the date of the enactment of this joint resolution), including any provision contained in any appropriation Act, unless such provision specifically authorizes the introduction of United States Armed Forces into hostilities or into such situations and states that it is intended to constitute specific statutory authorization within the meaning of this joint resolution; or (2) from any treaty heretofore or hereafter ratified unless such treaty is implemented by legislation specifically authorizing the introduction of United States Armed Forces into hostilities or into such situations and stating that it is intended to constitute specific statutory authorization within the meaning of this joint resolution.

(b) Nothing is this joint resolution shall be construed to require any further specific statutory authorization to permit members of United States Armed Forces to participate jointly with members of the armed forces of one or more foreign countries in the headquarters operations of high-level military commands which were established prior to the date of enactment of this joint resolution and pursuant to the United Nations Charter or any treaty ratified by the United States prior to such date.

(c) For purposes of this joint resolution, the term "introduction of United States Armed Forces" includes the assignment of members of such armed forces to command, coordinate, participate in the movement of, or accompany the regular or irregular military forces of any foreign country or government when such military forces are engaged, or there exists an imminent threat that such forces will become engaged, in hostilities.

(d) Nothing in this joint resolution—(1) is intended to alter the constitutional authority of the Congress or of the President, or the provisions of existing treaties; or (2) shall be construed as granting any authority to the President with respect to the introduction of United States Armed Forces into hostilities or into situations wherein involvement in hostilities is clearly indicated by the circumstances which authority he would not have had in the absence of this joint resolution.

Separability Clause

Sec. 9. If any provision of this joint resolution or the application thereof to any person or circumstance is held invalid, the remainder of the joint resolution and the application of such provision to any other person or circumstance shall not be affected thereby.

Effective Date

Sec. 10. This joint resolution shall take effect on the date of its enactment.

5

Congress: Defense and the Foreign Policy Process

1. The MX and Strategic Policy

Alton Frye

"If anything, the MX is a textbook case of how not to manage an important national-security issue." The words are those of former Sen. John Tower (R-Tex.), when he was chairman of the Senate Armed Services Committee. But that verdict is shared by most observers, whether proponents or opponents of the MX, whether members of the legislative or executive branch.[1] It is a judgment primarily about the political management of an important strategic project, although its shifting technical and strategic elements contributed to the impression of ineffectuality. As former Secretary of Defense Harold Brown said with characteristic understatement, " . . . more politically astute decisions in the past could well have produced a better solution."

Tower's personal exasperation with the prolonged and inconclusive process of fielding the missile was part of the wider discontent with legislative-executive relations on defense policy that prompted his decision to retire from the Senate in 1984. Yet the process illustrates strengths, as well as weaknesses, in U.S. decision making, particularly in the dynamic relationship between Congress and the president. If the policy-making system revealed a quality of indecisiveness, it also displayed a capacity to engage a healthy diversity of legitimate interests that deserved to be weighed and to compel deliberation on questions that deserved to be asked. Those who considered the "missile experimental" or MX an essential and urgent response to a rising Soviet threat

Alton Frye is currently the Washington director and a senior fellow at the Council on Foreign Relations. He also has served as a legislative and administrative assistant for Senator Edward W. Brooke and was a staff member of the RAND Corporation from 1962 to 1968. His published works include *A Responsible Congress: The Politics of National Security* (New York: Council on Foreign Relations/McGraw Hill, 1975).

would lament the protracted congressional discussions of the system. Those who questioned the need for the weapon welcomed such discussions, though many of them agreed that the United States ought to modernize its strategic forces.

To draw a balanced ledger sheet, one must place the complex MX story in the larger context of volatile public attitudes about nuclear arms and a markedly different congressional role in strategic arms policy. Disputes over MX have their political and technical roots in the late 1960s, where they find important parallels. Congressional debates and initiatives regarding antiballistic missile (ABM) systems and multiple independently targetable reentry vehicles (MIRVs) represented important consciousness-raising exercises for many legislators and their constituents. The souring of U.S. involvement in Vietnam was in part responsible for breaking the traditional pattern of deference to executive leadership in national security policy; issues of strategic policy and strategic weapons procurement faced greater congressional skepticism and prompted more energetic congressional intervention. Even without the searing controversies over Vietnam, one may well have seen mounting congressional activism on issues of nuclear policy, for they had already gained a place on the public agenda through such experiences as the Cuban missile crisis of 1962 and the Limited Nuclear Test Ban Treaty debate of 1963. But, whatever the basic genesis of the change in Congress's stance, the intense immersion in the arcana of ABM and MIRV contributed to enduring psychological and procedural changes in Congress.

Broadly speaking, the congressional system for reaching decisions on national security policy shifted from a relatively closed to a relatively open one, and from a relatively passive to a relatively active one. Decisions that were previously the province of a few committees operating in conjunction with defense officials attracted the interest of other committees and individual legislators who rarely had dealt with such matters. As personal, committee, and central staffs grew, the universe of those with access to classified information and outside networks of expert advisers expanded. With this diffusion of the necessary data and talent, sensitive strategic questions—once handled only in executive sessions of the Armed Services and Appropriations Committees—became part of everyday discourse in the halls of Congress. Accompanying this dispersal of knowledge and capability to deal with defense policy was a move toward what may be called more aggressive policy entrepreneurship by individual members of Congress interested in strategic weapons, arms control, and related subjects. Animated by a sense of the crucial importance of such matters and by a view that involvement in them could be politically worthwhile, many members of Congress took an active interest in strategic issues. Whether or not they had a specific committee assignment giving them direct jurisdiction, more and more legislators offered ideas, proposals, and bills touching these topics.

These changes in congressional participation in national security policy no doubt reflected the altered expectations members and their constituents had come to have about the proper role of Congress—and a diminished confidence in executive leadership in strategic affairs. Those expectations grew in part from the ABM and MIRV episodes, as well as the legislature's oversight of the Strategic Arms Limitation Talks (SALT) between 1969 and 1979, from which different people drew different conclusions. Some stressed that there would never have been a successful negotiation of the ABM Treaty of 1972 if Congress had not approved ABM deployment in 1969–1970, thus convincing the Soviets that the United States would move forward with a better defensive system than Moscow then possessed. Others argued that the administration would never have negotiated such a treaty if Congress had not applied pressure by giving ABM deployment the narrowest possible margin. That same tension of judgment—balancing incentives for Moscow with pressure on the incumbent U.S. administration to negotiate vigorously—would reappear in the MX case. In seeking to promote national security by blending prudent defense investments with sound diplomacy, such dilemmas are chronic.

Perhaps even more potent in shaping congressional attitudes toward executive proposals for MX was the tragic failure of congressional efforts in 1969–1970 to head off MIRV deployment through a mutual ban on MIRV flight testing and deployment. Spurred by Senators Edward Brooke (R-Mass.) and Clifford Case (R-N.J.), and boosted by Representatives Clement Zablocki (D-Wis.), Jonathan Bingham (D-N.Y.), and John Anderson (R-Ill.) among others in the House, the attempt to forestall a MIRV competition won approval in Congress—and little more than condescension in the administration. The Senate's endorsement of a revised Brooke resolution by a vote of 72 to 6 in April 1970 had no discernible impact on the course of the SALT I negotiations. Yet little more than three years later, U.S. negotiators were lamenting their failure to address the MIRV issue in a timely fashion. By the late 1970s when Soviet deployment of thousands of MIRV warheads spawned worries about the survivability of U.S. intercontinental ballistic missiles (ICBMs), almost everyone in U.S. political and strategic circles agreed that the decision to deploy MIRV without a serious attempt to obtain mutual restraints was one of the gravest errors of modern statecraft.

In retrospect, many in and out of Congress read the MIRV case as evidence not only of doubtful wisdom on the part of executive branch decision makers, but also of their resistance to wise strategic judgments when they arose in Congress. Thus, the MX would encounter in some congressional quarters skepticism both about such systems and about the judgment of those who, having ignored what they now acknowledged to be the more sensible MIRV policy Congress had advocated, were recommending the most advanced MIRV system yet devised. To frame the attitude baldly: MIRV proponents had botched the policy responsibility once. Were they doing so again with the MX? Having created the problem of ICBM vulnerability by proceeding across the MIRV threshold with too little foresight, were defense officials now compounding the danger of instability by raising the technological contest to a still higher level? The suspicion was by no means universal in Congress, but it lurked not far beneath the surface in the minds of many members.

Of course, the congressional stream of consciousness into which plans for the MX flowed included other perspectives as well. Most important, they included decidedly mixed opinions of the strategic arms control process and of the Soviet Union's performance during it. Senator Henry Jackson (D-Wash.) and others of like mind were perturbed that the United States had allowed its interest in arms control to sap its commitment to protecting its security through technological prowess. Jackson's prominence in the 1963 Senate review of the Limited Nuclear Test Ban Treaty owed much to his insistence that the United States safeguard its interest by an intensified underground test program. He brought the same point of view to evaluation of the 1972 SALT accords negotiated by Henry Kissinger, whose performance in the final phase of negotiation gave the senator deep qualms. Where others thought the United States had not pursued a MIRV agreement eagerly enough, Jackson and his allies thought that President Nixon and Kissinger had sought the SALT agreements all too eagerly.

This time, along with associates in the Joint Chiefs of Staff and other defense offices, Jackson was insistent that the administration commit itself to a number of technological hedges against the future. The senator was especially alert to the possibility that the interim SALT agreement on offensive weapons—among whose trade-offs were significant concessions to the Soviet Union's force of over 300 "heavy" missiles—might give Moscow future advantages in counterforce capabilities against U.S. missile silos. He was determined that U.S. missile development programs should compensate for what he considered a dangerous advantage conceded to the other superpower. If Soviet heavy missiles and throw-weight were not coming down dramatically, U.S. missiles should be refined to pose a comparable threat.

As one of the most influential legislators of his day, Jackson was in a position to coax matters in his direction, both by enlisting legislative support for his demand that future agreements accept no such inequalities as he found in SALT I and by spurring work on ICBM improvements for U.S. forces. Those improvements were contemplated already by air force planners. Even before the first-generation MIRVed ICBM, Minuteman III, began flight tests in 1968, there were concepts for improving its capabilities, particularly by better guidance and more lethal warheads to enhance its effectiveness against hard targets. Although early Soviet missiles had been rather "soft" targets, there was no reason to think they would remain such. To the extent that the United States wished to pose a threat of counterforce strikes against Soviet strategic systems, there would be an increasing requirement for more accurate and powerful U.S. warheads. President Nixon had assured Senator Brooke in a letter of December 29, 1969 that "there is no current U.S. program to develop a so-called 'hard-target' kill capability." Director of Defense Research and Engineering Dr. John Foster told the Senate Foreign Relations Committee on June 4, 1970 that he had cancelled a specific air force program for investigating such hard-target capability "to make it absolutely clear to the Congress and hopefully to the Soviet Union, that it is not the policy of the the United States to deny the Soviet Union their deterrent capability." Nevertheless, during the early 1970s, not long after senior officials testified that the United States did not seek destabilizing hard-target kill capabilities that might "be construed as" a first-strike capability, technologies that would provide vastly augmented capacity to destroy missiles in silos were moving forward. Foremost among them was an awesome ICBM that by 1973 was dubbed the MX.

To understand the tortuous evolution of the MX in the channels of legislative-executive relations, one again needs to take note of some of the earlier parallels that helped to shape congressional attitudes about such weapon systems. One important factor was the way in which the MX, like the ABM and the first MIRV systems, would move through the policy process under a variety of rationales and basing modes. For many observers in Congress and elsewhere, it was striking how rationales for weapons often dissolved, but the systems survived. In 1967 President Lyndon Johnson proposed deployment of the so-called Sentinel system, designed to provide a thin nationwide defense against possible attacks by long-range Chinese missiles, if and when they came into being. A decisive impetus for that anti-Chinese system, however, was the beginning installation of a limited Soviet ABM system around Moscow.

In early 1969 the Nixon administration abandoned the Sentinel configuration in favor of the Safeguard system to protect U.S. missile silos against a potential Soviet attack. Area defense gave way to hard-point defense, although the technology remained essentially the same. Whatever one's views about the respective merits of either deployment, the sequence left the impression that the objective of the ABM proponents was to deploy something, to get on with a system, any system, in order to have a foot in the door to shift U.S. posture toward primary reliance on the strategic defenses others considered unworkable, destabilizing, or both.

The inauguration of MIRV systems brought more than one line of argument to the Congress's attention. Having evolved for the most part from advanced work on penetration aids, MIRV was often presented as required to overwhelm the expected Soviet deployment of antiballistic missile systems. When the 1972 ABM treaty aborted such defenses, new rationales came to the fore as justifying continuation of MIRV. It was now a hedge against Soviet upgrade of its air defenses or a lever to move the SALT II negotiations or, in moments of candor, a cost-effective means to cover a far larger number of Soviet targets, many thousands in some calculations. As early as 1964, Professor Ted Greenwood reports that the "Golden Arrow" task force " . . . realized that the MIRV system it was developing could not be justified by any existing mission requirements . . . and made a conscious effort to find a strategic rationale." Once more in the 1970s, Congress harbored doubts about weapons that went forward even when their original justifications had faded. Congress overcame its doubts, but it did not forget them.

The prelude to the fierce congressional battles over MX took shape in 1973–1975 during the tenure of Defense Secretary James Schlesinger. A man of depth and experience, Schlesinger was identified philosophically with the position taken by Senator Jackson. Serving under Presidents Nixon and Ford, Schlesinger was insistent that something be done to handle the quantitative disparity in Soviet and U.S. missile carrying capacity. In National Security Council deliberations, he demanded that the U.S. SALT proposals force cutbacks in Soviet heavy missiles; failing that, he wanted to make clear that the United States would proceed with the large missile it already had under development.

One reason for Schlesinger's concern was his apprehension that Moscow might gain an important degree of intimidation over the United States if it exploited its missile throw-weight through MIRVing to place U.S. ICBM silos at risk. In congressional testimony, Schlesinger drew a scenario of a possible Soviet threat to destroy U.S. silos with a limited attack that might kill no more than a few hundred thousand Americans. His later estimates accorded more closely with those of an Office of Technology Assessment panel, convened at the request of the Senate Foreign Relations Committee, which placed minimum fatalities at several million. But a different outlook had emerged already between those, like Schlesinger, who felt that such a limited counterforce scenario might be plausible enough to lend political leverage to the Soviets, and those who thought such schemes too incredible to govern policy.

However improbable such an attack, in Schlesinger's view no less than in others', the secretary persuaded President Ford and congressional leaders in the key committees that the country required "essential equivalence" in strategic weaponry, not only in fact but also in the perception of potential adversaries. By June 1973 the MX had taken shape as a firm program component, and two months later Schlesinger made clear to the press that the United States would not abandon unilaterally the option to "acquire precision instruments that would be used in a limited counterforce role." A year later, the secretary signed a new Nuclear Weapons Employment Policy, laying the groundwork for the limited nuclear options strategy that Presidents Ford, Carter, and Reagan each would endorse. The centerpiece to implement that strategy was to be the MX.

A former official of the Carter administration later would describe the missile as "the illegitimate child of SALT," by which he meant the SALT II Treaty signed in 1979 and specifically negotiated to protect the U.S. option to build the MX. In truth the weapon was even more the spawn of the SALT I interim agreement on offensive forces. By capping the number of strategic missile launchers, but not restricting warhead totals, that agreement had the unfortunate consequence of inviting both countries to emphasize bigger missiles with more reentry vehicles. The interim agreement anticipated further accords within a five-year period that might have reduced both launcher and warhead totals. But the failure to constrain warheads and to reach agreement on reductions of offensive forces within the allotted time combined with growing anxiety about developments in Soviet forces to give life and momentum to the MX.

Schlesinger's support for the system won ready endorsement from strong majorities in the Armed Services and Appropriations Committees of both Houses. In 1971, few legislators had joined Sen. James Buckley (Conservative R-N.Y.) in his proposal to underwrite expanded counterforce efforts, but by early 1974 Secretary Schlesinger was able to invoke the start of Soviet MIRV testing in the summer of 1973 and the sheer breadth of Soviet missile development as a move by Moscow to acquire strategic superiority. He reversed the assurances offered by Nixon in 1969–1970, but did so with nuance and with the weight of fresh evidence, calling for "a more efficient hard-target kill capability . . . both to threaten specialized sets of targets with greater economy of force, and to make it clear to a potential enemy that he cannot with impunity proceed to threaten our own system of hard targets." It was the latter argument that almost surely carried the day for the MX in Congress, for no member was eager to concede that the Soviet Union should be allowed a monopoly on such power. Yet within the inner circles of the Armed Services and Appropriations Committees examining the program there were divided emotions from the outset.

As often happens in Congress, the legislative coalition that allowed the MX to proceed came together for quite divergent reasons. Armed Services Committee Chairman John Stennis (D-Miss.) had opposed the Buckley effort of 1971 to speed improvements in missile accuracy and yield, but by mid–1974 he had changed his mind. Sen. Thomas McIntyre (D-N.H.), on the other hand, remained opposed to an all-out counterforce competition, as did Senator Brooke; both opposed the Mk–12A warhead for the Minuteman III and the advanced guidance system to make it a "silo-buster." Yet they saw merit in developing a less vulnerable missile, as the MX development of a mobile option promised to provide. The signing of the Vladivostok accord in November 1974 excited new hopes for arms reductions and, coupled with delays in selecting a satisfactory mobility mode for the MX, led to substantial cutbacks in the program's funding. Still, it moved ahead with little legislative resistance and aimed for initial operation in 1981.

The menu of reasons for the system would change little in later years, although selections from it would vary. The Strategic Air Command (SAC) wanted the system to increase its overall firepower, especially for "time-urgent hard-target kill" missions, that is, taking out Soviet forces and command and control facilities in the early minutes of a strategic war. That function seemed reasonable and necessary to a number of legislators, including not only Jackson but Rep. Jack Kemp (R-N.Y.) and others who accepted the theory that nuclear war might be limited through discriminating counterforce techniques. Others were attracted by the quiet promise of greater survivability for U.S. forces. Some felt the system was necessary for bargaining purposes to elicit Soviet adherence to sensible arms control agreements.

Gradually, the evidence persuaded Sen. McIntyre that the air force was interested more in threatening the other side's silos than in making certain that U.S. forces survived as a credible retaliatory deterrent. An element in the senator's rising apprehension was the indication in early 1976 that the air force planned to field 300 MX, a number that could well place at risk virtually the entire Soviet ICBM force as projected at that time. Long having worried about the potentially destabilizing consequences of a hard-target MIRV competition with the Soviets, McIntyre had become convinced that the worst outcome would be one in which both countries possessed counterforce capabilities that were simultaneously lethal and vulnerable to each other. The senator was concerned about the large number of MX proposed, but even more about whether the system could be protected against attack. Articulating a view that would become accepted almost universally, though honored mainly in the breach, he argued that deployment of the MX would be prudent only if the missile itself could be made invulnerable.

Working with his key staff assistant on the Armed Services Committee, Larry Smith, McIntyre forged an unusual coalition to address this problem. Withdrawing his objections to the B–1 bomber, which was then the main interest of his committee colleague Barry Goldwater, McIntyre won the Arizona Republican's support for a package deal. Funds for fixed basing of MX were cut and the secretary of defense was directed to conduct a comprehensive study of the future of ICBMs. Parallel concerns had emerged in the House Armed Services Committee and the conference report for FY 1977 defense authorization bill set a standard against which all future MX proposals would be measured:

> . . . the rationale behind the development of a new missile system (M-X) is to provide a land-based survivable strategic force. The development of an alternate basing mode as opposed to a fixed or silo-basing mode is the key element in insuring this survivable force. *The conferees are in agreement that providing a survivable system should be the only purpose for this effort; that the design of this system should not be constrained for silo basing; that none of the program's funds shall be expended in fixed or silo basing for M-X; and that none of the program reductions shall reduce the Department's proposed investigations of mobile deployment.* [Italics added.]

McIntyre and his colleagues had set a sound standard, but one that would prove excruciatingly difficult and, in the end, impossible to meet. The conferees also called for a presidential clarification to accompany the study of the future of ICBMs, explaining the exact role of "silo-killers" in U.S. strategy. It was never forthcoming.

This congressional intervention would prove crucial to the fate of the MX. At the time, air force opinion remained relatively relaxed about the Soviet ability to target U.S. silos. Although planners thought there were clear limits to the feasibility of hardening silos against blast, electromagnetic pulse, and other nuclear effects—somewhere in the range of 2,000 pounds per square inch of overpressure—most of them were dubious that the Soviets could achieve the necessary accuracies to disable U.S. silos. Thus, the initial disposition at SAC had been toward placing the MX in silos, even though the Command's father figure, former Air Force Chief of Staff General Curtis Lemay, always had been reticent about how long missiles could survive in fixed emplacements. As the 1970s progressed, however, the air force saw more rapid improvement than expected in Soviet accuracies and came to respect the congressional preference for an alternate basing mode for the MX as the wiser course. Those committed to the proposition that only an invulnerable MX would be worth deploying soon realized that the problem could be intractable. As McIntyre stated in 1977, "The dilemmas of ICBM survivability are devilish. Most proposed solutions to this problem have at their center seeds of new dilemmas."

Closely related to the issue of MX survivability were questions of size, mission, and cost. On these matters, too, there were important intersections between legislative and bureaucratic politics. During 1977-1978, the Carter administration slowed the pace of the MX, partly in hopes that SALT negotiations might make it unnecessary to deploy it and partly to refine the Ford administration's plan to install the missile in a series of tunnels. Pressed by Rep. Les Aspin (D-Wis.) and others to consider a missile suitable for deployment both on land and at sea, DOD technical teams directed by Under Secretary William Perry took an active interest in the possibility of a common missile for the air force and navy. In contrast to the air force plan for a solid-fuel missile of 92-inch diameter, a rocket of 83 inches appeared to offer significant versatility for the missions of both services. In April 1978 Perry estimated that such an approach might save almost $2.5 billion while preserving ample options for hard-target capability and multiple deployment modes. Neither service was enthusiastic about a joint venture. In particular, the air force contended that the program would slip two to three years— and did not say what many of its leaders believed: that if the missile were small enough to go to sea, all of them might end up there.

To many participants, an MX too big for the submarine tubes became a virtual synonym for preservation of ICBMs as the most precise and controllable weapons in the strategic triad. That attitude was shared by Senators Strom Thurmond (R- S.C.) and John Tower, as well as by influential representatives like Jack Edwards (R-Ala.), William Dickinson (R-Ala.), and Samuel Stratton (D-N.Y.); they thought that the maximum capability afforded by the larger booster was needed to compensate for the sheer bulk of the Soviet missile force. Jackson joined Tower to defeat efforts by Committee Chairman Stennis and Sen. John Culver (D-Iowa) to encourage selection of the 83-inch design. To make the point stick, Jackson amended the FY 1979 supplemental appropriations bill to specify that the MX should not be limited to "a throw-weight less than the maximum permitted under strategic arms limitation agreements."

There was no dispute, however, that whatever the MX's size, it ought to be survivable, and its size posed severe difficulties for the most plausible route to survivability—mobility. During the late Ford months and early Carter months, basic U.S. policy shifted regarding mobile ICBMs, driven largely by perplexity over how to make the MX secure from attack. In the SALT I negotiations, the United States had wanted to ban mobile missiles on land because of the difficulties they would pose for verifying compliance with arms agreements. By the mid–1970s, Moscow displayed interest in precluding such systems, but by then the U.S. position was reversed. Mobility seemed necessary for the MX and the issue was recast to how such schemes could be incorporated in an arms control regime without effectively gutting the verification process.

If there was wide agreement that to purchase counterforce capabilities without survivability would damage strategic stability, there was also a spreading conviction that to purchase mobility without regard to verifiability would damage arms control—and that, in turn, could undermine stability. The latter view was less deeply ingrained and a number of prominent strategists and legislators in the military committees of the two houses believed that U.S. force planning should not be distorted by arms control considerations. For the Carter administration and its congressional allies, however, the search for MX survivability led to an interest both in mobility and in constraining that mobility by the requirement that it permit verification of the number of missiles actually deployed. A contest loomed among deception, mobility, and verification.

In addressing the arms control aspects of the MX and similar issues, the sharp senatorial attacks on Paul Warnke, the president's choice to head the Arms Control and Disarmament Agency, weakened the Carter administration at the outset. The confirmation battle over Warnke's nomination, orchestrated by Senator Jackson, brought to the fore the stern determination of a strong minority in the Senate not to allow the arms control process to impede vigorous pursuit of U.S. strategic programs. The Senate vote in early 1977 signaled that there were limits to how far the president could follow his obvious instincts to give nuclear arms control priority and to curtail U.S. strategic programs, as he was to do with the B–1 bomber cancellation and the stretch-out (at slower rate) of the MX and Trident submarine programs. Warnke and his allies in the administration did not find it prudent to fall on their swords on the MX issue, eventually judging that the new missile was a tacit price for gaining military and congressional support for the SALT II Treaty on which they were laboring. As the matter unfolded, the Joint Chiefs of Staff would not give their blessing to the SALT II Treaty until one week after the administration agreed to proceed with full development of the MX.

Congressional pressures, along with changing estimates of the strategic situation, also seem to have had a bearing on the notable shift in position of Carter's secretary of defense, Harold Brown. Well-known and highly respected by legislators who recalled his distinguished service in the Kennedy-Johnson administration, Brown took a more temperate view of the strategic balance than his immediate predecessors. Before the Senate Armed Services Committee in early 1977, Brown discounted the notion that limited nuclear war was feasible, given the tremendous dangers of escalation and loss of control. He consistently struck a balanced tone regarding the emerging threat to Minuteman silos, pointing out that even if it materialized it was far different from a threat to the entire U.S. deterrent. Agreeing with Perry's critique of the tunnel deployment design for the MX favored by the Ford team and doubting the imminence of the threat to Minuteman, Brown cut the air force's MX request in 1977 and 1978. In the spirit of the congressional guidance, he and Perry strove to keep missile and basing mode development moving in tandem, resisting service and some legislative demands to perfect the missile and then find a way to base it. Brown pulled the program back from the full-scale engineering development ordered at the end of the previous administration and, trimming more than half the funds, held the system in advanced development.

By April 1979, however, Brown was sounding a great deal like Schlesinger, telling the Council on Foreign Relations that increasing vulnerability of silos might create " . . . a perception of U.S. strategic inferiority that would have severely adverse political—and could have potentially destabilizing military—consequences." Several factors must have contributed to this evolution: new evidence of Soviet missile accuracy, congressional doubts that the administration was doing enough to build U.S. strength, and a rising understanding that neither SALT ratification nor Carter's reelection were in the cards unless the administration presented a firmer defense posture.

In the preceding two years the United States had examined many mobility options for the MX and had conveyed to the Soviet Union the decision to proceed with a scheme involving multiple shelters for the missiles. At the SALT discussions, Warnke had made the distinction between shelters and launchers—which could not be increased under prior SALT arrangements—assuring his counterpart that Moscow would be able to account for all missiles under such a deployment by enumerating the launcher-canisters that would move with the missiles. Many contentious exchanges had taken place in the technical and political circles dealing with MX basing. As the earlier trench concept had fallen into disrepute, interest turned to other plans for creating multiple aim points that Soviet missiles would have to attack to destroy the MX. A system of vertical shelters appeared to be most promising, although it might take 24 hours to move a missile from one shelter to another, giving it less mobility than tunnel or horizontal shelter concepts would afford, and although there was some anxiety that the Soviets would claim it violated SALT rules.

In the process of analyzing such ideas, many participants, including Michael May of Lawrence-Livermore Laboratory, began to favor smaller missiles that might lend themselves to greater mobility. But the MX was the missile ready for full development, and the decision process of 1978-1979 was focused on how to base a 92-inch, 190 thousand-pound rocket. At National Security Council meetings in June 1979, President Carter, despite strong personal misgivings, approved the big missile, but ordered further work to define a horizontal multiple protective shelters (MPS) plan that could be more verifiable, yet comparably survivable to the vertical shelter design. In early September a so-called racetrack scheme was approved, expected to cost about $33 billion for 200 missiles movable among some 4,300 shelters in Nevada and Utah.

Throughout this period the dominant opinion in Congress had been to urge the administration to get on with the job of modernizing U.S. missiles by building the MX and devising a suitable basing mode for it. When President Carter finally reached his decision to approve it, however, the sturdy ground of congressional support on which the MX seemed to rest began to shift unexpectedly. Suddenly, the MX was embroiled in an extraordinary stew of constituent displeasure from areas scheduled to receive the missiles, congressional reactions torn between those who feared the system would undermine the chances for arms control and those who felt that the superior basing mode had been sacrificed to arms control, and wider political interests preoccupied with the place of the MX dispute in the upcoming presidential election.

Ironically, two of the missile's strongest proponents in the Congress, Senators Paul Laxalt (R-Nev.) and Jake Garn (R-Utah), proved formidable adversaries to the decision. In a manner not dissimilar to the public uproar over the first ABM deployment plans in 1967–1968, the citizens of Nevada and Utah were reluctant to receive the MX. Originally, the governors of both states had welcomed the planned deployments of the MX, and the governor of another Western state had even complained to senior air force officials about not receiving some of the MX. But visions of dollars and jobs soon paled before alarm over possible environmental and social dislocations. Regional resistance, including that from within the Mormon Church, prompted the Western senators to lead the charge against the MPS plan, just as they had figured prominently in the demand for early action to deploy the MX.

Laxalt's role was decisive on several fronts. From his place on the Military Construction Subcommittee he arranged hearings in early 1980 that brought into play sharp critics of the MPS. The senator skillfully deployed witnesses from utterly divergent orientations. Retired Admiral Thomas Moorer thought new missiles should be deployed on surface ships, an idea praised in print by former Secretary of Defense Melvin Laird. Gen. Daniel Graham (USA, Ret.) denounced the notion that the United States should build shelters to soak up enemy warheads the MX should be designed to attack. Professor William Van Cleave of the University of Southern California objected to shaping U.S. deployments to accord with a SALT process he considered more damaging than helpful to U.S. security. Physicist Sidney Drell advocated putting the missiles in small submarines, operating close to the U.S. mainland. Their reasons and purposes varied astonishingly, but the senator's array of witnesses wrote the same bottom line: The MPS "shell game" approved by Carter was a bad idea. Thus fortified, Laxalt prevailed against the MPS, not directly in congressional action but through persuading the Republican presidential nominee, Ronald Reagan, to applaud the MX, reject the Carter administration's MPS design, and promise to reexamine the issue once he was in office.

Although public reactions to the MX were largely negative, some of the legislators most familiar with the issue were persuaded that the MPS was in fact the best of the rather bad options available. Senator Tower and Representative Dickinson hoped that, once elected and given fuller information about the need to insure the weapon's survivability, Reagan would modify his campaign stance and move forward with some kind of MPS deployment. Meanwhile, those responsible for the system in the executive branch worked overtime to meet the objections that had been raised. By June 1980, a Defense Science Board study led by Lt. Gen. Glenn Kent (USAF, ret.) had framed important changes in the deployment, using a system of linear roads to minimize the amount of land required and a simplified design for the transporter-erector-launcher. Additional environmental analyses sought to guard against the excessive diversion of water in the arid region and to moderate other side effects. These program adjustments would have little weight in the MX deliberations of the new administration.

The seeds of future difficulty were apparent in congressional votes during 1980. Superficially, the MX and some form of the MPS seemed to be acceptable to majorities in both Houses, but the visible majorities for the Carter program disguised significant regional and partisan cleavages. In May 1980, for example, the House beat back attempts to block the program. A motion by Rep. Ron Dellums (D-Calif.) to kill the MX was swept away by a vote of 319–82, 18 votes more than had defeated a similar Dellums proposal the preceding year. A more revealing vote came on a floor amendment submitted by Rep. Paul Simon (D-Ill.) to cut $500 million for developing the MPS basing mode. Simon's initiative also lost (250 to 152), as did a related effort by Rep. Dan Marriott (R-Utah), but the record indicated almost two to one opposition to the plan among northern Democrats—and mounting reluctance among representatives in the West, including not only Marriott, but Democratic Rep. Jim Santini of New Mexico.

In the Senate there was little floor discussion of the MX, except for John Glenn's (D-Ohio) proposal to study basing the system on trailers operable on the interstate highway system, which was rejected 80 to 9. The Senate Armed Services Committee, responding to the concerns of Laxalt and Garn, already had included a provision to split MX basing by limiting to one-half the number of shelters to be built in Utah and Nevada. Senator Tower was expressing a willingness, if necessary, to accept some of the MPS deployment in Texas. House-Senate conferees authorized all $1.6 billion requested for the MX and the MPS, but left open the option for the air force to spread the basing further among other states to minimize the dislocation and hardship. At no time during 1980 did the MX opponents garner more than 40 percent of the votes in the House.

Yet while the MPS was moving forward in Congress as the "most militarily acceptable and cost effective" solution to the MX vulnerability, the wider public debate was acquiring a different complexion. The Republican platform promised "the earliest possible deployment of the MX missile in a prudent survivable configuration"—but it neither approved the MPS nor indicated what other basing scheme would meet that standard. Despite Paul Warnke's vivid denunciation of the MX program as "an unworkable and expensive solution to a virtually non-existent military threat," the Democratic National Convention resisted efforts to oppose the deployment. Once debate had moved to this wider theater, however, the MX-MPS began to suffer subtle erosion. The shell game imagery invited cartoon attacks, sharp ridicule from both Left and Right, and deep inner doubts on the part of ordinary citizens. Carter's initial reaction to the MPS had been to call it "the craziest idea I've ever heard." It took long and close analysis to persuade oneself that it was the soundest of the available options. But what would the country do about the MX if the soundest military option for basing it proved politically unacceptable?

As that question took shape in 1981, the ironies of the situation were profound. A president natively opposed to nuclear weapons had worked through the MX problem and convinced himself that it should go forward in the MPS deployment. His successor, natively supportive of the MX and an enhanced nuclear posture, had committed himself to find an alternative to the MPS, without considering that his options might be militarily unacceptable and no more popular politically. Congress had established the clear and proper requirement that the MX be survivable, but had not established the preferred military solution to the problem. The early months of the Reagan presidency were a swirl of intense and confusing activity to sort out the MX issue and meet the president's commitment.

At his confirmation hearings, Secretary of Defense-designate Caspar Weinberger made clear that he opposed silo basing for the MX and his deputy secretary to be, Frank Carlucci, said that he thought the system would have to be mobile. The MPS approach, however, struck Weinberger as having "an element of the unreal." During the next few months a technical panel appointed by Weinberger and headed by the physicist, Charles Townes, reviewed force vulnerability generally, quickly settling against the suggestion that the MX could be based securely on ships. It also concluded that the MPS might be overcome by increased numbers of Soviet warheads, unless actively defended.

Meanwhile, Laxalt had assumed the chairmanship of the Military Construction Subcommittee and produced a report contending that the MPS was vulnerable; the report urged a shift to silo basing combined with hard-point ballistic missile defenses. Other congressional voices were calling for MX deployment on submarines, a concept endorsed by Senate Appropriations Committee Chairman Mark Hatfield (R-Ore.). An Office of Technology Assessment study commissioned by Rep. Morris Udall (D-Ariz.) and Sen. Ted Stevens (R-Alaska) questioned whether the Soviets might not be able to find the MX among the multiple shelters and pointed out that, without the limits imposed by the unratified SALT II agreement, Soviet warheads could increase to saturate even the thousands of shelters planned. Townes and his associates recommended further study of possible air-mobile deployment, stationing the MX on continuous airborne patrol aboard big new aircraft, as well as examination of deep underground facilities to protect the MX as a strategic reserve. Secretary Weinberger reportedly took a special interest in air mobility, but its costs and other characteristics won little sympathy in the air force. Old ideas and new came into view, none into favor.

The procedure provided no real opportunity for senior air force officials to present the case for the MPS to the president. Air Force Chief of Staff General Lew Allen had only a limited occasion to do so at a meeting of Townes with the president and the National Security Council in Los Angeles in mid-August. Deeply disturbed that Reagan was not hearing from those best able to evaluate MX basing options, Senator Tower and Representative Dickinson flew to California a week later to argue that the president should go with a modified MPS plan for 100 MX in 1,000 shelters. But within a month Laxalt and Garn also had met with Reagan and countered that the more limited MPS would be more vulnerable and that it was merely a foot in the door for an expanding shelter system later. Confronting the central decisions on his major strategic program package, the president, new to the office and to the issues, was caught in a bruising crossfire on the MX—Tower and Dickinson versus Laxalt and Garn, his military professionals versus his secretary of defense, strategic requirements versus political feasibility. Under the circumstances, the president's decision may have seemed sensible to him, but it stirred a veritable firestorm in Congress.

On October 2, Reagan announced a far-reaching program to modernize all elements of U.S. strategic forces. Embedded in the announcement was a decision to produce the MX but to kill MPS basing and install the first 36 missiles in "superhardened" silos, while the search continued for a permanent solution. Legislative action on the several defense authorization and appropriations bills during 1981 had granted funds for the MX but reserved to Congress the right to review the president's pending decision on basing. There appeared to be a reluctant majority prepared to tolerate the MPS, if the president found it necessary, but there was a vehement majority lurking in the wings to denounce the idea of placing such lethal weapons in fixed silos, no matter how hard. The learning experience through which Congress had passed in recent MX deliberations may have been imperfect, but it had taught one idea very well: silos were no place for the MX.

Chairman Tower immediately and uncharacteristically derided the Reagan proposal as less satisfactory than the Carter plan, because it would place "more lucrative targets in already vulnerable fixed silos." He complained publicly that the decision was made "within a small circle, without coordination of the best military expertise." The Armed Services Committee would investigate the matter. Tower's Senate opponents relished the turn of events. Thomas Eagleton (D-Mo.) declared that "if President Carter had recommended this [MX plan], Senator Tower would have called for his impeachment." Senator Goldwater and Rep. Jack Edwards loyally supported the president, as did Senate Majority Leader Howard Baker (R-Tenn.), but disgruntlement with the decision flowed through both Houses.

While supporting the overall Reagan strategic program, the Joint Chiefs of Staff chairman, General David Jones, made clear that the professionals still preferred the MPS—and that without it, the MX would be a lower strategic budget priority than bombers. In November, House and Senate conferees showed their displeasure by cutting back the MX authorization, inserting additional funds to study shuttle basing possibilities, and barring use of any funds for research on airmobile systems for the MX. Following the president's mid-November arms reduction proposals to the Soviets, the administration request for MX funding squeaked through the House Appropriations Committee by a vote of 25 to 23, but it lost such stalwart Democratic defense proponents as Congressmen Jamie Whitten of Mississippi and William Natcher of Kentucky, as well as Republicans Lawrence Coughlin of Pennsylvania,

Virginia Smith of Nebraska, Carl Pursell of Michigan, S. William Green of New York, and John Edward Porter of Illinois.

To save the situation in the Senate, the administration agreed to explore possible deceptive basing of the MX in conjunction with an ABM overlay, which was an appealing package for a number of Republicans, notably John Warner of Virginia. But the central message came through loud and clear in an amendment crafted by Senators William Cohen (R-Maine) and Sam Nunn (D-Ga.) discouraging installation of the MX in silos and urging work on more survivable modes. It passed 90 to 4. Three weeks later the final appropriations measure prohibited contracts for work at any specific sites until Congress received detailed plans regarding the locations, costs, and survivability of superhardened silos.

Within three months the administration dropped its suggestion of superhardening Titan silos and proposed to base the first 40 MX in existing Minuteman silos. The fiscal 1983 budget submission foresaw a 13 percent increase in defense spending, a surge that brought pointed demands for cuts from Senate conservatives like Finance Committee Chairman Robert Dole (R-Kans.) and Budget Committee Chairman Pete Domenici (R-N. Mex.). Much of the increase lay in defense, where, among other items, the administration proposed to procure the first nine MX missiles. In the spring of 1982, the Senate Armed Services Committee deferred $1.45 billion for MX procurement, approving funds for development and denying those for any silo basing. Members were worried that to present such a vulnerable basing plan to their colleagues might jeopardize the entire program. On the Senate floor, John Glenn proposed to drop the MX and move to the development of a smaller and truly portable ICBM, but his amendment was tabled 65 to 29. There was also inquiry into possible reliance on the large Trident D–5 submarine-launched ballistic missiles (SLBM), but Tower fought hard for the view that a triad including the MX was still essential. (A minority of the Townes panel had suggested abandoning the MX in favor of the more survivable sea-based counterforce weapon, in part out of apprehension that trying to make the MX invulnerable could lead to evisceration of the ABM Treaty.)

In the House, however, a narrow 212 to 209 vote retained some production money after Representative Stratton added language forbidding its expenditure until 30 days after Congress was notified of a permanent basing decision, which Reagan now promised to make by December 1982. Rumor had it that the president was gravitating toward a wholly novel deployment called closely spaced basing (CSB) or "Dense Pack," in which missiles would be tightly bunched and rely on Soviet attackers to destroy themselves through an effect known as "fratricide."

In November, in what had come to seem almost an annual fall ritual, the president unveiled the CSB as his definitive response to the MX dilemma. The missiles would go into Warren Air Force Base near Cheyenne, Wyoming. If confidence in the scheme's technical merit was tentative, confidence in its political appeal was high. It would take little land, create no distinctive environmental problems, and confine the missile to an existing military base.

Seldom has a presidential initiative on national security received such a scathing response from Congress. Some defense professionals even suspected that the administration offered the proposal in the expectation that Congress would refuse it and take on the responsibility for killing the MX. That surmise gained plausibility when it was learned that three members of the Joint Chiefs had opposed the plan. Interesting technical arguments could be advanced, but most legislators found inherently implausible the thesis that, after billions of dollars and years of effort to protect the MX against the vaunted Soviet threat, the United States now would propose to base its viability on the theory that the incoming warheads simply would kill themselves off. Jack Edwards conveyed the pervasive exasperation of MX proponents in the House. "I am supposed to be one of the hawks on the committee," he mentioned in the Defense Appropriations Subcommittee, "but I swear the more I sit here and listen to this, the more I wonder what in the world we are up to . . . I sit here and think that this whole world has got to be foolish...This sounds like Dense PacMan." Rep. Norman Dicks (D-Wash.) told Defense Department witnesses bluntly, "You are never going to be able to sell this to the American people. If you think you had problems with multiple protective shelters, this thing is going to be much more difficult, because it sounds stupid. . . ."

On December 7 the House voted against appropriations for procuring the first MX. One of those opposing the funds, Les Aspin, summarized the situation by saying that Congress is "still for the MX, is undecided but skeptical about dense pack, and is against procurement of the missile until you've decided on the basing mode." Desperate to fend off defeat of all procurement, the administration welcomed a compromise put forward by Senator Jackson requiring a presidential report on Dense Pack and its alternatives in spring 1983. In the end, amid fierce squabbling between Armed Services and Appropriations Committee leaders, Congress deleted money for procurement of the first five MX, but granted $2.5 billion for research and development (R&D) on the missile and its basing. Over half a billion dollars could not be spent until Congress approved a permanent basing mode after receiving the president's report. The measure also forbade flight tests until Congress agreed to a basing arrangement.

Clearly, if there was to be an MX, it would require a fresh strategic and political synthesis to justify it. To shore up the collapsing congressional coalition on the MX, the White House adopted a strategy it had used on other issues and that had been recommended by Senators Cohen and Warren Rudman (R-N.H.) during the frantic MX scramble of December 1982. The president appointed a bipartisan commission chaired by a former national security adviser, Lt. Gen. Brent Scowcroft (USAF, Ret.). The Commission on Strategic Forces would frame an approach to the MX that transformed the context in which it was considered and, in a remarkable feat of political legerdemain, persuaded an agonized Congress to authorize what it had judged anathema—deployment of a limited number of MX in silos.

The commission's work proceeded at a time of remarkable disarray in the president's national security team. By early 1983, Reagan had lost in quick succession his first assistant for national security affairs, his first secretary of state, and his first Arms Control and Disarmament Agency (ACDA) director. A bitter battle erupted over confirmation of Kenneth Adelman as the new ACDA director, simultaneously with movement toward a protracted brouhaha in the House over a resolution demanding a "mutual, verifiable freeze on the testing, production and deployment" of nuclear weapons. As one shrewd senator observed, "Half the guys up here don't trust the Russians—and the other half don't trust Reagan to negotiate seriously." Into this inauspicious setting the 11-member commission, together with its senior advisers (including four former secretaries of defense and two former secretaries of state), sought to inject a policy framework that could earn broad consensus and endure the many years required for strategic program definition and completion.

In its April report, the commission tried to take account of both political and strategic realities. It tempered the alarmist formulation about ICBM vulnerability by noting the survivability characteristics of the triad and proposing a significant reorientation of U.S. forces for the future. It urged movement away from high-value, multiple warhead ICBMs that tended to decrease stability and toward eventual reliance on smaller, single-warhead missiles as the main component of the ICBM force. Equally important, the commission stressed modifying U.S. arms control proposals to comport with that goal, relaxing the previous demand that missile launchers be cut to 850 on each side and focusing primarily on reductions in warhead totals. In the context of these major shifts in strategic and arms control policy, the commission still found a limited deployment of the MX worthwhile as a transitional force until the single-warhead was available. But, having found no satisfactory way to make the MX truly survivable, the commission concluded that 100 of them should be placed in existing Minuteman III silos—not enough, it thought, to be a provocative first-strike threat against the Soviets, but quite enough to demonstrate U.S. determination to remain in the contest with Moscow. "Cancelling the MX when it is ready for flight testing, when over $5 billion have already been spent on it, and when its importance has been stressed by our last four presidents, does not communicate to the Soviets that we have the will essential to deterrence." Demonstrating that will, the commission averred, was the surest method of inducing the Soviet Union to negotiate stabilizing reductions in their own large missile force.

Congress disputed many of the commission's arguments, but in its totality the report provided a blend of policy with much appeal on Capitol Hill. The MX could not stand on its own, but coupled with the objective of de-MIRVing the force long favored by such congressional leaders as Rep. Albert Gore (D-Tenn.) and with a more constructive approach to arms control, it was able to survive tenuously as the least palatable part of a package deal. During the next several weeks, legislators sought to pin down the president's commitment to the whole package, making clear that their approval of even a limited start on MX production was contingent on Reagan's good faith pursuit of the single-warhead missile and explicit adjustment of the Strategic Arms Reduction Talks (START) proposals. Only after extending the president's personal pledge in writing to launch the so-called Midgetman single-warhead missile program and to put forward a mutual build-down proposal—under which more warheads would be retired than deployed by the United States and the Soviet Union—would the administration obtain initial approval to proceed with the MX.

The MX had become the object of intricate political maneuvering in both chambers. A group of moderates led by six senators and congressmen—Cohen, Nunn, and Charles Percy (R-Ill.) in the Senate and Aspin, Gore, and Dicks in the House—held the balance of power. Thoroughly dissatisfied with the administration's performance on arms control and strategic arms programs, they saw the Scowcroft Commission Report as a vehicle for moving the executive branch toward more reasonable positions on both fronts. With that objective in mind, a number had advised the commission on both the tactics and substance of its report. The report had been delayed to let the air clear after the seven-week House imbroglio regarding the freeze resolution and in hopes that some members would find it advantageous to balance their pro-freeze vote with a "pro-defense" vote on the MX. For congressional Democrats the MX posed a tough choice: If they killed the MX, would the president merely go through the motions on arms control and, failing to gain an accord, blame the Democrats for having undermined his diplomatic efforts by aborting his main strategic program? If they authorized the MX, would they be in a better position to hold the administration's feet to the fire in a genuine quest for negotiated restraints? It was a risky business either way.

Swayed by this gang of six, the House and Senate swallowed hard and reversed their prior prohibition on silo deployment of the MX. The change was most striking in the Democratically controlled House. The House that on May 4 passed a softened version of the nuclear freeze resolution, on May 24 approved MX testing and basing by a vote of 239 to 186; 44 members who opposed the MX in July 1982 now voted for it, as did 55 freeze supporters. Many members were uneasy about the deal. The tentative nature of the arrangement was best captured by a letter from Cohen and 18 other Republican senators on May 25, emphasizing that the MX vote represented a bargain, not a consensus. They would allow the missile to go forward as long as the administration kept its part of the deal.

To make sure that it did so, Gore and Aspin offered language tightly tying MX to parallel work on the Midgetman. Gore's provision cut the initial MX buyback to 21 from the 27 requested, and Aspin, along with House Armed Services Committee Chairman Melvin Price (D-Ill.), drafted language phasing progress on the single-warhead missile with specific milestones in the MX. Senator Nunn added a requirement that any future procurement request detail the number of that year's MX production actually slated for deployment and describe the expected impact of that increment on strategic stability. Throughout the deliberations there was deep suspicion of the administration's true attitudes on arms control.

That suspicion reared its head in June when Arms Control Director Adelman wrote the Senate Foreign Relations Committee indicating that the MX would be bargained away only if the Soviets dismantled their entire existing force of large MIRVed ICBMs. Nunn and Cohen openly scoffed at such a nonnegotiable proposition and Sen. Joseph Biden, Jr. (D-Del.) characterized it as meaning "we'll give up something if they'll give up everything." Republican Charles Mathias said the letter "really brings into serious question the basis on which several of us cast our vote," and he upbraided Deputy Secretary of State Kenneth Dam with the warning that "the administration has made impossible demands . . . that the Soviets will not consider seriously and which threaten to wreck the arms control process." Sen. Patrick Leahy (D-Vt.) said the United States was "offering to swap a moo for a cow." Hostility toward the claim that the MX would afford diplomatic leverage was no less pronounced in the House, where Rep. Byron Dorgan (D-N. Dak.) would say that in his state they knew "the difference between a bargaining chip and a cow chip." The abundance of ridicule on so serious a subject showed how corrosive the atmosphere had become. Yet slender majorities in both houses hoped that the MX would energize the negotiations with the Soviets. As Senator Rudman remarked, "They don't really know whether this is the first 100 or the last 100."

The summer doldrums of 1983 bred nagging doubts among congressional moderates, as the administration appeared to drag its feet on defining the strategic build-down proposal promised by the president, and the air force seemed content to move promptly on the MX and lethargically on the Midgetman. Looking ahead to MX votes late in the year, the gang of six prepared and presented a joint program to National Security Adviser William Clark in the latter part of September. Reluctantly, and after occasionally bitter interbranch dialogue, the president embraced the group's eight principles and undertook to make further changes in the START negotiating proposals. One had the impression that the long wrangle over the MX, strategy, and arms control had been a learning experience for Reagan. He seemed to recognize now the inequity and nonnegotiability of his earlier proposals to demand the greatest reductions in ballistic missile forces, where the Soviets had concentrated 75 percent of their weaponry. In early October he publicly committed the United States not only to the build-down principle for missile warheads and bomber platforms, but also to fair trade-offs between U.S. advantages in bombers and Soviet advantages in ballistic missiles.

Unfortunately, the significance of these adjustments was lost to the Soviets in the cloud of propaganda and animosity surrounding the introduction of Pershing II and ground-launched cruise missiles (GLCMs) into Europe. The intermediate nuclear force (INF) controversy, aggravated by hostile emotions aroused by the Soviet destruction of a Korean airliner in September, dominated East-West relations. Soviet termination of the INF negotiations was followed by their refusal to set a new date for continuing START negotiations. Pro-arms control legislators had exploited the MX as their bargaining chip to force constructive changes in U.S. strategic plans and arms control offers. But the tortuous domestic politics of the MX could not control the larger movements of international politics.

Those striving for a new balance in U.S. policy were trapped in no-man's-land: pairing MX deployment with ultimate de-MIRVing through the Midgetman system was feasible only if arms control succeeded in curtailing the number of warheads allowed each side. With the arms control process stalled—perhaps for years if the Soviets refused to bargain with a Reagan administration they distrusted totally, but which Americans would return to office—the MX was moving through tests and toward initial deployment in 1986, but there was little chance of achieving the benefits for which Congress had bargained. The moderates could only struggle to advance the Midgetman in tandem with the MX in order to keep the deMIRVing option alive and to hold open the possibilities for meaningful arms control for a reasonable interval, trying to persuade the Soviets that it would be mutually advantageous to resume negotiations.

Senators Cohen and Biden accepted an invitation from the Soviet Academy of Sciences and visited Moscow in February 1983 to explain details of the build-down concept. Their reception was courteous, and discussions seemed to advance Soviet understanding that the build-down proposal was more than just a Reagan "plot." Soviet participants described build-down as "not a bad idea," although it had been "contaminated" by Reagan's embrace of it; a senior official emphasized that "anything negative we have said about build-down applies only to the opening presentation of the idea in Geneva and specifically not to the concept outlined by the senators." There seemed reason to believe that the build-down approach to making possible fair trade-offs between the two sides' forces could provide a basis for worthwhile negotiations, if and when START resumed. But Moscow was already forming its ranks for a wholesale denunciation of the Reagan administration that was bound to make difficult any future business with it.The Soviets believed that the administration still was bent on the goal of military superiority proclaimed by the 1980 Republican platform; they cited the MX as one of many signs of that intention, appearing even more alarmed about the president's "Star Wars" initiative, the INF weapons, and sea-launched cruise missiles (SLCMs). In the short run, at least, all evidence indicated that the Soviets were more inclined to match any U.S. buildup than to be compliant in negotiating mutual restraint.

Thus, spring 1984 found Congress once again in a quandary over the MX. Should it continue to authorize deployment of a weapon system about which most members were anxious and which no member felt would be more survivable than existing ICBMs in silos? If it did, would the legislators be rewarding Moscow for having walked out of the talks and reducing their incentive to resume negotiations? With all leading Democratic contenders for the presidency calling for cancellation of the MX, would rejection of the system only guarantee that perpetual partisanship would displace the enduring bipartisan coalition for which the Scowcroft Commission and its congressional allies had worked so hard? Was there any realistic prospect that continuing the MX would help revive arms control after the election?

Responding to these concerns, once more the gang of six tried to strike a balance that would earn their colleagues' endorsement. They moved to reduce, by one-half or more, the 40 MX the administration proposed to procure and, in the House, to fence that procurement by relating it to resumption of good faith talks at START. In a motion offered by Representatives Aspin and Joel Pritchard (R-Wash.), the House agreed to hold off further MX procurement for six months; if the Soviets returned to START, the delay might continue for another period, subject to a presidential determination. It was an acknowledged maneuver to buy time. If the election brought a Democrat to office, the MX was dead; if Reagan were reelected there was at least some hope that the Soviets would decide to resume negotiations and that a modest delay in the MX would encourage them to do so.

Derided by MX opponents, most of whom had no faith in the willingness or ability of the Reagan team to conduct fruitful negotiations with Moscow, the holding action held for less than a week in the House. In a series of votes largely along party lines, House members denied authorization for further MX production by a single vote, but indicated they would reconsider the matter six months later in light of developments on the negotiating front.With the Republican Senate expected to approve perhaps 21 missiles for the next fiscal year, the stage was set for serious division between the Houses. And in 1984 the MX was an even sharper electoral issue than it had been four years before, as Democratic nominee Walter Mondale directed much of his fire against the incumbent's record on nuclear arms and negotiations.

Reagan would not waver in his commitment to a defense buildup including the MX, but he did moderate his anti-Soviet rhetoric and emphasize his desire for progress in arms control. He admonished the Republican national convention to temper its previous platform call for military superiority over the Soviets and began to move toward more active negotiations in his second term. He and Secretary of State George Shultz managed to coax the Soviets back to the bargaining table in 1985, as Mikhail Gorbachev took the reins of power in Moscow. His continuing demands, however, for MX development as an essential element in U.S. leverage fell on ever less receptive ears in Congress. In 1985 the legislators capped deployment in silos at 50 MX, though they left open the possibility for additional weapons if the administration finally devised a more credible basing scheme. Particularly if the two nations agreed on the dramatic force reductions being proposed by both Reagan and Gorbachev, there would be little room and even less rationale for more substantial MX deployment. The 300 MX planned by the air force in the mid–1970s had dwindled to the 200 proposed by Jimmy Carter and the 100 urged by Ronald Reagan. It seemed unlikely that any of those numbers would ever be achieved.

In Conclusion

The convoluted, incomplete, unfinished story of the MX reveals much about legislative-executive relations in our time, but it permits no neat conclusions. One can note the crucial interventions Congress made and offer preliminary judgments about them. Perhaps most surprising is the discrimination and steadiness of purpose that the legislature has shown on the larger principles involved. Congress has reflected, articulated, and refined ideas that, although not always the first instinct of executive decision makers, often seemed wiser as matters unfolded. Indeed, many of those who have managed the MX would concur in the view that the recurrent delays and policy shifts that have afflicted the MX stemmed more from intra-executive and wider political sources.

Immersion in the MX question brought Congress to a firm collective verdict that counterforce weapons in vulnerable bases were unwise. That verdict in turn led to constraints on MX basing that produced the plan for multiple protective shelters, but the public and congressional outcry over the "shell game" deployment led to an executive—not legislative—decision to abandon what most analysts considered the least bad of the available options for survivable basing. The record indicates that, had President Reagan chosen to proceed with the MPS, Congress would have supported him. Congressional rejection of the administration's ideas for the MX in silos, air-mobile basing, and closely spaced basing prompted the far-reaching Scowcroft Commission inquiry that placed the MX in a broader and more sophisticated context for evaluation. For the first time, the MX was measured critically against alternative strategic concepts, arms control requirements, and the vital condition for any effective national security policy, a durable domestic consensus.

Out of the Scowcroft Commission and its interaction with Congress came basic turning points, toward preference for more survivable and less destabilizing single-warhead ICBMs and a fresh start on arms control centered on the build-down principle and comprehensive trade-offs between U.S. bomber advantages and Soviet missile advantages. From this perspective, the MX became the fulcrum by which the de-MIRVing principle and build-down concept—both devised in Congress and against the grain of executive planning—came to prevail in declaratory policy. In essence, the events of 1983 represented belated executive ratification of the Senate's 1969–1970 judgment that U.S. security would be served better by precluding an open-ended competition in MIRV missiles and unbounded increases in strategic nuclear warheads. But those events did not resolve the lingering questions: Would congressional acquiescence in limited MX deployment energize diplomacy to render such destabilizing systems less numerous in the future? Or would it feed a continuing technological contest portending even greater instability in the coming decade?

Notes

1. Readers are entitled to assess what follows in light of the writer's own opinion about the MX: I believe the system is strategically unwise, but I respect the position of those who feel that limited deployment is tolerable as part of a political bargain that might shift the United States—and perhaps the Soviet Union—away from large MIRVed ICBMs and toward negotiated restraints on the scale and characteristics of the two nations' strategic forces.

In gathering my data, I owe a particular debt to the meticulous reporting of Pat Towell in the *Congressional Quarterly* and Michael Gordon in the *National Journal*, as well as to John Edwards's book, *Superweapon: The Making of MX* (New York: Norton, 1982).

2. The AWACS Sale to Saudi Arabia

I. M. Destler

On Wednesday, October 28, 1981, the United States Senate voted 52-48 *not* to block the sale to Saudi Arabia of five airborne warning and control system (AWACS) aircraft, together with various weapons designed to enhance the effectiveness of the F–15 fighter planes provided under the Carter administration.

On the surface and in the headlines, it was a dramatic victory for Ronald Reagan, a foreign policy feather for the presidential cap to match the plumes won earlier that year in congressional combat on spending and taxes. In fact, it was nothing of the sort. At home, what Reagan accomplished was mainly to avoid becoming the first president to have a sale vetoed under the Arms Export Control Act. Abroad, the protracted debate offended the Saudis, and the outcome upset the Israelis. And the time and attention the president and his administration had to devote to this narrow—if important—issue postponed the development of a serious, comprehensive Middle East policy, one that might have averted the war that broke out the following June.

What are the lessons of this particular case? What does it tell us more broadly about the executive-legislative politics of arms sales, and the now-defunct legislative veto through which Congress sought to exert leverage? This paper will begin by setting forth the specific background in executive-legislative, as well as Saudi and Israeli, relations. We will then move to description and analysis of the AWACS case itself, before concluding with some thoughts about the broader problem of congressional involvement in the operational choices of foreign policy.

Domestic Background: The Arms Sales Veto

The early 1970s brought congressional foreign policy assertiveness on a scale unseen since World War II. One cause was reaction to Vietnam; another was the related broader wave of reform that was cresting on Capitol Hill. A major result was legislation constraining presidential foreign policy making, particularly in the use of military and paramilitary instruments.[1]

I. M. Destler is a senior fellow at the Institute for International Economics. From 1977 to 1983, he was a senior associate for executive-congressional relations at the Carnegie Endowment for International Peace. He also has been a senior fellow in Foreign Policy Studies at The Brookings Institution. His numerous publications include *Presidents, Bureaucrats and Foreign Policy* (Princeton, N.J.: Princeton University Press, 1972).

The movement peaked during congressional consideration of the Foreign Assistance Act of 1974, in the early months of the Ford administration. Over strong presidential objections, Congress attached to that bill such restrictions as a prohibition on covert Central Intelligence Agency (CIA) operations unless and until the administration notified appropriate congressional committees of their nature and scope, a requirement that the bulk of food aid be allocated to countries on the United Nations list of those most in need, and a partial embargo on arms sales to Turkey in response to the invasion of Cyprus.

Also included in the 1974 foreign aid bill was a broader restraint on arms exports. Overcoming the resistance of leaders in both branches, Senator Gaylord Nelson, a member of neither the Foreign Relations nor the Armed Services Committee, managed—in alliance with Rep. Jonathan Bingham—to win adoption of a proviso requiring the president to notify Congress in advance of major arms sales. It further specified that if Congress passed within 20 days a concurrent resolution disapproving a sale, it could not go forward. There were various exceptions—sales to NATO countries and certain Pacific allies and sales below a certain dollar threshold amount. And the law (Section 36 of the Arms Export Control Act) was refined in 1976 to allow Congress more time, 30 calendar days, to act on a sale and to strengthen the process in other ways. But the legislative veto by concurrent resolution was maintained.

From December 1974 when President Ford reluctantly signed the original bill to June 1983 when the Supreme Court declared legislative vetoes unconstitutional, three presidents protested the arms sales veto in principle but acquiesced in practice. Though it had been imposed by one branch on the other, it was, in its actual operation, a moderate form of congressional control, allowing far more executive flexibility than the detailed country programming characteristic of foreign aid legislation, for example. It gave the president leeway but forced him to consider possible congressional reaction. And legislators, having fashioned themselves a new policy tool, employed it sparingly. Objections from Capitol Hill did force delays and changes in a handful of proposed arms sales. But Congress did not flatly disapprove a single one.

Two sorts proved controversial, however. One was sales of arms to Arab adversaries of Israel. The second was the provision of weapons whose technology the United States did not wish to fall into Soviet hands.

Foreign Background: AWACS and Saudi Arabia

In the summer of 1977, President Jimmy Carter notified Congress of his intention to sell AWACS to the shah's Iran. Led by Senator John

Culver (D-Iowa), critics protested that this risked defense secrets and might also upset the balance of power in the Persian Gulf. After the House International Relations Committee recommended a veto, and the Senate Foreign Relations Committee was about to do the same, Carter withdrew his notification. When he resubmitted it the following September, the proposal was revised to exclude sensitive secret coding and communications equipment. The threat of veto receded, though the shah was to fall from office before any AWACS were actually delivered.

The following spring, Carter proposed to sell 60 F–15 fighter aircraft to Saudi Arabia, as part of a package including planes for Israel and Egypt as well. U.S. friends of the Jewish state, led by the American-Israel Public Affairs Committee (AIPAC), mobilized to oppose the Egyptian and Saudi components, especially the latter. But in what was perhaps its most effective congressional lobbying operation on a foreign policy issue, the Carter administration prevailed in the Senate, 54–44. The foreign credibility it gained from this success, from proving the United States could help Arab friends despite Israeli objections, contributed to conclusion of the Camp David accords the following September.

In the course of the spring congressional campaign, Secretary of Defense Harold Brown had offered written assurances that the Saudis would not be supplied with certain equipment—auxiliary fuel tanks, bomb racks, an aerial refueling capacity, and Sidewinder (AIM, 9L) missiles—that would increase the range of the F–15s and enhance their utility for offensive use against Israel. And Assistant Secretary of State Douglas J. Bennet, Jr., in a letter to House Foreign Affairs Subcommittee Chairman Lee Hamilton (D-Ind.), declared that "an F–15 sale will not lead to the sale of E–2C or E–3A (AWACS)" surveillance systems.[2]

However these words were viewed on Capitol Hill, the Saudis did not regard any of these assurances as final, for they expressed growing interest in both AWACS and F–15 enhancement during 1979 and 1980. At the technical level, air force officials in both countries developed detailed plans and rationales. At the political level, Saudi officials pressed their case with Brown and National Security Adviser Zbigniew Brzezinski. The attractiveness of the AWACS as both a weapon system and a political symbol became all the greater when, in the spring of 1979 and again in the fall of 1980, the United States deployed the aircraft to Saudi Arabia in response to the specific threats of the Yemeni civil war and then the war between Iran and Iraq.

As part of its broader response to what it called the "changed situation in the Gulf since 1978," specifically the Iranian revolution and the expanded Soviet threat, the Carter administration reversed itself.[3] It concluded, late in 1980, that Saudi Arabia should receive promptly certain previously denied F–15 enhancement equipment and, in the near future, an aerial surveillance system. Simultaneously, the U.S. Air Force had determined that AWACS was the surveillance system the Saudis needed. The Saudis knew this, but as former Secretary of State Alexander Haig writes in his memoirs, "I did not know it, and I do not believe that Muskie or Brown knew it, either. The judgment had been made by men deep in the American bureaucracy talking to counterparts in the Saudi defense establishment on the basis of technical needs rather than political considerations."[4]

Thus, as the Reagan administration prepared to assume power, U.S. foreign policy was moving in a direction bound to cause trouble on Capitol Hill. Saudi Arabia was pushing very hard for an arms package combining the same two elements that had separately caused trouble in prior years: "threat to technology" and "threat to Israel." The campaign was far enough advanced that anything short of the AWACS would be interpreted as a rebuff. But even with the most careful executive branch management, an AWACS sale was bound to be serious trouble on Capitol Hill.

The new Reagan team was thus dealt a difficult hand. It was to play that hand disastrously, making AWACS a case study in how not to manage a politically volatile foreign policy question.

January–September 1981: Digging a Deep Hole

The Reagan people were first presented the AWACS and F–15 issue by Carter's secretaries of defense and state, Brown and Edmund Muskie, who offered to share the burden on Capitol Hill, perhaps even present the actual sales proposal to Congress before Reagan's January 20 inauguration. Not surprisingly, this offer went unaccepted. New administrations seldom want to share concrete policy responsibility with their predecessors. Nor do they readily commit themselves to continue previous policy lines without the new look to which they feel their election entitles them. And in this particular case, the Reagan people had little respect for either the substance of Carter policies or the political effectiveness of the administration.

It made sense, then, to spurn the offer of help—the Carter political strategy was unpromising. What did not make sense was to develop no serious political strategy at all. But this, essentially, is how the Reagan administration handled AWACS for its first eight and a half months.

The primary reason was internal disorganization. There was no fundamental disagreement on whether to proceed with some form of sale of the F–15 equipment and AWACS. But the Reagan administration lacked, in 1981, any effective means of establishing and enforcing coordinated policy. The national security adviser had been downgraded, but Secretary of State Alexander Haig had been rebuffed in his efforts to establish alternative, State Department centered policy procedures.

The result was an executive branch acting like two separate governments. Secretary of State Haig maneuvered, from January through March, to work out—with the Israeli government and on Capitol Hill—a tacit agreement to move quickly with a specific sale of F–15 enhancement equipment (excluding bomb racks) to the Saudis, while deferring action on an unspecified surveillance aircraft system until somewhat later.

The fact that a majority of senators was already on record against selling all of these items to Riyadh underscored the need to move with care. But Secretary of Defense Caspar Weinberger was busy reinforcing the air force's hell-bent approach: together the Pentagon bureaucracy and its new civilian leadership plunged ahead, with little heed to either foreign or domestic sensitivities. Leaks from the Pentagon indicated, before any administration decision, that the AWACS was to be offered to Saudi Arabia. This leakage served to narrow the administration's options—for other surveillance systems or for delay or for the sort of joint ownership and management under which AWACS was operated in NATO—and to force the thumbs up-or-down choice that fit the Saudi definition of the issue as a litmus test of the U.S. commitment.

On April 1, the National Security Council overrode Haig and recommended to the president a massive, $8.5 billion sales package, which included AWACS, tankers to refuel AWACs aircraft, and a number of F–15 enhancement items. Reagan, in the hospital recuperating from the assassination attempt, agreed. The White House did not announce the package publicly until April 21. But it leaked to the press on April 2, just as Secretary Haig was preparing to depart for the Middle East where he hoped, among other things, to mitigate Israeli opposition with security assurances and offers of offsetting aid. Israeli Prime Minister Menachem Begin, his instinctive opposition reinforced by the upcoming Israeli election in June, went public also, declaring to Haig that the proposed sale presented "a very serious threat to Israel."

The Reagan administration had committed itself to a foreign policy action for which opposition was strong and growing. Between March 24 and April 7, "44 senators and 78 House members made floor speeches denouncing the sale."[5] Prominent among the opponents were Republican Senators Bob Packwood of Oregon and Roger Jepsen of Iowa, and Rep. Jack Kemp (R-N.Y.). Outspoken congressional support came only from Senate Armed Services Chairman John Tower (R-Tex.). And the administration had made this commitment with little White House and Pentagon consciousness of the magnitude of its political problem. But having committed itself, it now needed to move quickly to counter the opposition.

Instead, the White House did next to nothing through the spring and most of the summer. It made sense to defer, on Senate Majority Leader Howard Baker's recommendation, the formal notification of Congress that would start the 30-day clock ticking, in the hope that detailed arrangements could be reached with the Saudis to assuage the senators' security concerns. But instead of using the time gained from delay to mobilize domestic support, the administration effectively yielded the playing field to the sale's adversaries for several crucial months. In fact, foreign policy officials were specifically barred by the White House from presenting senators and representatives with the substantive case for the sale: they could urge solons to remain uncommitted and promise that when they finally heard the administration case they would like it. But they could do no more. And as one Republican senator put it in retrospect, "Just to wander around here and say, 'As soon as you see the whole thing, you'll be satisfied,' which was what we were hearing from National Security Adviser Richard Allen for months, is not an appropriate way to handle an issue of this magnitude."[6]

Why was the administration fighting with both hands tied behind its back? The best explanation is the second deep organizational gulf in the early Reagan administration—that between the president's trio of close White House aides and its foreign policy leadership, Haig in particular.

The first group was giving absolute priority to the president's budget and tax proposals, and the White House Congressional Relations staff under Max Friedersdorf was working overwhelmingly on this economic program. Reagan's senior advisers, particularly White House Chief of Staff James Baker, were determined not to repeat Jimmy Carter's error of seeking too many things at once, spreading political resources too thin. They wanted to be sure that nothing would threaten the general public support the president needed to win the big showdown votes on economic policy and nothing would complicate bargaining with specific representatives.

In fact, a strong AWACS lobbying effort, led by the departments and targeted at the Senate, would not necessarily have undercut the economic lobbying, which was focused mainly on House members. But its leader would have had to be trusted by the White House to defer to its political priorities, and Haig was not. He and his department had already muddied the public waters by shining their spotlight on El Salvador. So the White House kept them on a tight leash on AWACS until the economic battles were won.

As a result, the executive branch went through several months of wheel spinning. At first, Under Secretary of Defense for Policy Fred Iklé was given responsibility for briefing skeptical legislators. As his effort won mixed reviews, Haig and Weinberger went to Counselor Edwin Meese in June to urge a strong White House effort, but instead of choosing Vice President George Bush—Haig's apparent suggestion to lead the campaign—Reagan designated Richard Allen. Allen took on this unhappy task with a fuzzy connection to the president and limited experience in lobbying the Hill. In due course three teams were formed (labeled "Red," "White," and "Blue") and were headed by Allen, Iklé, and Under Secretary of State James Buckley. The teams were essentially unconnected to the White House congressional relations staff that was winning a formidable reputation for its economic policy successes. Only Buckley, a former senator, won favorable Hill reviews.

The result was hardly surprising. Legislators were faced with one-sided pressure orchestrated by an AIPAC under adroit new leadership. The administration had then exacerbated this pressure by upsetting the Israeli government. And the administration was offering the targets nothing with which to counter the pressure. Thus not only did Democrats overwhelmingly join the anti-AWACS banner—as a majority had bucked Jimmy Carter on F–15s in 1978—but a substantial minority of Republicans did also. Maverick moderates like Senators Bob Packwood of Oregon and Rudy Boschwitz of Minnesota were joined by Orrin Hatch of Utah, William Cohen of Maine, and even, in an impressive AIPAC coup, Jepsen, a hard-line conservative. In all, 20 Republicans joined 34 Democrats in a June 24 letter to the president urging that he "refrain from sending this proposal to Congress." Three months later, on September 17, 18 Republicans joined 32 Democrats in cosponsoring the Packwood resolution of disapproval. Sentiment in the House was even more negative, as that chamber's ultimate 301–111 vote to block the sale would show.

AIPAC had more going for it than an adroit leadership and an effective national network of supporting organizations that could put pressure on members from where it counted. It had a persuasive array of policy arguments, extending beyond U.S.-Israeli relations. It is difficult for an interest group to prevail on a foreign policy issue unless it can join its cause to a broader national interest theme. In this case, the substantial core of reliable friends of Israel could be expanded through concern about the security of military secrets in the hands of a nation that might, to paraphrase President Reagan, "become an Iran." The earlier, unconsummated AWACS deal seemed an apt warning. Senators like John Glenn (D-Ohio) would seize upon the concern over military technology and press for a "joint control" arrangement in which the United States would have explicit coresponsibility through the 1990s. When this approach was rejected, Glenn joined the opposition.

A third source of opposition was the U.S. public's resentment of the Arab's oil power. In the words of one State Department official at the time, there was a widespread feeling that "the Arabs are jerking us around too much," and we ought to call a halt. Many felt that the United States was being blackmailed, squeezed into making concessions to Arab countries while getting nothing substantial in return—no solid political commitments, no clear recognition of Israel or even its right to exist within pre–1967 borders. This created a market for attacks on Saudi Arabia during the course of the debate that, inevitably, cut into the political gains sought from the sale in the first place.

Supporters of the sale had answers to all of these arguments. They could explain that a Saudi AWACS, even if a potential threat to Israel, was one Israel could easily counter, and that the sales package (e.g., no F–15 bomb racks) was designed to limit that threat. This could not, of course, assuage the Israelis' political concern that if a U.S.administration would make such a commitment to an Arab nation with whom Israel had not come to terms, then there might be real limits on what the United States might do on Israel's behalf in a crisis. Advocates could show how certain components of the U.S. AWACS—those at the technological frontier or with offensive potential—were not being included in the Saudi package. This, however, would only confirm the charges of Glenn the technocrat that the United States was providing a second-rate AWACS, rather than the first-rate system—under joint U.S.-Saudi control—that the situation demanded.

Eventually, the administration would make all these arguments, and more. But in the months from the White House announcement in April to the preliminary notification to Congress in August, and the formal notice on October 1, it was the critics who dominated the debate. As Secretary of State Haig prepared to present the proposal to the Senate Foreign Relations Committee, the political problem was all too clear. The House was bound to override; Senate vote counts were on the order of 12 in support of the administration and 65 against. And an absolute majority—enough to veto the sale—were on record in opposition.

One way to turn the tide would be to extract visible concessions from Saudi Arabia. In the fall of 1977, as criticism grew over the security provisions of the Panama Canal treaties, the Carter White House had invited Panamanian President Omar Torrijos to Washington and won his assent to an "understanding" that met the concerns of key senators. The following spring, this language enabled senator after senator to declare that his tough scrutiny had resulted in improvements that made it possible, now, for him to support ratification. Individual senators had also crafted their own reservations, to which Panama reluctantly assented.

But the Saudis would not—perhaps could not—play this rather humiliating American game. The very things senators needed—constraints on military autonomy, overt ties with the United States, and steps toward Israel—would undercut the balance the desert nation was seeking to strike between de facto security links to the United States and its independent standing within the Arab world. So the efforts of the divided administration to secure Saudi concessions served only to discredit it further. Allen made the rounds of Capitol Hill with Prince Bandar bin Sultan and worked with Howard Baker to see whether a senatorial mission to Saudi Arabia might culminate in a policy package that could serve as the domestic vehicle for the delivery of AWACS. But this effort was not advanced by public reports that Haig was vociferously resisting it and that the secretary did not want "blankety-blank senators making American foreign policy." In the end, in any case, the Saudis turned thumbs down on any congressional mission that would discuss restrictions on the use of AWACs.

If senators were unable to extract concessions from the Saudis, a political alternative was to provide benefits for the Israelis. As suggested by former State Department Congressional Relations Chief Brian Atwood, the administration was making much of the new stategic relationship it was building with Israel, and it could have "allowed members of Congress to claim credit for that kind of security enhancement."[7] But this possibility went unexploited, perhaps even unexplored. Nor was this card played with the Israelis, although there was apparently an intent to do so. Menachem Begin, his election now safely behind him, visited Washington in early September, and, according to press reports at the time, the administration decided to make it clear to him, in person, that the new relationship depended on a muting of opposition to AWACS. But nobody was chosen to bell the cat. Instead Begin reiterated to the Senate Foreign Relations Committee, in response to members' questions, the strength of Israeli objections. This precipitated, in turn, a scramble within the administration to determine whether the president's guest had violated his promise not to lobby personally against AWACS on American soil.

So when Haig came to testify on October 1, it was clear that Reagan's foreign policy team had failed. The secretary claimed that the sale was now conditioned on strong, recently negotiated assurances, but no one outside the administration camp could find them: the specifications he conveyed seemed no different than what lower-level officials had been communicating in the weeks before. And if the substantive case for the sale found few Senate takers, the judgment on administration management was lower still. Senator Sam Nunn (D-Ga.), who ultimately backed the president, remarked that if his colleagues were to vote on how the administration had handled the matter, the tally would be negative by about 97 to 3.

October 1981: Climbing Out of the Hole

The foreign policy team failed. Taking over now was the political team, which had contributed to that failure by the severe constraints the White House had imposed. The new team had three primary players. One, Senate Majority Leader Howard Baker, had been engaged for months, trying vainly to sensitize the White House to its Hill problems, to probe in all directions for political leeway, to buy time, to keep open the possibility of a positive outcome. The other two—Ronald Reagan and his Chief of Staff James Baker—were getting into the issue seriously for the first time.

Their task was simple to state but, in the apt words of columnist Mark Shields, "the most difficult of all" to accomplish—"to persuade [legislators] to change positions on an issue publicly."[8] The political team would have to turn several senators around. And beyond the general rewards they could offer those who went with the president on a tough issue, the resources they could draw upon were limited. But they deployed them with remarkable effectiveness.[9]

One resource was party loyalty. The Saudi sale was not the sort of issue to be cast in partisan terms: for one thing, it was too unpopular. Reagan therefore had to stress broad national interest arguments in his policy appeals. But 20 Republicans had signed the Packwood letter of June, and many of them were junior members of the party that the Reagan election of 1980 had swept into majority Senate status. He had claim to their loyalties, and he asserted that claim.

The first sign of success came in the Senate Foreign Relations Committee, which, despite the backing of Chairman Charles Percy (R-Ill.), had been cool to the administration case. Three of the panel's nine Republicans had signed the June letter and two had cosponsored the September resolution of disapproval, but only one of them, Boschwitz, voted on October 15 to veto the sale. The big surprise was the successful White House wooing of Larry Pressler (R-S.D.) the day of the vote. The resulting 9–8 committee margin for disapproval was a moral victory for the administration, as a stronger anti-AWACS vote had been expected.

But the split also signaled how much AWACS was becoming, in the senators' alignments, a partisan issue. Responding perhaps to pressure from his colleagues, Minority Leader Robert Byrd (D-W. Va.) came out against the sale a week later, disappointing Baker who had, under Carter, teamed with Byrd on Panama (though not on SALT II). And in the final tally, northern Democrats would break 28–4 against AWACS.

To supplement the claim on partisan loyalties and to reach out to the diminishing number of Democrats still on the fence, there was also some brokering in policy substance. Senators now wishing to shift their position needed a rationale: few cared to admit, as did one prize Reagan convert, that "nothing much has changed but me." It was better to be able to assert that one had pressed serious policy concerns, and they had been accommodated. Changes in the U.S.-Saudi arrangements were ruled out; Riyadh would not accept them. But the president might make a unilateral explanation to Congress of the security assurances and constraints governing the sale, and there was some slight leeway in the words he employed. Senators could, for credit-claiming purposes, exaggerate this leeway, and the White House could encourage them in this game.

Hence the Reagan administration, working with sympathetic and fence-sitting senators like Nunn, John W. Warner (R-Va.), Dan Quayle (R-Ind.), and Slade Gorton (R-Wash.), devised a new vehicle for policy bargaining, the ever-changing presidential letter. An explanation of the terms of the sale was drafted, and redrafted, and redrafted. Senators invited to the White House had access to the draft and were invited to participate, to insert their own phrases and sentences, and to declare publicly how they were toughening the terms. A number availed themselves of this opportunity. It proved a remarkably successful charade, a bridge enabling senators to walk credibly from opposition to support. And since the final draft, under Reagan's signature, was not transmitted to Majority Leader Baker until the day of the showdown vote, there was little time even to check the final language against senators' specific contributions, much less give the letter the sort of broad analysis that would have shown how little new it contained.[10]

The third resource was the president himself. Ronald Reagan opened up his office to the targeted senators, meeting them again and again. He made AWACS his overriding personal policy enterprise for a full month. Unlike Jimmy Carter on Panama, Reagan did not seek to out-argue the legislators on substantive detail, though his grasp of the basics reportedly improved in the course of October. And though he was, objectively a supplicant, arguing against congressional action that would "cut me off at the knees," he somehow managed not to come across as weak in making this appeal—again in contrast to his predecessor. In fact, the president would win on AWACS because—above all—senators were not willing to repudiate their president in his first year on an issue he had made a litmus test of his foreign policy credibility. This was the ultimate argument from weakness. But it was a tribute to Reagan's art that it did not come across that way.

All of these efforts came together, finally, in the last week of October. As late as the day before the Wednesday vote, the *New York Times* reported 53 senators declared against the sale and only 38 in favor. But that Tuesday the fruits of the Reagan-Baker-Baker campaign were revealed. Senator after senator shifted from opposed or uncommitted to favorable. The most dramatic and surprising switch was Jepsen of Iowa, until then a leader of the opposition. This switch caused one anti-AWACS lobbyist to declare, in a postmortem with an administration official, "The next time we get into a fight, we're going to start out with Jepsen on *your* side!"

By the time of the final 52–48 vote (two more on his side than the president needed), Reagan had won the support of no less than 10 signers of the June letter, 9 of them Republican. Two more were believed ready to switch if their votes were absolutely required. In the end, only 12 of Reagan's party stood against him: not as impressive as the virtual unanimity Senator Baker had achieved on the summer's budget and tax issues, but a remarkable accomplishment given the count on October 1. The majority leader's touch was, by all accounts, critical to the president's success: Senator Baker responded to the needs of the un-committed, helped those who might be willing to switch find ways to do so, exerted continuing suasion, yet stayed on speaking terms with those whose votes he could not get for this one but would need another day.

Congressional Involvement
in Operational Choices

The AWACS vote was a personal victory for Ronald Reagan. It was not a major policy accomplishment for his administration. The president had avoided humiliation, and his own efforts had been crucial in this avoidance. But that outcome was hardly unusual: except in the atypical period of 1973–1975, postwar presidents have almost always won their foreign policy showdowns on Capitol Hill. Even Jimmy Carter was victorious on every major issue—Rhodesian sanctions, Panama, arms for the Middle East, Turkey, nuclear fuel to India—that came to a thumbs up-or-down vote. What was notable on AWACS was not that Reagan came out ahead, but that his administration had put him so far behind.

Moreover, Reagan's victory did not lead anywhere. Unlike Jimmy Carter's arms sale of May 1978, an important step toward Camp David, the AWACS sale did not build a base for future policy accomplishment. In fact, it proved counterproductive. The protracted U.S. domestic struggle laid bare the deep tensions between two nations crucial to U.S. Middle East policy. The glaring spotlight on Saudi military dependence was exactly what the sensitive U.S. relationship with that nation did not need. Relations were exacerbated with Israel in general and Prime Minister Begin in particular. In the effort to salvage an operational decision made without recognition of its political volatility, the administration lost time that broader Middle East policy badly needed. That time would run out the following June.

The purpose of this paper is not, of course, to evaluate policy per se: either the wisdom of the AWACS package deal or of the overall Reagan approach to the region. But the unfortunate results were the product, in part, of a process that brought this arms sale to particular prominence. Specifically, Section 36(b) of the Arms Export Control Act—the legislative veto—created a political hurdle that the administration had to surmount and that opponents could use to thwart its plans. It forced the confrontation, which in turn brought the publicity, the rubbing of salt into Israeli and Saudi wounds, and the incredible drain on presidential time. It brought about the disproportionate attention both branches paid to what was, in the end, an operational matter, a question of foreign policy implementation.

It was, of course, an important operational matter: the largest arms sale in U.S. history, with an important impact on the overall U.S. approach to the region. It would have been controversial in any case, and even without a Nelson-Bingham amendment on the books, critics could still have mobilized against it, pressing their cause through the regular legislative process. Amendments would have been proposed to foreign aid authorizations or appropriations and very likely approved by at least one House. This would have complicated the administration's broader legislative program, as officials debated how to kill such an amendment without losing the overall bill.

But in all probability, the AWACS issue would have been less the center of attention, more one of several hard issues along with Angola and El Salvador. And the president's bargaining position would have been stronger. To prevail on the issue, critics would not only need to win in both Houses. They would have to attach the prohibition to a bill that the president had to sign, or else achieve the two-thirds majority necessary to override his veto.

AWACS would have been politically volatile in any case, but the existing process made it the big issue, the event of 1981 in the interbranch politics of foreign policy. This exposed a significant weakness of the legislative veto as a power-sharing device, a drawback inextricably linked to its substantial virtues.

Advocates of the veto, this writer included, have argued that its advantages lie in the threat, not its employment.[11] It serves as a club in the closet. The executive branch knows it is there and that it might be taken out and used, so to avert this, foreign policy leaders find it prudent to move carefully, take advance soundings, and make vetoable decisions on controversial issues only when there is a political strategy for sustaining them. The virtue of the veto is that it encourages consultation and compromise before the political and policy lines have hardened, before the prestige of the president and a foreign government is staked to a specific outcome.

It did not turn out this way on AWACS, for one simple reason: the Pentagon leaders and White House aides who dominated the April 1 decision were insensitive to the threat. And in any bargaining situation where one party ignores the other's sanction, a natural counter is to escalate. The administration was treating congressional views and pre-rogatives with contempt, ignoring them. Its opponents were sophisticated; their initial goal was not victory but a place at the bargaining table. But the administration was acting as if it thought it could roll over them. It was doing so, moreover, without the sort of mandate it could claim and without the public support it could mobilize on, say, its economic program.

Reagan could claim electoral sanction to tilt foreign policy in a more militant, overtly anticommunist direction, as his 1981 success with the Weinberger defense budget demonstrated. But AWACS did not really fit in with that mandate either. The sale was more in the unpopular mainstream of the efforts of predecessor administrations to balance the primary U.S. commitment to Israel with measures that built military ties with moderate Arab regimes. The most attentive and organized segment of the Middle East policy public—the U.S. Jewish community—generally opposed such efforts. No comparable force in U.S. politics supported them. Any adminstration whose behavior was insensitive to this fact of life would pay a substantial cost. So the Reagan administration paid, "victory" notwithstanding.

AWACS is now history; so is the legislative veto. In June 1983 the U.S. Supreme Court declared it unconstitutional, in an opinion impressive in its scope and impact if not its logic. So for those concerned with Congress and foreign policy operations, today's question is not, "Is the legislative veto a good thing?" It is, rather, "What might Congress devise to replace it, and will that be better or worse?"

As dissenting Justice Byron R. White wrote, the *Chadha* decision confronts Congress with a "Hobson's choice," on arms sales as well as other areas of policy. There is little doubt that they fall within the legislature's constitutional power "to regulate commerce with foreign nations." But without the legislative veto as a sanction for policy oversight, Congress must, following White's formulation, either legislate on them in greater detail than before or "abdicate its lawmaking function to the executive branch."

Which should Congress choose? The choice each of us wants will depend in part on how much each thinks Congress should influence foreign policy, and on how—more generally—each would make the trade-off between two good things that often compete in practice: democratic participation and credible national security action. On arms sales one can think of several general control devices, some of them presently in operation: overall ceilings, "report and wait" requirements, or a joint resolution veto (requiring, in practice, two-thirds of each House). Each of these allows greater executive leeway than the law that existed from 1975 through mid–1983. They tilt Congress toward abdication.

But Congress could also restrict executive leeway by insisting on preauthorizing specific arms sales in advance, by country amounts, or by requiring that each sale above a certain dollar amount be submitted to the Congress for specific statutory approval. To win on an arms sale under that rule, a president would have had to carry both Houses. Ronald Reagan would have needed, in addition to the miracle he wrought with senators, to get the votes of at least 96 of the representatives who went against him on AWACS.

The choice we get will depend, over time, on whether presidents avoid forcing a replay of the interbranch confrontation of 1974 that produced the Nelson-Bingham amendment in the first place. In the short run, the Court has given presidents greater leeway on arms sales, and legislators are not rushing to constrain him—many would have been delighted, in fact, to be spared the yes-or-no choice on AWACS. But if, as 12 years ago, an administration persistently presses arms sales on a scale that alarms a congressional majority, and seems unresponsive to that alarm, restrictions will come again. Their exact form cannot be predicted. But it could well make future executive leaders nostalgic for the leeway that Nelson-Bingham provided their predecessors.

Foreign policy operations present Congress with a dilemma. In general they are the sort of detail that the U.S. national legislature handles badly and should avoid. Ideally, Congress should stick to influencing broad policy. But what if the details, taken together, add up to policy, defined as what the U.S. government actually does in the international arena? And what if certain operational choices, like the AWACS sale, are large and consequential in and of themselves? How can Congress affect them without imposing the sort of item-by-item controls that would put executive branch leaders in a straitjacket? Can it keep the executive flexible without rendering itself impotent?

Like most dilemmas, this one has no simple resolution. And much congressional activity on specific foreign policy issues is "noise," position-taking, and playing to domestic constituencies rather than seeking to exercise real responsibility. But recent experience suggests that if an administration ignores strong and persistent congressional signals—as

did the Nixon-Ford administration in 1973–1974, and Reagan's in 1981—
it will pay a price. And so will U.S. foreign policy.

Notes

This essay draws substantially on *Congressional Quarterly* and other contemporary sources and on research and writing the author carried out in 1981 as
director of the Carnegie Endowment's project on executive-congressional relations
in foreign policy. I am grateful for the comments of Congressman Richard
Cheney (R-Wyo.) and other members of the project's steering committee.

1. For a fuller discussion of this congressional resurgence, see I. M. Destler,
Leslie H. Gelb, and Anthony Lake, *Our Own Worst Enemy: The Unmaking of
American Foreign Policy* (New York: Simon and Schuster, 1984), chapter 3.

2. See U. S. Senate. Committee on Foreign Relations. *The Proposed AWACS/
F-15 Enhancement Sale to Saudi Arabia: A Staff Report* (Committee Print) 97th
Cong., 1st sess., Sept. 1981, p. 3.

3. Letter from Edmund Muskie and Harold Brown to Senator Carl Levin,
April 1, 1981, quoted ibid, 5.

4. *Caveat: Realism, Reagan, and Foreign Policy* (New York: Macmillan, 1984),
175.

5. *Congressional Quarterly Almanac, 1981*, vol. 27 (Washington, D.C.: Congressional Quarterly, 1982), 130.

6. Ibid., 135.

7. Ibid.

8. *Washington Post*, November 30, 1981.

9. For a fascinating discussion of how six senators determined their stand
on AWACS see Richard F. Fenno, Jr., "Observation, Context and Sequence in
the Study of Politics," *American Political Science Reviews*, forthcoming 1986.

10. For details on how this device was developed, see "Executive-legislative
Consultation on US Arms Sales," by Richard F. Grimmett, Congressional Research
Service, *Congress and Foreign Policy Series*, no. 7, House Foreign Affairs Committee
Print, December 1982, 28–34.

11. See I. M. Destler, "Dateline Washington: Life After the Veto," *Foreign
Policy* 52 (Fall 1983): 181–186.

Commentary: On the MX
and AWACS Debates

Richard Cheney

Frustration resulting from the Vietnam and Watergate experiences served as a catalyst in transforming the U.S. Congress as an institution, altering the foreign policy relationship that had existed with the executive branch since World War II. A significant lack of confidence in the executive branch's ability to formulate effective foreign policy spurred Congress to assume a more active role in its development and implementation.

At the same time, Congress became a more decentralized body with diffused power. As such, institutional change has magnified the role of individual members and their staffs and compounded the difficulty of the executive branch in coordinating its relations with Congress. As a result, traditional constituent pressures on individual members further aggravated the relationship, making foreign policy more vulnerable to national mood swings. The MX and AWACS case studies illustrate the complexity of legislative-executive relations and provide insights into those aspects of the process where adjustments could improve the effectiveness of U.S. foreign policy.

Given the increased assertiveness of Congress in the foreign policy process, a relevant question to be considered is where to draw the line between legitimate congressional oversight and congressional intrusion. Congress is in the unique position of being both critic and coworker, partner and adversary in the national security arena. Such creative tension and debate can contribute to policy review. Ultimately decisions can reflect more accurately public values and interests.

The MX Debate

The MX has been an extremely complex and multifaceted issue. Congress became increasingly involved in the MX debate because of the mounting skepticism regarding the quality of executive decision making on strategic issues. The evidence suggests that had the Reagan

Richard Cheney has represented Wyoming in the U.S. House of Representatives since 1978. In 1975–1976, he served as White House chief of staff under President Gerald Ford following a year as deputy assistant to the president. Currently the chairman of the House Republican Policy Committee, Representative Cheney serves on the House Committee on Interior and Insular Affairs and the Permanent Select Committee on Intelligence.

administration held fast to the multiple protective shelter (MPS) basing mode proposed by the Carter administration, Congress would have acquiesced. Nonetheless, the administration created a problem for itself by eliminating the MPS system and deserves criticism on this point.

Another important parallel between the debates is the impact of congressional reaction to constituent pressures. Important constituent uprisings occurred over the MX as people contemplated the placement of 4,300 shelters in Nevada and Utah. An obvious parallel is drawn with the 1967–1969 period when the prospects of a substantial deployment of antiballistic missile systems around the country triggered public pressure from a significant number of people, frightened by the thought of having missiles in their backyards.

Despite constituent pressure, the most striking aspect of the debate is that had the MPS approach to the MX deployment been followed, it probably would have been passed by Congress. That multiple protective shelters would have been a defendable political stance is indicated by the fact that, during the key voting periods in 1980, never more than 40 percent of the House voted against the MX even though constituent attitudes were rising against it in key areas. In 1980–1981 the evidence indicates that, had the MPS stayed on track in the executive branch, deployment of the MX probably could have been sustained in Congress.

Although President Jimmy Carter was reluctant to advocate additional nuclear deployments, he was persuaded finally that the MX and a multiple protective shelter scheme were necessary. When Carter initially recommended it, he won the early congressional test votes. Following the 1980 election, President Reagan, who supported a strong defense and substantial nuclear deployments, was reluctant to go forward with the particular MPS deployment mode of his predecessor. Ironically, President Reagan vetoed the most militarily sound deployment mode and unintentionally undercut the necessary political base for deployment of a system that he strongly favored. This is another example of the lack of continuity in U.S. foreign policy, resulting from a president's unwillingness to be associated with the policies of his predecessor.

Congress, following the lead of the executive branch, had established a fundamentally sound principle in 1976 when it said that the MX, if it were to be deployed, had to be deployed in a survivable basing mode. Yet, by the time the issue matured in the 1982–1983 period, Congress was distressed to find itself presented with a silo basing scheme about which it had expressed doubts since the mid–1970s as a vulnerable basing mode. The irony is that a Congress that had set a sound standard for survivable basing found itself reluctantly accepting the very basing mode it had identified as unacceptable in 1976.

Alton Frye argues that the MX was not a "bungled job," but rather an extremely complex issue with many facets. In evaluating this statement, it might be useful to consider whether the country would have been served better by the originally proposed, unscrutinized deployment of the MX. Many would agree that Congress forced to the surface a variety of complex issues. Thus Frye concludes that, as imperfect and unsatisfactory as the scheme has seemed to be sometimes, the United States is served by having had this type of evolution, with all its pains. The alternative is seen as an unexamined, single-minded drift toward a monolithic deployment of a weapon system.

Although I agree with many of the points raised by Frye, my own comments provide a different perspective on how the issue was decided. I would support the proposition that the congressional-supported proposal for a "build-down" of nuclear weapons on each side, plus some of the other concepts that ultimately became part of the basic compromise with the White House, were generally positive. We should not overlook the contributions made by Congressmen such as Albert Gore (D-Tenn.), Norm Dicks (D-Wash.), and Les Aspin (D-Wis.) to the debate over arms control and what U.S. strategy ought to be. These congressional specialists in the area of security affairs had a considerable impact on administration thinking and performed a useful function throughout the entire process. Congress should pay even more attention to the informed opinion of its members, especially in foreign affairs. In addition, it should give greater consideration to the roles of committees—the Foreign Affairs, Armed Services, and Intelligence Committees.

Congress should also implement a number of procedural changes with regard to foreign policy questions. To limit the ability of less informed members from adding tangential or negative amendments to foreign policy bills, the bills should be sent to the floor with closed or modified closed rules. Such a procedural adjustment would certainly strengthen the role of the informed committees in foreign policy issues.

My own philosophical disagreement with Frye can be indicated in two principal areas—in congressional involvement in diplomacy and in the U.S. approach to arms control. Although a large portion of Congress's involvement was motivated by the desire to play an active role in the arms control process, much also was motivated by the basic law of political constituent considerations. The effect of constituent pressure upon a representative body like Congress must not be underestimated. Also, the heart of the battle on the MX revolved around whether the United States needs a counterforce capability. Therefore, on the issue of full force procurement, the emphasis was on the kind of force required.

The Reagan administration, prior administrations, and the Commission on Strategic Forces (Scowcroft Commission) have judged the MX missile to be necessary as a negative incentive to accomplish what a decade of arms control negotiations had been unable to accomplish—moving the Soviets away from their proclivity for large, silo-busting ICBMs. Congress, on the other hand, consistently has opposed the development and deployment of a counterforce weapon like the MX. The technical issue of basing, so heavily emphasized by Frye, has at times been used as a surrogate for the deeper distrust and antipathy of Congress toward the destabilizing potential of counterforce weapons. At times, the basing argument is employed for purposes other than questioning the basing mode itself.

There is fundamental historical disagreement between Congress and the Reagan administration that involves differing perceptions of the nature of the Soviet Union and the place that arms control has in the question of national security policy. Congress views the arms race as resulting from the absence of arms control agreements and therefore perceives arms control as a necessary condition for improving relations between the United States and the Soviet Union. The administration, on the other hand, sees the arms race as a symptom of differences between the United States and the Soviet Union that are deeply embedded in fundamental and sometimes irreconcilable approaches to how both sides view the world. The administration therefore has a more limited view of what arms control can accomplish compared to Congress's more expanded view. Diminished congressional confidence in the administration's approach to arms control has led to a serious effort to seize the initiative from the executive through such devices as the nuclear freeze resolution, holding the MX hostage, and trying to tie up the arms procurement process through various arms control schemes.

Frye appears to see the extent of congressional involvement as more favorable than I do. From my perspective, it poses two specific dangers. First, the endless debates that have taken place in Congress over the MX and arms control reflect, in part, the weakening of congressional will and resolve to follow through on decisions, especially those that have to do with modernizing the U.S. land-based ICBM force. Second, congressional involvement has allowed the Soviets to influence major U.S. defense programs. The terms of the May 1984 House vote "fenced in" the MX money, pending a Soviet return to Geneva and arms reduction talks. The reasons the Soviets had for not returning were irrelevant; nevertheless, by showing up they could, in effect, kill the MX program. The reluctance of Congress to go forward with the MX and the general resistance to it were tied, at least in part, to the same kind of feeling that for a time led the Dutch to try deferring the deployment of ground-launched cruise missiles in their country. At least an element of successful Soviet intimidation was present in both cases. In addition, there has been a lack of political will on the part of Congress to go forward with basic decisions on land-based ICBM forces.

It is also difficult to be optimistic about the future of the Midgetman missile program. Although a number of members of future of the Midgetman missile program. Although a number of members of Congress have said that they are for the Midgetman but against the MX, there is a tradition in congressional debate of opposition to the system about to be deployed, but support for the one that has not yet been tested. Midgetman in its current (1985) configuration will never be deployed. I find it impossible to conceive of there being enough congressional districts in the country willing to accept Midgetman, and I speak as a congressman from Wyoming where Cheyenne is home to the MX. Congress will display no more will in the future deployment of Midgetman than it has with the MX.

Obviously there are many people in the United States who honestly believe that it is wrong to build nuclear weapon systems. This segment of society always will exist, and it will continue to be a significant percentage, not only of the rank and file voters but also of groups and organizations such as the Catholic church, which in Wyoming has taken the lead and successfully organized the opposition against the MX.

Another important aspect, however, is that the United States does appear now to be vulnerable in the face of Soviet capabilities. In the early 1960s it was easy to sell the old Atlas system because the Soviet forces did not constitute a serious threat. When the missiles were based near Cheyenne, few people were concerned that Cheyenne was a target that actually would be hit. Today, however, they are concerned. There is a subliminal reaction to the fact that the Soviets have capabilities that make the United States vulnerable. It is relatively easy for the opponents of weapon systems to organize opposition, but it is unlikely that a group will lobby for deployment in their district. A significant portion of the recent debate on the MX has dealt with these concerns.

Political will comes if it is perceived as necessary. Generating the perception of a definite threat is difficult, especially when this revolves around the hypothetical possibility that some day the United State might conceivably need to use the weapon. It is much easier to talk about the need to send additional military support to Central America and have people regard it as a crisis situation than it is to persuade the public that there ought to be a Midgetman cruising up and down the interstate highway.

Although lack of will is also an important consideration in terms of the future of Midgetman, there are those who feel that some states would be prepared to carry part of the responsibility for basing as long as they would not be required to carry it disproportionately. If the evolution toward Midgetman were to continue, members of Congress conceivably would have some protection against constituency anxieties by being able to say that, in the context of a dispersed deployment, a particular state would take only its fair share of the burden. Many feel, however, that while it might still have been possible in the early 1980s to have organized a lobbying effort that could have argued successfully for deployment, that time has passed. With the history of the missile deployment issue as extensive as it is, a number of opposition groups already are mobilized.

The AWACS Debate

In contrast to Frye, who covers a 10-year period, I.M. Destler has presented a "snapshot"—a more detailed look at a particularly ignominious episode.This paper raises perhaps more difficult problems than Frye's about what broader lessons can be drawn from it. It is fascinating as a history of a new administration—one well organized on legislative tactics—grappling with an issue in its first year. Clearly mistakes were made, along with some brilliant recouping of mistakes.

Since the 1983 Supreme Court *Chadha* decision that ruled the legislative veto unconstitutional, the institutional framework within which AWACS occurred no longer is applicable. The AWACS case does, however, provide a means of evaluating how to deal with large operational questions, although this is not the kind of question that Congress handles particularly well. It was a misuse of presidential time for President Reagan to spend the month of October 1983 on an arms sale. Nevertheless, it was a consequential action in terms of the U.S. posture toward the Middle East.

The overall thrust of Destler's paper is on target, but more emphasis should be given to two factors. First is the extent to which the domestic political agenda—the economic agenda, the budget agenda, and the tax question—dominated the early months of the Reagan administration. Viewed from the perspective of Capitol Hill, by someone who was involved in the process, the decision to delay pursuing the AWACS sale was made to avoid having anything else cluttering up the legislative agenda that might interfere with the domestic political program. Although the general argument for postponing of AWACS and concentrating on the economic package was understandable, it seems implausible to some of us that serious efforts could not have been made with some of the 20 Republican senators who signed the AWACS letter and then the resolution. The administration's judgment can be called into question because opponents of AWACS were allowed free rein for several months, and then Republican senators were forced into the embarrassing position of switching their votes. Ultimately, for the package to be passed, the administration had to hold 190 Republican members of the House in line while persuading 40 Democrats to join their ranks.

The executive branch believed that Congress was best capable of focusing on one issue at a time and did not choose to pursue AWACS when it thought attention would be distracted from the central priority of the economy. On the key budget vote in August 1981, the Republicans prevailed by a slim margin of three votes on the floor of the House. It is entirely possible that, if something like the AWACS controversy had interfered, the vote might have gone differently. The administration deserves high marks for its sense of timing. Another important influence was the sense of momentum. The assassination attempt upon President Reagan in April 1981 contributed to the administration's success because an enormous outpouring of sympathy helped create an advantage in the tax and budget fights.

The second factor that required greater emphasis was one not touched upon at all by Destler: as was true of previous administrations, the administration at the outset identified a problem with what its predecessor had done and then tried to organize its way out of the problem by changing the White House structure. The problem that the Reagan administration sought to deal with was the perceived historical conflict between the Department of State and the National Security Council (NSC).

This issue is related to the administration's disorganization in the national security area with regard to the AWACS case. In this context, there are two separate but overlapping problems. One involves relationships within the national security apparatus: Who is leading? What is the role of the national security adviser vis-à-vis the secretaries of state and defense? The second involves the relationships between national security officials and the "political team." Both sets of relationships were faulty in the Reagan administration, but perhaps the more serious problem was the lack of effective connection between the two teams. It made sense politically for the administration to defer AWACS, but it was counterproductive to have leaked to the press an NSC decision that airplanes were to be sold to Saudi Arabia. Within the NSC, there was not only a lack of coordination but also a lack of connection between the operational and the political priorities set by the administration. Virtually all administrations have had this difficulty, and national security advisers—whatever their other assets and liabilities—have in general not been particularly sensitive to congressional politics.

In attempting to deal with conflict between the NSC and the Department of State, the Reagan administration buried the NSC so far down inside the White House organization in 1981 that the NSC lost its effectiveness as a mechanism for coordinating other agencies and departments. Deciding that they did not want conflict between the NSC and the Department of State almost guaranteed that that would ultimately occur—and it did. The Defense Department, particularly the air force, got involved and aggressively pursued the AWACS sale without looking at what the sale might mean from the standpoint of the State Department and congressional politics. This happened because of the weakness of the NSC, a weakness that was not in personalities, but reflected some of the problems that the administration encountered. One indication of these problems is that this administration had three NSC advisers in less than four years.

Conclusions

The Frye and Destler studies raise the broader question of the kind of foreign policy role Congress can effectively play. Because power is so diffuse within the institution, Congress is extremely ill equipped to identify or develop a coherent policy. The executive branch must perform this management function. Because the legislative process does not lend itself to the day-to-day conduct of foreign policy, the congressional burden becomes one of contributing to policy formulation, providing informed consent, and helping to educate the public. The fact that Congress represents diverse public opinion can have both positive and negative effects upon debate and the decision-making process.

Both studies should give greater emphasis to importance of constituent and parochial considerations when Congress formulates arms decisions. Also, there is a tendency for the debate, especially in the arms control area, to focus (as Frye does) on congressional elites, those members like Aspin, Gore, and other experts who are involved heavily and who are knowledgeable about the issue in question. This tendency ignores the political pressures that come to bear on the rank and file who do not know that much about the substance, but who are fairly responsive to local groups.

The lesson that comes out of both studies, especially Destler's on AWACS, is the extent to which the executive branch can make problems for itself, as with the Reagan administration's decision to bury the NSC and with the tendency for the foreign policy apparatus in any administration to emphasize that it makes policy and does not deal in politics. Like much of the rest of the national security bureaucracy the NSC is compartmentalized and lacks political understanding, political skills, and empathy for the kinds of issues and concerns that have to be addressed to get Congress to support a package. With almost all of the controversial foreign policy and national security issues in recent years, at least as important as the content of the policy itself has been the ability of the administration to generate political support not only in Congress but all across the country. These two processes cannot be divorced, although in practice they often are.

The MX and AWACS are cases in which Congress has challenged two separate executive policies; and in the MX case, Congress tried to shape an affirmative arms control policy in the face of a generally unwilling and unaccepting administration. The lesson of both cases is that the executive branch needs to pay attention to potential congressional opposition and to develop in advance an effective strategy. Destler presents the Reagan administration as initially not doing this effectively with AWACS. In focusing on economic issues, the administration allowed the opposition to mobilize and initially to control the AWACS issue.

To avoid remodeling the governmental system established by the Constitution, alternatives must be developed to improve attitudes and relations between Congress and the executive branch. Formulating national security policy in a complex and multipolar world never will be simple. Creative tension between the two branches, as well as congressional debate and policy review, can bring about decisions and actions that are better able to serve the interests and values of the American public. To meet the objective of improved, ongoing consultation, an informal congressional briefing system should be established. It should incorporate key members of the State and Defense Departments, as well as other members of the executive branch. On a regular basis, general and specific issues should be discussed. Possible alternatives and options should be presented prior to the development of a crisis situation. The ideas, opinions, and counsel of members of Congress should be welcomed and considered in the executive decision-making process. In addition, the president could meet monthly with congressional leaders and key committee members to discuss the world situation in general and problem areas in more detail. Bipartisan discussion of national security principles and objectives, transcending specific administrations, could provide greater continuity and coherence of policy. Congressional involvement in the policy-formulation process may help to preclude congressional overinvolvement or intrusion in the policy execution phase.

6

Foreign Policy Making
on the Hill

Alvin Paul Drischler

Edwin S. Corwin once described the sharing of foreign policy powers between the president and the Congress in the Constitution as "an invitation to struggle for the privilege of directing American foreign policy."[1] In recent years a new element in this ongoing struggle has emerged as the Congress has shifted from the traditional, free-standing, foreign assistance authorization and appropriation bills to continuing resolutions and supplemental appropriations as its principal legislative mechanism for affecting foreign affairs. This shift has enhanced the power of the Appropriations Committees of the Congress, which manage this legislation, at the expense of the foreign affairs committees, which do not. In addition, it has affected the overall role that the Congress plays relative to the executive in the formulation of foreign policy:

- by forcing tougher trade-offs with domestic programs;
- by forcing the foreign policy leaders in the executive branch to be more cognizant of U.S. domestic political requirements;

Alvin Paul Drischler, former principal deputy assistant secretary of state for congressional relations, is a senior vice president of Black, Manafort, Stone & Kelly, a government relations consulting firm, and a fellow at the The Johns Hopkins Foreign Policy Institute. He is an adjunct fellow at CSIS and originally wrote this article for the CSIS Legislative-Executive Relations Project.
Reprinted from *The Washington Quarterly* 8, no. 3 (Summer 1985): 165–177 with permission from MIT Press Journals, Cambridge, Massachusetts.

- by reinforcing the tendency that Congress already had to micro-manipulate rather than oversee broad policy outlines for U.S. foreign policy.

Control over legislative vehicles is an important determinant of congressional power. Certainly personality, seniority status, and partisan positioning play a role, but of more fundamental importance is the ability to originate legislation, manage it through the process, and ultimately see it enacted into law. Attention from the executive branch and the media, as well as the ability to affect foreign policy, follow from this power to enact legislation.

Paralysis

In recent years, free-standing foreign affairs bills have not been enacted. Instead, they have faced almost insurmountable obstacles including those general obstacles faced by all legislation and by those more specific barriers relating directly to the fact that foreign policy questions are now among the most controversial facing the Congress.

In general, congressional circuits are overloaded, diffusion of power and decentralization of the committee structure are pervasive, customary norms of deference to institutional and party structures have broken down on the floors of both Houses, and the budget process has all but collapsed. Accordingly, despite the occasional heroic exception, it is now fair to say that Congress only gets done what it cannot otherwise avoid.

This paralysis has the effect of sharply curtailing the ability of the foreign affairs and the Appropriations Committees to produce free-standing legislation and it has very nearly made continuing resolutions and supplemental appropriations the only viable legislative mechanism for affecting foreign policy. Indeed, since 1980, only one foreign assistance authorization bill and one free-standing foreign operations appropriations bill have been enacted. In contrast, over the same period, there have been 19 continuing resolutions and supplementals with foreign operations chapters.[2]

Partisan cross-currents have played a role in holding up free-standing foreign affairs bills because House Democratic leaders, who for years had been shouldering the political burden of unpopular foreign assistance programs, have been less willing to do so for the Reagan administration. They have insisted on significant support from their Republican colleagues, which frequently has been difficult for the administration to muster.

Beyond partisan differences, general system overload has made it difficult for the Congress to get anything done. The effects of the institutional revolution of 1974, which propelled into the sunlight a previously closed system, are covered in detail elsewhere. Staff growth, proliferation of subcommittee assignments, intensified media scrutiny, access by junior members to levers of power, and the overall diffusion of congressional power have all been discussed.[3] Whether Congress has ever worked very well in an organizational sense may be debatable; that it now has an even greater difficulty transacting the nation's business is undeniable.

The basic political calculus of the younger members of Congress has aggravated the problem. This new breed of political entrepreneurs is no longer willing to serve time in the "seniority protégé apprenticeship system." They see no particular advantage to working within the system to affect legislation. Instead they are looking for early acquisition of public platforms, staff, and above all, immediate media attention.[4]

Deferential norms have been particularly eroded in the Senate. The informal inhibitions against challenging the leadership on the floor are not only gone, but they have been replaced by positive incentives for those seeking greater media coverage to engage in floor fights. Where to strike the balance between dispersing power and accomplishing legislative business is, of course, difficult, but overall it is hard to avoid the impression that power in Congress has become so diffuse that getting anything done is very difficult.

Problems associated with the budget process have further compounded congressional immobility. Former Senate Majority Leader Howard Baker (R-Tenn.) described the budget problem as a kind of three-layered cake that resulted in serious managerial problems for the Senate leadership. Controversial issues, even if settled in one stage of the process such as the authorization bills, keep coming back as budget resolutions and appropriations bills move through Congress. Because of this multiplicity of decision points, issues refuse to die. Members dissatisfied with the outcome on particularly contentious issues keep reopening lost battles, consuming precious floor time, and making it difficult for the Senate to get anything else done.[5]

Indeed, in recent years, it is fair to argue that the progress that has been made on fiscal issues has come in spite of the formal budget process. In 1984 the extent to which the process worked was the extent to which it was honored in the breach. The first budget resolution for FY 1985 was passed only in the last few days of the session. Those FY 1985 appropriations bills that were enacted got through only because of an informal agreement reached between the House and the Senate budget conferees that each House would use its own resolution as a guideline for appropriations purposes. What is more, in conjunction with the passage of the Energy and Water Appropriations Bill, the House approved a blanket budget waiver for all FY 1985 appropriations.[6]

Foreign Policy for All

The diffusion of power, the breakdown of traditional deferential practices, and a budget process that consumes more in the way of time and attention than it produces in the way of constructive product all constrain the ability of Congress to transact the nation's business. While the impact of general congressional immobility has affected the entire legislative process, free-standing foreign affairs bills have been particularly hard hit, owing to their increasingly controversial nature and the openness with which these issues have been handled. In addition, the Supreme Court has further transferred effective legislative authority for foreign affairs to continuing resolutions and supplemental appropriations bills with the 1983 *Chadha* decision striking down the legislative veto. In sharp contrast to the immediate post-World War II period on Capitol Hill, foreign policy issues are now open to all. In the past, Congress tended to go along policy issues are now open to all. In the past, Congress tended to go along with the executive branch and its own leaders on foreign policy questions. Floor leaders worked with committee chairmen and the executive branch to deliver the rank and file membership.

In the post-Vietnam, post-Watergate period, rank and file members have access to information, staff resources, and personal expertise not available to their predecessors. They also see political benefits from taking highly visible leadership roles on foreign policy issues such as Central America and arms control, which were not as readily available in earlier days. Members in both Houses are now free agents and their votes are not effectively deliverable by anybody.

Accordingly, free-standing foreign affairs legislation must move through the general log-jam of congressional immobility, in addition to which it must be able to secure support from rank and file members, who have far more active political agendas of their own. Moreover, experiences with the SALT Treaty, Vietnam, the Panama Canal Treaties, and many other foreign policy issues of the last decade have given rank and file members a much greater sense of confidence as well as a reduced willingness to trust committees, or anyone else for that matter, as the repository of knowledge in an arcane field. The foreign policy game is now so open that virtually anyone who wants to can play. Because many do, the demands on an already overloaded system result frequently in stalemate and paralysis.

The fate of the FY 1985 foreign assistance authorization bill (S.2582) on the Senate floor in July 1984 is a good case in point. Despite a maximum effort on the part of the administration and heroic efforts in the House just prior to the adjournment for the July recess, S.2582 faced up to 15 threatened filibusters on the Senate floor from the left and the right. Debate would have been far too long and divisive for the Senate leaders to consider scheduling it. The leadership, practicing a form of political euthanasia, killed it.[7]

By striking down the legislative veto, the Supreme Court has had the effect of transferring another major piece of free-standing foreign affairs legislative turf to the domain of continuing resolutions and supplementals. Particularly with respect to the Third World, arms transfers are among the most significant instruments of U.S. foreign policy. With the privileged concurrent resolutions that emanated from the foreign affairs committees under Sec. 36(b) of the Arms Export Control Act of 1976 stricken by the Court, the only practical legislative vehicles now available for Congress to effect arms transfers issues are riders on continuing resolutions and supplementals. This was clearly indicated in March 1984 when the administration decided to withdraw the proposed Stinger sale to Jordan under pressure from Senator Kasten who, with a large number of the Senate cosponsors, proposed a rider to the Emergency Food Aid for Africa Supplemental, H.J. Res. 492, which would have prohibited the sale.[8]

Power to Appropriations

Free-standing foreign assistance authorizations and appropriations bills are not getting through, but continuing resolutions must be acted upon because they provide funding required for the continued operation of the government. Supplementals can be just as essential because they contain emergency funding for such domestic programs as pay raises, food stamps, summer jobs or emergency assistance for poor people.

Control over these legislative vehicles confers enormous power on the Appropriations Committees. The power to manage the only viable foreign affairs legislative vehicles has given appropriations dominance in shaping policy on the Middle East, on arms sales, on Central American funding levels, nuclear nonproliferation matters in South Asia, and many other issues.

The effect of this shift to appropriations vehicles is also self-perpetuating as able politicians in both Congress and the executive branch recognize this trend and choose to fight their battles and cut their deals on vehicles sure to be enacted. It is not surprising, for example, that in its haste to enact urgent military assistance for El Salvador in FY

1984, the administration chose to bypass both the authorizing committees and the foreign operations subcommittees with an amendment in the full Senate Appropriations Committee to the Emergency Energy Supplemental, H.J. Res. 493. Although the effort failed in this instance, the vehicle itself was a sure winner that went on to prompt enactment.

If policy influence is now conferred by continuing resolutions and supplementals rather than free-standing authorization and appropriation bills, what does that mean for foreign policy formulation on the Hill and how will it affect the role the Congress plays or should play, relative to the executive branch in the overall foreign policy process? On balance, foreign affairs legislation by continuing resolutions and supplementals has beneficial effects because it tends to strike more direct programmatic trade-offs on foreign policy resource questions with pressing domestic priorities. It also diminishes executive branch parochialism with respect to U.S. domestic political needs, but legislation by continuing resolutions and supplementals also means a reduction in influence for the thoughtful overview process characteristic of free-standing bills. Thus it does nothing to assist the Congress in performing the broad overview, education, and domestic support functions that are particularly important to the overall process of formulating and sustaining U.S. foreign policy.

The procedure for dealing with free-standing foreign affairs legislation that has emerged since World War II has been a kind of symbiosis between the House Foreign Affairs Committee and the Senate Foreign Relations Committee on the one hand and the two appropriations subcommittees on foreign operations on the other. Beginning with the secretary of state's traditional kick-off appearance before each body in the early spring, an extended hearing process distills literally hundreds of hours of oral testimony and thousands of pages of written documentation from all sides of contending issues.

There is a combination of thoroughness and creative tension here that is quite healthy for the process. The foreign affairs committees and their counterparts on appropriations, the foreign operations subcommittees, are a repository of expertise and attention. They have the expertise, interest, and time to devote to exploring thoroughly the many ramifications of foreign policy issues that come before the Congress.

Senator Mark O. Hatfield (R-Ore.) set forth the ideal role for the authorization committees in his testimony before the Quayle Committee largely by lamenting its absence.

> I think frankly one of the major things that's lacking in the legislative process today is oversight,and that oversight is not performed by-and-large because we are too busy with the current day's problems. I would like to see the authorizing committees sit back and project into the future

and review the past. We do not get that perspective today in the whole legislative process.[9]

The appropriators' function is complimentary. Although their role has been considerably eroded in recent years, the traditional purpose of appropriations has been to counter spending pressures across the board both from the executive branch and the Congress. The appropriators are supposed to be Congress's fiscal watchdogs. As such, they focus on programmatic specifics. Each of the 13 subcommittees is structured and staffed to look in detail at the programs submitted to it in the annual budget estimates from the various federal agencies. The appropriators work by adjusting the needs of program claimants both from the executive branch and the authorizing committees against their view of the requirements of fiscal responsibility.

The mechanism for doing this is the subcommittee structure and the full committee. First, each of the 13 subcommittees examines the budget estimates in its area of responsibility. It then submits its recommendations to the full committee. At full committee, 55 of the most senior members of the House and 29 of the most senior senators sit in judgment of the fiscal priorities of the entire federal government when they consider in turn the 13 separate bills as recommended by the subcommittees.[10]

The idea is that there should be a kind of creative tension between the two processes, authorizations and appropriations. The authorizers provide broad policy guidance and oversight in specific areas in which they specialize while the appropriators ensure that authorized programs are efficiently and economically structured.

When the free-standing authorization-appropriation process is in place, this system of pressures and cross-tensions works fairly well. When the authorization precedes the appropriation, Congress's expectations are clearly set forth. The appropriators then have their parameters set. After due deliberation, Congress has established that money should be made available for authorized programs, the appropriators then are to determine how to do it at the most efficient rate possible. Frequently, the "zone of discretion" for effective cuts then ends up being between last year's appropriation and the next year's budget request. The Appropriations Committee can then focus on programmatic specifics within that zone.[11]

Foreign affairs legislation by continuing resolutions and supplementals means that both careful deliberation and authorization guidance are frequently absent, with the result that this creative tension breaks down. Of course, in a system as flexible as the Congress, there are few hard and fast rules; increasingly both the foreign affairs committees and the foreign operations subcommittees are attempting to adapt by making use of continuing resolutions and supplementals rather than free-standing bills for their own purposes.[12]

Even so, an inescapable consequence of foreign affairs legislation by continuing resolutions and supplementals is more direct budgetary trade-offs on resource issues between domestic and foreign policy because continuing resolutions and supplementals contain both foreign policy and domestic subject matter. For example, in FY 1984 the administration lost its funding for the anti-Sandinista guerrillas in Nicaragua largely because the Senate could no longer delay funding for summer jobs in the Emergency Food Supplemental Aid for Africa, H.J. Res. 492. On the other hand, the administration won on the Omnibus Supplemental, H.R. 6040, largely because the House leadership could not delay a vote on additional military assistance for El Salvador, because the Food Stamp program was running out of money.

Aside from the benefits gained in setting budget priorities in a more comprehensive way, direct trade-offs on resource issues with domestic programs also have the beneficial effect of breaking down the parochialism inherent in the foreign policy establishment of the executive branch. This is of tremendous importance in that in a very fundamental sense foreign affairs begin at home and no U.S. foreign policy can succeed without the support of the Congress and the American people. Trade-offs between domestic and foreign policy issues force the National Security Council, the State Department, and others who had been more attuned to foreign than to domestic constituencies to consider the necessary bases of domestic support for foreign policy.

In general, the foreign policy establishment tends to be ineffective in structuring its proposals to secure support from the Congress. It is not good at thinking about the domestic political costs of its policies. It is composed of bright, capable people who can learn, but as Leslie Gelb put it, "the inescapable ethos of the building [meaning the State Department] is to look outside the United States, not inside."[13] The hard trade-offs with domestic programs inherent in dealing with supplementals, continuing resolutions, and an increasingly powerful Appropriations Committee will force a healthy change in that ethos, forcing the foreign policy leadership to look inward as well as outward.

The negative side to foreign affairs legislation by continuing resolutions and supplementals is that it can encourage the promotion of U.S. domestic interests at the expense of the central foreign policy questions by those people who have marginal interest, little expertise, and virtually no time to devote to foreign policy matters. However imperfect the lengthy hearing process of the foreign affairs committees and the foreign operations subcommittees might be, it is a model of thoughtful deliberation compared to the trade-offs and compromises, many made literally in the dead of night, that characterize continuing resolutions and supplementals.

The exclusion of the deliberative process is perhaps the most serious problem with foreign affairs legislation by continuing resolutions and supplementals. It eliminates whatever chance Congress may have to distill the executive branch's bureaucratic tendencies toward fire fighting and incrementalism into something coherent and sustainable over time. As Leslie Gelb put it, "there is an ingrained tendency in bureaucracies to subordinate overall policy to the requirements of immediate action. Policy then gets made by doing without any structural or long-term direction."[14]

The daily demands of fire fighting, crisis management, and routine problem solving consume the waking hours of program managers within the bureaucracy. The temptation to make policy by doing, if for no other reason than there is so little time to make it any other way, is often overwhelming. To the extent that Congress plays a constructive overall role in foreign policy, it should be to counteract this tendency toward incrementalism on the part of the executive branch by infusing into the process domestic political factors, sustaining values, and long-term coherence.

Toward a Policy Perspective

Congress should insist on and contribute to a carefully thought-out policy. Former Senate Foreign Relations Committee Chairman William Fulbright (D-Ark.) delineated the ideal role for Congress in the foreign policy process when he said that Congress should pursue a coherent, purposive U.S. foreign policy, well grounded in political support, reflecting sustainable U.S. values. As he put it, "The essential Congressional role lies in the authorization of military and major political commitments and advising on broad policy directions while leaving to the executive the necessary flexibility to conduct policy within the broad parameters approved by the legislature."[15]

Legislating on foreign affairs by continuing resolutions and supplementals makes it more difficult to play this role. While Congress should be contributing perspective and domestic support to the foreign policy process, it fails without the careful deliberation inherent in the free-standing authorization and appropriations process. Instead, it tends to engage in the day-to-day attempts to manipulate foreign policy, pejoratively referred to as "micromanagement."

Congress is congenitally weak in dealing with policy implementation, and its insistence on specific statutorily imposed conditions, certifications, and limitations can result in policies that are both delayed and counterproductive for all concerned. The congressional weakness for micromanagement of foreign policy is well known. The Congress is 1) too slow, 2) too blunt, 3) too public, 4) too short-termed and parochial in its interests, 5) lacking in the necessary expertise and information, 6) sporadic, eclectic, and focused on flash points rather than sustained and systematic in its applications, 7) too narrow in its focus on problems and not understanding of their full complexity and interrelated nature, and 8) lacking unity of leadership.[16]

It is also true that Congress cannot and does not conduct foreign relations in the sense of providing an alternative to executive policies. Too often it simply keeps the executive from acting. Congressional involvement can be a recipe for confrontation and stalemate if Congress gets too deeply into detail. By describing the specifics of policy and implementation and retaining for itself the power to block in one form or another executive branch actions not in conformity with congressional interpretations of policy, Congress can turn the problem of its inability to formulate an alternative policy into no policy at all.

Encouraging the Congress to move beyond micromanagement toward a coherent long-term foreign policy strikes at the heart of what Congress's role in the process is, or should be, all about. As Zbigniew Brzezinski told the Senate Government Operations Committee, the congressional role in foreign policy involves "the essence of a democracy functioning in a nuclear age; it concerns how we reconcile our most precious possession which is our democracy with our most vital interest, which is our security."[17]

This is where a Congress anchored in domestic politics and focused on the big picture can contribute. Congressman Lee Hamilton summarized the essence of these strengths as those that should emerge from a kind of creative tension between the branches. As he put it, "Debate, tension, and review can lead to decisions and actions which stand a better chance of serving the interest and reflecting the values of the American people."[18]

Congress's accessibility to the people, its representativeness, can provide positive input to the executive branch in formulating policy. Some of the positive functions that the Congress can perform in setting the outlines and gaining necessary domestic support for U.S. foreign policy would include providing support for presidential initiatives and warning the executive branch in advance of those that may not get support, as well as conveying the views of the people to the president and informing and educating the people on presidential foreign policy initiatives.

What might be referred to as the elucidation function is particularly important. Senator Fulbright applied it to foreign policy when he cited with approval James Madison in "The Federalist no. 10." Congress as an educational forum would "refine and enlarge the public views by passing them through the medium of a chosen body of citizens whose wisdom may best discern the true interest of their country, and whose patriotism and love of justice will be least likely to sacrifice it to temporary or partial consideration."[19]

Although executive branch witnesses at difficult hearings may not always quite see it that way, when properly focused, Congress is better able to sense and reflect changes in popular thinking than the executive branch. It is also an effective forum for testing ideas, and because it is more broadly continuous as well as more representative than the executive branch, it can help design long-term policies that are sustainable. In that vein, it is also well to remember that many senior members of Congress have seen numerous administrations of both parties come and go. Their personal experience is, in many ways, the institutional memory of the U.S. government on numerous foreign policy questions, and their wisdom and expertise can be quite useful to the executive.

To Restore the Balance

As Senator Fulbright put it, "The trouble with the resurgent legislature of the late 1970s is not so much that it has gone too far as that it has gone in the wrong direction, carping and meddling in the service of special interests but scarcely asserting itself through reflective deliberation on the basic issues of national interests."[20]

Foreign affairs legislation by continuing resolution and supplemental appropriation and the more assertive Appropriation Committees that have emerged from it are healthy in that they ensure that the necessary bases of domestic support for U.S. foreign policy get covered. What is not healthy is the resulting exclusion of the careful deliberation and overview characteristic of the free-standing legislative process. Short circuiting the established authorization and appropriations process in foreign affairs weakens Congress's ability to play the broader role contemplated for it in the Constitution. If, as Corwin says, the shared foreign policy powers are indeed an invitation to struggle for the privilege of directing U.S. foreign policy, then surely the congressional role should be to pitch this struggle on the highest plane possible to ensure that the resulting policy is reflective both of the national security interests and the sustaining values of the American people.

Notes

1. Harold W. Chase and Craig R. Ducat, eds. *Edwin S. Corwin's The Constitution and What It Means Today* 14th edition (revised) (Princeton, N. J.: Princeton University Press,1978), 673.

2. 3rd Cont. Res. FY 80, H.J. Res. 440 (P.L. 96–123) Supplemental FY 80, H.R. 7542 (P.L. 96–304);

1st Cont. Res. FY 81, H.J. Res. 610 (P.L. 96–369);
2nd Cont. Res. FY 81, H.J. Res. 644 (P.L. 96–536);
Supplemental FY 81, H.R. 3512 (P.L. 97–12);
1st Cont. Res. FY 82, H.J. Res. 325 (P.L. 97–51);
2nd Cont. Res. FY 82, H.J. Res. 368 (P.L. 97–85;));
3rd Cont. Res. FY 82, H.J. Res 370 (P.L. 97–92);
Final Cont. Res. FY 82, H.J. Res 409 (P.L. 97–161);
Supplemental FY 82, H.R. 6863 (P.L. 97–257);
1st Cont. Res. FY 83, H.J. Res. 599 (P.L. 97–276);
2nd Cont. Res. FY 83, H.J. Res. 631 (P.L. 97–377);
2nd Supplemental FY 83, H.R. 3069 (P.L. 98–63);
1st Cont. Res. FY 84, H.J. Res. 568 (P.L. 98–107);
2nd Cont., Res. FY 84, H.J. Res. 413 (P.L. 98–151);
Supplemental FY 84, H.J. Res. 492 (P.L. 98–332);
Supplemental FY 84, H.J. Res. 493 (P.L. 98–248);
Supplemental FY 84, H.R. 6040 (P.L. 98–391);
1st Cont. Res. FY 85, H.J. Res. 648 (P.L. 98–473).

3. See, for example, Thomas E. Mann and Norman J. Ornstein, eds., *The New Congress* (Washington, D.C., American Enterprise Institute for Public Policy Research, 1981), 400; Thomas M. Franck and Edward Weisband, *Foreign Policy by Congress* (Oxford: Oxford University Press, 1979), 400; Second ed.; Lawrence C. Dodd and Bruce I. Oppenheimer, eds., *Congress Reconsidered* (Washington, D.C.: Congressional Quarterly Press, 1981), in particular the chapter on the conflict between the executive and legislative branches in foreign policy formulation by I.M. Destler.

4. Roger H. Davidson in Mann and Ornstein, eds., *The New Congress*, 107.

5. U.S. Senate. Temporary Select Committee to Study the Senate Committee System Hearings, August 2, 1984, testimony of Senator Howard Baker, Jr. Washington, D.C.: USGPO, 1984.

6. *Congressional Quarterly Report* (Washington, D.C.: Congressional Quarterly Press) August 4, 1984, p. 1875.

7. Ibid., 1884.

8. *New York Times*, March 10, 1984, p. 1. Of course, the Supreme Court did not specifically address arms transfers in the *Chadha* case. What is more, the Reagan administration has agreed to abide by the reporting and notification provisions of Section 36 (b) of the Arms Export Control Act of 1976. Consequently, it is not at all certain what would happen if a concurrent resolution of disapproval of a specific arms sale were to be passed by the Congress under Section 36 (b). It is also true that the Congress could pass a free-standing bill prohibiting a specific arms sale should it choose to do so. The point here is that in an uncertain legislative and political environment with supplemental appropriations and continuing resolutions moving through on a regular basis, these vehicles are likely to be selected for riders prohibiting arms sales as Senator Robert W. Kasten threatened to do with the proposed Stinger sale to Jordan in 1984.

9. U.S. Senate. Temporary Select Committee to Study the Senate Committee System Hearings, August 2, 1984, testimony of Senator Mark Hatfield. Washington, D.C.: USGPO, 1984.

10. This is, of course, a theoretical depiction of how the system is supposed to work. In practice, subcommittee dominance is so strong in both Appropriations Committees that their work is usually ratified with very little change by the full committees.

11. Allen Schick, *Congress and Money* (Washington, D.C.: The Urban Institute, 1980), 417–418.

12. See *Congressional Quarterly Weekly Report* (Washington, D.C.: Congressional Quarterly Press) 1983 Almanac, 528; *Congressional Quarterly Weekly Report* (Washington, D.C.: Congressional Quarterly Press, October 20, 1984), 2737. On the 2nd Cont. Res. for FY 84 (P.L. 98–151) the foreign affairs committees were able to attach a stripped down version of their foreign assistance bill for FY 84. On the FY 85 Cont. Res., on the other hand, the exercise failed. That the foreign affairs committees have almost literally had to go hat in hand to the Appropriations Committees to get their legislation considered is both tangible evidence of the power of the Appropriations Committees on foreign affairs questions and the extent to which continuing resolutions and supplementals have become the dominant legislative vehicles for foreign assistance. It is also true that much of the appropriations hearing process is preserved when foreign operations bills are attached to continuing resolutions as has been the practice in recent years, but this at best preserves only half the process as the authorization committees are still effectively excluded.

13. Leslie H. Gelb, "Why Not the State Department?" *The Washington Quarterly* 3, no. 4 (Autumn 1980): 27.

14. Ibid., 38.

15. J. William Fulbright, "The Legislator as Educator," *Foreign Affairs* 54 (Spring 1979): 726.

16. Representative Lee Hamilton, "Congress and Foreign Policy," *Presidential Studies Quarterly* 12 (Spring 1982): 136.

17. Zbigniew Brzezinski, in testimony before the Senate Governmental Affairs Committee, on the relationship between Congress and the executive branch in the formulation of foreign policy, July 31, 1984, Washington, D.C.

18. Hamilton, "Congress and Foreign Policy," 134. Of course, tendencies toward micromanagement are also present in the free-standing process. The point here is that by largely excluding that process from meaningful involvement in foreign affairs legislation and focusing instead on continuing resolutions and supplemental appropriation, Congress will have an even more difficult time focusing on broader problems associated with the oversight of U.S. foreign policy.

19. Fulbright, "The Legislator as Educator," 730.

20. Ibid., 727.

Commentary: On Hill
Foreign Policy Making

Clarence D. Long

That there has been a recent shift to the use of the continuing resolution (CR) and supplemental and away from the old freestanding foreign assistance authorization and appropriation bills, as Alvin Drischler maintains, conforms to my own perception as former chairman of the Subcommittee on Foreign Operations of the House Appropriations Committee from 1976 through 1984. I am not certain, however, that I would agree with him entirely on the precise reasons for that shift or on its implications for foreign policy.

It is difficult to document in a brief account the historical background of the shift to CRs and supplementals and away from freestanding authorization and appropriation bills. Drischler singles out the "system overload" caused by the "institutional revolution of 1974." This revolution, he contends, had an onerous effect on "staff growth, proliferation of subcommittee assignments, overwork on the floor, access by junior members to levers of power, and the diffusion of congressional power." He asserts correctly that the institutional revolution of 1974 resulted in a congressional diffusion of power, but it is stretching to link the diffusion to the shift to CRs and supplementals in the area of foreign assistance legislation. Congress has witnessed a decline in the number of freestanding authorization and appropriation bills passed in recent years. Such legislation, nonetheless, successfully navigates the congressional process on regular bases, and the woeful record of foreign aid bills by no means approximates that of other freestanding bills.

The congressional diffusion of power within Congress is what the constitutional forefathers sought, but it has not been achieved until now. Drischler views this turn of events with a doubtful eye perhaps because the development has weakened the executive control compared to Congress's, but he neglects to mention that the developments of a decade ago and the resultant diffusion of power were largely a reaction to executive branch war policy on Vietnam and the executive abuse of power involving Watergate.

Clarence D. Long was the Democratic representative from Maryland's second district from 1963 to 1985. He served on the House Appropriations Committee as chairman of the Foreign Operations Subcommittee. He also has taught economics at The Johns Hopkins University and is the author of numerous books and articles on unemployment, wages, economic fluctuations, and the labor force.

But if the shift to CRs and supplementals cannot be attributed solely, or even mostly to the congressional diffusion of power within Congress, then what has caused this shift in the area of foreign assistance and why has it occurred since 1978? In briefly passing over the role of "political crosscurrents," Drischler asserts that House Democratic leaders, who for years had been shouldering the political burden for unpopular foreign assistance programs, were unwilling to continue to do so in the absence of significant support among their Republican colleagues, support that was not always easy for the administration to muster. There is certainly some truth to this. Politics has had an impact. Foreign aid has never been popular, and the shift to CRs and supplementals actually began, not with Reagan, but late in the Carter administration.

Diffusion of congressional power, the unpopularity of foreign aid, and a Republican administration working with a Democratic House all have contributed to the shift to CRs and supplementals. The shift has occurred primarily because of congressional fear of the voters and as a response to the rise of the budget process. In the past, before there was any budget limitation, the average member of Congress had no objection to voting for foreign aid because more money for foreign aid did not mean less for domestic programs. Foreign aid has had weak congressional support because it lacked a large domestic constituency, but voting in favor of foreign aid had occurred mainly because of pressure from groups who contributed to the campaign of either the member or his opponents. The rise of the budget process changed this and caused a sudden shift of support away from freestanding bills. Voting for foreign aid shifted money away from more popular domestic programs. Obviously, foreign assistance could not be done away with, but neither could it be faced head-on in a freestanding bill. Thus, the shift was made to CRs and supplementals because foreign aid could be slipped through along with other bills in the stopgap funding bills.

This became clear late in the summer of 1979, prior to the end of the fiscal year, when Senator Edmund Muskie moved the budget limitation of foreign aid. As a result, the congressional leadership was unwilling to let the foreign aid bill come to the floor for a vote, not because the bill was over the budget, but for political reasons: the Appropriations Subcommittee chairpersons—other than myself—did not want to be seen by the voters as cutting domestic programs in favor of foreign aid. I pleaded with the leadership that I had never lost a foreign aid bill on the floor. I wrote letters to the House leaders, signed by many majority members of the Foreign Operations Subcommittee, urging them to allow the conference report go to the floor for a vote. I got nowhere. I was met with the argument that with elections coming up the members did not want to vote for foreign aid when that would cause domestic programs to suffer. The distinction here is important: Congress was not against foreign aid programs as such, but it was against making domestic programs second to foreign aid programs. This is the problem, and before budget ceilings were put on, this problem did not have to be met.

Since budget ceilings were instituted, the FY 1982 foreign aid bill has been the only freestanding bill passed by the House, and even that was imperiled by foreshortened debate and limited time for'amendments. The shift to CRs and supplementals caused by the budget process is not confined, incidentally, to foreign assistance. Defense has gone even longer than foreign assistance without getting a freestanding bill.

Drischler's conclusion, that freestanding foreign aid bills have given way to CRs and supplementals because of the congressional diffusion of power, the unpopularity of foreign aid, and partisan politics, is therefore perfectly valid. But the timing of the shift resulted from the rise of the budget process.

Regardless of cause, the trend to CRs and supplementals has occurred. The question remains about the consequences of this shift, and here Drischler leaves himself open to criticism.

Drischler credits the shift to CRs and supplementals with giving greater power to the Appropriations Committees and their chairpersons and reducing the power of the authorization committees. I would agree that the House Foreign Affairs Committee's thoughtful, systematic study of foreign aid is vital to any well-thought-out foreign policy. I have never done anything but welcome the actions of the committee, and I would be delighted to have it act. The fact that it does not act, however, enhances the power of the Foreign Operations Subcommittee, as Drischler suggests.

Yet the subcommittee would have this power in any event, even with a dynamic and commanding House Foreign Affairs Committee, because of what I like to call the golden rule: They who have the gold make the rules. In other words, the Foreign Operations Subcommittee dispenses the money. The story of Congress is that the executive branch's concern for the foreign policy activity taking place in Congress is not focused until the question of money arises. This would be true no matter how the process operates, whether through CRs and supplementals or freestanding bills.

The Nixon administration's experience with the Vietnam War illustrates the prominence of money as a factor in executive-legislative relations. The administration held policy discussions in the Senate Foreign Relations Committee ad infinitum and was opposed by the powerful, influential, and eloquent chairman J. William Fulbright. But the administration did not take congressional opposition to the Vietnam War seriously until

1973 when the Appropriations Committee cut off the funds. Prior to this and despite years of fierce opposition by Senator Fulbright, the administration had gotten everything it really wanted on Vietnam.

The Foreign Operations Subcommittee was thus already a focus of power before its power was further augmented by the shift to CRs and supplementals. Critics argue that the Foreign Operations Subcommittee, particularly its subcommittee chairpersons, has acquired disproportionate power, which in a highly decentralized Congress is bad for the system. It is not always with approbation that Clarence Long has been labeled the "secretary of state from Baltimore."

What power I did possess for FY 1982-FY 1985 derived largely from the subcommittee's temporary composition. The subcommittee during FY 1982-FY 1985 consisted of seven hawks and seven doves. My vote represented the balance of power; whichever way I voted, not on all things but on most issues, made a subcommittee majority. My power as chair of the subcommittee was not an institutional power, but an accident of this particular time and place and this particular subcommittee.

Similarly, the Foreign Operations Subcommittee derived its power less from CRs and supplementals than from the fact that the subcommittee receives the strong backing of the Appropriations Committee because it has always been the style of the Appropriations Committee to support its subcommittees' actions.

Given the shift from freestanding bills to CRs and supplementals and the resultant shift of power from the authorizing to the appropriating committees, what have been the negative consequences? Has the shift to CRs and supplementals been detrimental to either foreign aid or congressional consideration of foreign aid? Has the power shift from the authorizers to the appropriators brought about unfortunate foreign policy results?

The fact is that, given the budget process as noted above, foreign aid benefits from the shift to CRs and supplementals. If foreign aid were not part of a larger, more encompassing bill, it either could not pass or, if passed, could not pass intact. In addition, funding foreign aid by CR, while not the optimal method of funding, does not necessarily signal an end to the deliberative process. For FY 1985, for example, the Foreign Operations Subcommittee in the House held extensive hearings on all aspects of the foreign aid program. There was a full subcommittee markup. The deliberation normal to a freestanding bill occurred. All that was missing was the final floor vote.

The Foreign Operations Subcommittee has adapted to the realities of funding by CR by adapting to the CR itself, with its marked-up bill being added to the CR in toto. The CR for foreign aid is nearly identical to a regular bill; it does not employ numerical formulas applied to other spending. Hence, funding by CR has not altered the substance of foreign aid funding materially.

It is more difficult to assess, however, what harm has been done in the shift in power from the authorizing to the appropriating committees. Drischler furnishes little sense of what it is about the House Foreign Affairs Committee that provides "broad policy guidance and oversight." But this is something that the Foreign Operations Subcommittee can and does perform, and surely Drischler is not suggesting that the subcommittee ignores broad policy and oversight. Drischler asserts a bit vaguely that Congress, presumably in the form of the authorizer, should provide "long-term perspective." But it has always been said that Congress is the last place to look for long-term, thoughtful, coordinated policy perspective. Congress is more of a barometer of the sentiment of the moment. In my own experience, I do not know of any example of Congress determining long-range, thoughtful policy in any committee.

A legitimate argument can be made that the distinction between the authorizing and appropriating committees should be one of policy considerations on the one hand and monetary considerations on the other. This forms the theoretical division of labor between the authorizers and the appropriators. If the system functioned perfectly, the executive branch, as the initiator and controller of foreign policy, would work through the authorizing committees as the repositories of policy in Congress. The administration would not focus its policy on the Appropriations Committee, presumably because policy that is all money oriented is bad policy.

Of course, the system does not function perfectly, nor can it be made to. It is impossible to separate money from policy and because power naturally gravitates toward the appropriators, policy follows as well. This is especially true in an era when resources are limited, the congressional focus is on the budget, and the congressional thrust is on setting priorities and making choices.

This is not the fault of the appropriators. Even in those instances where the foreign affairs authorizers have possessed strong leadership and have attempted to take a dominant role, they have been ignored and circumvented by the executive branch if their respective policy positions are in direct opposition. The foreign affairs committees simply lack the power that comes from control of the purse to stand up to the executive branch. As noted above, Senator Fulbright's lack of success in opposing the administration on Vietnam is a prime example. A more recent example was the conflict between the Reagan administration and the House Foreign Affairs Committee, and in particular Mike Barnes (D-Md.), chair of the Subcommittee on Western Hemisphere Affairs, over policy toward El Salvador. When the administration and Representative Barnes could not agree on a policy toward Central America, the administration attempted to form a coalition within the committee to oppose Representative Barnes's subcommittee. When this did not work, the administration established a coalition on the floor to accomplish the same thing, and the House Foreign Affairs Committee was effectively bypassed.

The latter committee has been accused of being excessively liberal—too far to the left of the political disposition of the average member. This is why, it is said, the committee has been dealt out of the foreign policy process. This is simply not true. The problem for the committee is that it is out of tune not only with the rest of Congress, but also with the executive branch. The fact is that if there is disagreement between the executive branch and a congressional committee, it is the committee that is out of tune. In the 1960s no committee was in greater discord with the congressional constituency than the Senate Armed Services Committee. The committee was in tune with the Defense Department, however, and therefore it had legitimacy. But if tension develops between a committee of Congress and the executive branch, then it is said that the committee is out of tune and somehow not doing its job or is ideologically off on a binge.

The Foreign Affairs Committee's relative power position is eroded further by a jurisdictional problem: The committee does not exercise control over all aspects of foreign policy. The committee deals with foreign aid and defense programs. But economic policy and international trade also are part of foreign affairs. These cause as much irritation in foreign affairs as anything else, but jurisdiction is exercised by authorizing committees as various as Ways and Means, Energy and Commerce, and Banking and Currency. The Foreign Operations Subcommittee, by contrast, does deal with economic policy and international trade issues.

For a variety of reasons—the shift to CRs and supplementals, the power of the purse, and jurisdiction over a broad expanse of foreign affairs issues—the Appropriations Committee has transcended its authorizing counterpart in the review of foreign affairs issues. But this is a limited transcendence, limited in degree, and, more important, limited to Congress. Despite what many critics say, the Foreign Operations Subcommittee simply does not possess that much power relative to the executive branch.

In foreign aid, the administration still gets the bulk of everything it wants. From FY 1982 through FY 1984, the Foreign Operations Subcommittee recommended cuts of more than $2 billion from the administration's budget request. But this is only about 4 percent of the total, and of this, less than half came out of the House-Senate Conference.

The administration thus gets all but 2 percent of its requests. For a committee charged with cutting spending, a 2 percent cut is hardly excessive or in any way an abuse of power. In the case of El Salvador, the administration did not get more than half of what it asked for. The appropriation for El Salvador in 1984 is still about nine times what the 1981 level was. By any measurement, this is a big increase for a country as small as El Salvador, and it is by no means certain that El Salvador could absorb any more aid effectively. Congressional testimony has been given that most of the guerrillas' weapons have come from government troops and are turned over by sale and surrender, and, if this is true, what positive good would more military aid do? Yet, El Salvador is one of the few exceptions to the near-total fulfillment of the administration's wish list on foreign assistance—and this is assuming that the administration does not pad its El Salvador aid requests in anticipation of congressional cuts. Despite the unpopularity of foreign aid, the executive branch receives the bulk of what money it wants.

The administration's quarrel, and perhaps the basic factor underlying Drischler's discontent, is that the executive branch does not get everything it wants from Congress. Because the Appropriations Committee is the one denying it, the committee bears the brunt of the administration's fury. It is, admittedly, more than a question of 2 percent. The executive branch wants more control than it already has. It wants to conduct a war in Central America as it did in Vietnam. It wants to put U.S. troops into Central America. One of Congress's roles is to frustrate policy if it thinks that policy is wrong. Congress did not do this during the Vietnam War; for many years it gave the executive branch everything that it wanted; only after 10 years did the Congress suddenly rebel with a cutoff resolution. Recently, however, the administration has not been given everything. This does not mean that the Foreign Operations Subcommittee is less effective or is somehow in the wrong. Many of the things that the administration wants to do in foreign policy are wrong and ought to be frustrated. And the way for Congress to frustrate the committee is through its constitutionally dictated control of the purse.

One of Drischler's complaints is that Congress resorts to micromanagement on individual policy issues. Perhaps there is some validity to the claim that Congress has interjected itself at times in too much detail or at the wrong time, but Congress has not been drawn into the details of foreign policy without reason. It can be argued fairly that Congress has been pushed into it by the action or inaction of the executive branch and has resisted entering into the details on many occasions.

The executive branch encourages Congress to become involved in such details by its poor communications with the Hill. Often Congress is told that it will be consulted on decisions, but consultation has come to mean that Congress finds out just before—or sometimes just after—the media. And this is by no means a partisan matter; lack of communication consistently crosses party lines, with an administration frequently alienating its most fervent supporters. The lack of communication is particularly acute in the area of foreign affairs. The executive branch's foreign policy establishment is outer-directed, in fact directs its attention worldwide. It does not look to the Hill; it thinks of the Congress as a necessary evil, as a stumbling block, and as an obstacle. The foreign policy establishment shares as little information as possible with Congress. But the foreign policy bureaucrats in the executive branch not only look outward, but they also have an idealized version of what foreign policy should be. Congressional involvement, instead of being a positive reinforcement in shaping policy as it is on domestic issues, is resented and resisted.

Drischler very correctly points out that Congress has a closer ear to the voice of the American people and is therefore more likely to avoid unpopular foreign policy action. Normally, Congress will go along with almost anything that the administration proposes. When it balks, it is usually because the public has expressed a contrary view. In Central America, for example, the executive branch would like to have sent troops, but because this would have cut against the wishes of the American people, Congress rose up in opposition. The members of Congress owe primary allegiance to the interests of the country, but their secondary allegiance is to the voters and not to the administration. In my own political situation as a Democrat, I had to be elected from a district that the Democratic candidate for president has carried only twice since 1860—once in 1936 with Roosevelt and once in 1964 with Johnson. Yet, my position on El Salvador—as well as Lebanon—was well known, and it was not politically detrimental for me. It is true that I lost in 1984, but by only 1 percent—compared with Mondale who lost by 30 percent to Reagan.

The tensions between the executive branch and the Congress are therefore real and are not simply the product of a recalcitrant Congress. Whenever national administrations misinformed and misled Congress, I had, as chair of the Foreign Operations Subcommittee, no alternative but to be wary of leadership agreements between the Hill and the White House. Congress has been burned too often, including in Vietnam, the turning point of congressional involvement in foreign policy. For better or for worse, no better long-term policy comes out of the executive branch than comes out of Congress—which is a reflection more on executive branch policy-making than on congressional expertise.

Lebanon is a fine example. One month the American people and Congress were told that U.S. involvement in Lebanon was vital to our interests. The next month the administration said that it was nonessential, thus justifying the administration's transfer of money from Lebanon to build an airport for civilian traffic in Grenada. Does this manifest a sense of long-term policy planning? Does condemning the spread of communism in general, with particular reference to Latin America, while beginning a trip to negotiate with Communist China and providing grain, sophisticated technology, and loans to the Chinese that may never be repaid, bespeak a policy easily understood by the American people?

El Salvador remains the last and best example, if only because the lines between the Foreign Operations Subcommittee and the administration have been drawn so sharply on the issue. The level of aid the United States gives this small nation is almost unprecedented in percentage terms. As mentioned above, Drischler complains about the micromanagement of foreign policy. If he means, with reference to El Salvador, examples such as the Long-Specter amendment that withheld 30 percent of military aid until a trial and verdict could be reached on the question of guilt in the case of the killers of the American nuns, then I plead guilty to the charge of micromanagement. The same is true for naming a special ambassador to negotiate for peace in Central America. The subcommittee has used conditionality to insist on improvements in human rights, because the death squad activities are too serious to be ignored, as the administration even now concedes. The improvements in human rights as a result of this conditionality have been that Mr. Duarte was elected, he is making a valiant effort to make reforms, and I was very happy to offer my public support.

The good old days when the leadership ran Congress and made its deals with the White House are what Drischler seems to lament. But this was what enabled the Vietnam War to continue, until Congress finally rebelled in the CR of 1973 at a time when President Nixon was virtually a prisoner in the White House. Is this the kind of situation the State Department should see as ideal? Is a compliant Congress and an imperial presidency an essential combination for a bipartisan foreign policy?

The framers of the Constitution did not intend to establish an imperial presidency. On the contrary, theirs was an ideal of checks and balances, of—to use Madison's term in Federalist no. 51—"auxiliary precautions," with the president's role as formulator of policy emanating from his explicit role as commander in chief, while Congress's responsibility was to declare war, to appropriate money consistent with military requirements, and to advise and consent on treaties and appointments. The Constitution gave the president little explicit constitutional power over foreign policy. It is by stretching his presidential power as commander in chief that his foreign policy role has been expanded.

The tension has left a no-man's-land between the two branches of government. One of the founding fathers wrote that "a certain inefficiency is a cheap price to pay for liberty." Preserving liberty was the principle behind the separation of powers and the reason why maintaining democratic procedures in U.S. institutions is always more important than quibbling over policy outcomes. Perhaps our system may not be able to survive a world under threat of nuclear war, but what a pity if it cannot do so. Had the German government maintained—as it does today in West Germany—an inviolable separation of power, Adolph Hitler would never have been able to transform his election into a dictatorship. The day may be coming when World War III explodes because some president may prevail over a Congress insufficiently powerful and too poorly structured to restrain a president ready to "cry havoc and let loose the dogs of war."

For the moment, however, Congress has been successful in checking some of the excesses of the executive branch. Congress has accomplished a good deal in its objection to Lebanon, although the crucial congressional vote was lost on the floor by a narrow margin. In El Salvador the amount of aid has increased ninefold, but at least the key to the treasury has not been given away—as happened in Vietnam. And, more important, U.S. troops have been kept out of open combat. The administration should be glad that Congress is saving the administration from the consequences of its adventures.

Congress is not perfect. It functions neither as a rational entity nor as a well-oiled machine and fails to offer much room for change and improvement. But with regard to Drischler's contention that the system has suffered because of the shift of power away from the authorizing committees and from the standpoint of either internal congressional organization or executive-legislative relations, it is not certain that much has been lost by this transition. On the contrary, perhaps the system has evolved to the point where it might be useful to merge the authorization and appropriations committees. It might be helpful to centralize further the foreign affairs function in Congress by creating a committee that could serve as a liaison to the administration, possibly along the lines of Clement Zablocki's suggestion for a Joint Committee on National Security Affairs. This would be beneficial to the administration, and it would be advantageous for both the House and Senate to have their leaders in regular contact with the president on foreign policy.

Tinkering with congressional reform is not the answer to the overall problem of foreign affairs in executive-legislative relations. In the final analysis, it is not Congress that needs to change, but the successive administrations that need to understand better the process and to use it more adroitly. If the executive branch cannot learn to do this, it does not matter how good Congress is, because the system is not going to work as well as it needs to.

7

Interest Groups and Lobbying

Norman Ornstein

If there is one word that characterizes Washington over the past two decades, it is "change." Both Congress and the White House have expanded, diversified, and decentralized. Outside forces, including trade associations and interest groups of every stripe, along with law firms and innumerable advocacy groups, have proliferated in number and activity.

Change and growth in government size and activity, and growth in outside group numbers and activity, are interrelated. These changes are important because they have had major impact on what government does and how it does it, along with an impact on the relationship between the executive branch and Congress. First, I will explore some of the reasons for growth inside and outside government, especially during the 1970s. Then I will turn to some speculation on what the consequences of these changes have been.

Lobbying in Washington: Two Eras

Interest groups have been a part of U.S. life since the beginning of the Republic. The most prominent of the Federalist Papers, No. 10, was devoted to a discussion of the importance of groups in political life. James Madison, who called the groups "factions," said that their inherent problems—the "mischiefs" of faction—must be dealt with by allowing all such factions to grow and operate, so that the narrow interest or

Norman Ornstein is currently a resident scholar at the American Enterprise Institute. He has served as staff director of the Senate Temporary Select Committee To Study the Senate Committee System, and he has been staff assistant to Senator George McGovern and Representative Donald M. Fraser. His numerous published works include *Interest Groups, Lobbying and Policymaking* (Washington, D.C.: Congressional Quarterly, 1978).

"ambition" of one faction would be diluted by setting it against the selfish interest of other factions. In other words, Madison viewed groups and their impact on government in terms of the checks and balances that are the basis of the U.S. political system.

Before and after Madison's time, groups flourished in the United States and were active in trying to influence the U.S. government. The word "lobbyist" was coined in the late 1820s and was commonplace in Washington by the 1830s. Lobbying and interest groups were an ever-present fact of national political life in the United States. What was true in the 1830s was even more true by the 1930s. In the interim century, Washington, D.C. had been institutionalized and expanded as the government town. Although lobbies came and went with the part-time Congress of the 1830s, groups and their representatives had become permanent fixtures when, in an expanded Washington, Congress moved to essentially year-round operation.

These groups were a mixture of profit and nonprofit, public and private, economic-based and other interests, but in the 1930s and following several decades all of them shared an ability to operate within the "closed system" that characterized Washington, and especially Congress, at the time.

The significant operations of Congress, in large part, were conducted behind closed doors, whether they were votes, mark-ups, or strategy sessions. The policy agenda was predominantly in the hands of the chairs of the standing committees, who had the power to dominate their bodies—controlling the subcommittees through their jurisdictions, memberships and chairmanships, hiring and firing the staff, deciding when and on what subjects the committees would meet. Their selection was automatic and they were virtually immune from removal or retribution. Party leaders also had considerable authority. They acted as brokers between committee chairmen and between the barons and the rest of the chamber; they managed and orchestrated the floor agenda; they held a great deal of sway over rank and file members through control and selective use of perks and punishments. Rank and file members went along to get along—because virtually all the incentives for those concerned about their congressional careers existed inside the chamber and were controlled by the leaders.

This closed system was reinforced by the limited nature of the media coverage of Congress before the 1960s. Even if network television had wanted to cover Congress, it could not because nearly all activities on the Hill were "off limits" to cameras. Print media attention was greater, but was still selective and limited and was focused on the committee barons and party leaders. With little media attention paid to congressional wheeling, dealing, power-brokering, or decision making, the closed system was able to operate without significant external pressure and with junior lawmakers lacking the resources outside the chamber to influence behavior inside.

Interest groups were also captives of the closed system. A successful lobbyist had to be able to wheel and deal within the closed system, which meant having access to party leaders, committee chairpersons, and their senior allies for the most part. Many potential groups lacked the resources to do so; others were not mobilized at all or could not operate without the substantial public attention and outside pressure that comes through active and wide-ranging media coverage, especially television.

Congress changed first in its membership, thanks to political trends that started with the 1958 election and were reiterated in 1964, in part because of the natural generational change that followed World War II. The result was that from the mid–1960s through the 1970s, Congress became much younger and much more junior, expanding the size and relative strength within the majority Democratic Party of its northern liberal wing. A younger, junior, more northern, and more liberal congressional membership put enormous strains on the closed congressional system. Not surprisingly, a system dominated by seniority and with a top-heavy power structure that gave great leverage to the more conservative southern Democrats was directly threatened by a mass of new and active members who were not at an advantage in this system.

In the 1970s, northern Democrats were able to change the system by changing the rules, especially in the House, taking power from committee chairs and spreading it outward and downward to subcommittee chairs and to rank and file members. Formerly protected committee chairs were exposed to individual secret ballot votes every Congress, and their powers over subcommittees, policy agenda, and staffs were taken away and given to others. The number of subcommittees was increased, membership was made automatic, and subcommittee chairmanships were taken away from the discretion of the committee chairs. The subcommittees were given virtual independence.

At the same time, reforms dramatically expanded congressional staffs in subcommittees and in the offices of the individual members. From 1965 to 1980, the number of committee staff employees in the House quadrupled while increasing nearly threefold in the Senate. In the same period, personal staff allowances for each House member more than doubled. Rules changes also opened up congressional deliberations, virtually eliminating closed sessions of committees and subcommittees by the mid–1970s. Mark-up sessions, the key meetings for making policy in Congress that uniformly had been closed to all but members and a handful of privileged staff in the Congress, were opened to public, press, and interest group representatives. Previously closed votes on amendments to bills on the House floor were also opened during the reform movement of the 1970s.

These congressional changes were paralleled by important changes in the U.S. mass media, the most striking of which was the movement in 1963 by television networks to a 30-minute nightly newscast. As additional congressional reforms exposed more of Congress to cameras, congressional deliberations often made stories on the evening news. Evening news coverage of Congress and Washington increased dramatically after Watergate and the impeachment; this in turn meant a dramatic expansion in the Washington bureaus of major newspapers, local television stations, and other news outlets and an expansion in the amount of national media attention paid to all Washington activity.

With all of these changes, the basis of the closed system—incentives for individual members kept internal to Congress and controlled by a small number of power brokers—could not hold. Expanded media coverage of Washington and Congress meant more public attention and more opportunity for individual members to get national publicity and recognition, which provided for career and power outlets outside congressional structures themselves. The new Congress—fluid, decentralized, and democratized—was an open system.

These changes, especially the congressional reforms, did not come about solely because of congressional membership or mass media changes. Outside groups, national issues, and presidential-congressional relationships all contributed significantly to creating changes in the structure and nature of interest group lobbying in Washington. One key to all of this change was the Vietnam War.

Vietnam and the Antiwar Lobby

The Vietnam War had a direct impact on Congress. In the late 1960s and early 1970s it became a dominant and divisive issue that split the membership along much the same lines as the issues of reform or nonreform. Following the 1968 election it became the major element of tension between the new, aggressive, and conservative Republican president, Richard M. Nixon, and the Democratic Congress, especially its liberal antiwar members. But Vietnam was also important in changing lobbying groups and lobbying itself during the 1970s.

The Vietnam War was like its Korean counterpart in the 1950s in many ways, but it brought about a different, organized response from the public than the earlier Korean conflict. From the mid–1960s through the early 1970s, massive antiwar demonstrations were accompanied by the organization of a number of visible pressure groups that experimented with a range of tactics, traditional and new, to persuade U.S. political institutions and actors to pull out of Vietnam.

Mass demonstrations, grass roots lobbying efforts, and attempts to pressure Congress directly—elements that were almost entirely absent from the Korean conflict—emerged during the Vietnam War for a number of reasons. First, of course, the baby boom created a large group of young people who were becoming eligible for the draft at just the point when their numbers were needed for military service. But this fact was not enough to explain the antiwar movement. In the 1950s and 1960s the civil rights lobby had used these same techniques to dramatize its moral stance and were given, for the first time, widespread visibility and credibility by the new national medium, television. The impact of nonviolent mass demonstrations and other organizing tactics were displayed on television screens night after night, at just the time when the baby-boom generation was paying attention to policy and to television. Not surprisingly, the antiwar forces mobilized and adopted the same tactics for their moral crusade.

The antiwar lobby that emerged and expanded in this period built a base for future involvement by others in foreign policy. It also had an enormous impact on other elements of the process: It encouraged and influenced change and reform in U.S. political institutions, including the congressional reforms I have discussed; it shaped the recruitment of individuals to political life and public office for a future generation; and it brought about a new cadre of trained individuals who understood political pressure techniques. These changes directly affected the number, scope, and direction of group activity in the decades that followed, as well as generating the counterlobbying that further resulted in an expansion of group activity.

These emerging antiwar lobbying groups and their leaders joined with antiwar members of Congress in both their policy and process agendas. When the members became frustrated with their inability to shake the existing congressional power structure to bring forward their anti-Vietnam War agenda, or even to get votes in committees and on the House floor, they pushed for institutional changes that would help their cause. Reform of the seniority system, the recorded teller vote in the House that required many more issues to be decided on the record, and proposals to open mark-up sessions and conference committees were aided by the efforts of outside lobbying groups, including direct antiwar and public interest groups like Common Cause, formed out of the systemic dissatisfaction precipitated by Vietnam.

Once the congressional reforms were under way, there were many growing reasons for interest groups in general to become involved in the national political process. An open, fluid, decentralized, democratized, and well-staffed Congress provided hundreds, even thousands, of new points of access for groups or individuals to enter the legislative process. A large number of independent subcommittees meant greater opportunity to get a hearing, to introduce legislative ideas, and to have an official policy forum. A Congress that relied less on committee products and more on floor amendments and that gave additional formal and informal clout to rank and file members meant groups previously lacking entry into the policy process now had new opportunities.

Add to these institutional changes a series of outside changes and the formula created a dramatic expansion in interest groups. As U.S. involvement in Vietnam began to decline in the mid-1970s, a large infrastructure of the antiwar movement was left behind. Many individuals who had been trained in techniques of political organizing and had built their careers on that basis were left without a cause or a job. While some went back to school or moved into other careers, a number used the skills that they had developed to form other groups for political movements in Washington like the environmental movement—expanded greatly with the anti-warlike technique represented by Earth Day in 1970— the consumer movements, the anti-defense spending movement, alternate energy groups, and citizens public interest movements.

With the new openness and accessibility in Congress, new causes and trained people to advance them, and fewer expensive resources required to build a niche inside the policy process, there was every reason to expect an expansion in the number, scope, and role of interest groups.

Because this new, open system in Washington and Congress was activist in its orientation, and because the vast number of rank and file members, especially the newer ones, were ambitious and energetic, the interests of the issue-oriented groups with ideas and agendas meshed with the entrepreneurial lawmakers looking for ideas and themes. This symbiosis sparked a dramatic increase in congressional activity. Throughout the 1970s, roll-call votes rose sharply, meetings and hearings of committee and subcommittees more than doubled, and Congress broadened its agenda in both the domestic and foreign policy arenas. The outcome—public attention focused on such areas as environmental regulation, consumer protection, and energy costs, combined with considerable new legislation mandating regulations in these and other areas— began to have an immediate and dramatic effect on business and other traditional interest groups during the mid–1970s.

Counterlobbying: Growth
in the Business Sector

Many of the traditional lobbying groups, especially businesses and trade associations, enjoyed substantial success and stability during the

1950s and 1960s in the old, closed environment of Washington. When dramatic changes began to take place, however, they were slow to understand or appreciate them. But when the effects of change became apparent and tangible, business was forced to react. A proliferation of groups and group activity resulted, as business, commerce, and industry extended their presence in Washington to compete on the newly expanded playing fields.

Throughout the 1970s, national trade associations came to Washington to establish their national headquarters at the rate of more than one per week, reaching a total of more than 2,000 by 1980, thus making Washington the national capital of trade associations. From 1975 to 1980, the U.S. Chamber of Commerce doubled its membership. The number of major corporations with at least one full-time representative in Washington doubled during this period to more than 500, with a total staff increase of at least 300 percent. In addition, as the Greater Washington Research Center reported, related and auxiliary group activities also expanded, triggered by the lobbying growth:

> Corporations, trade associations, regulatory agencies, executive departments, Congress, state and local government organizations, consultants, and citizen activist organizations alike require extensive professional assistance. They need help to interpret, plead, litigate, lobby, administer, enforce, account for, or amend the flood of laws, court decisions, benefit programs, regulations, mandates, contracts and grants. Not surprisingly, therefore, attorneys, accountants and associations now (in 1980) occupy 40 percent of Washington's downtown office space compared with only 20 percent in Los Angeles and 19 percent in Chicago.
>
> Thirty-five new accounting firms appeared on the Washington scene between 1970 and 1976, and established firms doubled and tripled in size. Membership in the D.C. Bar nearly doubled from 16,800 in 1973 to 32,200 in 1980. Most of the nation's largest law firms now have Washington branch offices. In only the past five years, the number of out of town law firms with Washington branches increased from 79 to 175, and the number of lawyers employed by these branches increased from 672 to 1,791.[1]

From the early 1970s through the early 1980s Washington saw an unprecedented boom in commercial building. Privately owned office space, nearly all geared to monitoring and influencing the federal government, has more than doubled since 1970 and now totals more than 40 million square feet in the District of Columbia alone.

Change in the Executive

Obviously the executive branch was not static. While Congress increased its staff to alter its internal power structure and to give it the
resources to combat what it saw as a hostile executive, the White House
under Richard Nixon also expanded its staff and adjunct agencies to
combat what it saw as a hostile bureaucracy and a threatening Congress.
The core White House staff nearly doubled, and the Executive Office
of the President also expanded substantially. For example, under Nixon
an Office of Public Liaison was designed for outreach to the public and
constituency groups and was then expanded, beyond its own office
throughout the White House, to create specified individual staff conduits
into the White House for an array of important groups, from ethics to
business and labor. And, of course, more channels of access into the
White House further encouraged the growth and establishment of interest
group efforts in Washington.

The executive branch was affected directly by the change taking place
in Congress. Increased congressional activity meant longer laws, more
omnibus legislation, and more sets of directions for executive branch
agencies and White House officials. As the congressional workload
mushroomed, executive branch regulatory activity increased in a parallel
fashion. From 1970 to 1980, pages in the Federal Register increased
nearly 450 percent. A more lengthy Federal Register reflected more
government regulation, of course, but it also ensured more discretionary
power vested in executive agencies. Thus interest groups witnessed an
expanded and important outlet for their pressure activity.

White House congressional liaison officials, like other lobbyists, no
longer could rely on the handful of committee chairs and party leaders
who had dominated the agenda in the old, closed system. In the 1970s,
they had to pay attention to all 535 members of Congress from the
most junior on up, as well as a growing group of powerful congressional
staffers both in personal offices and in committees and subcommittees.
They were also pressured by outside groups to pay greater attention to
a wider range of issues and to put more items on their priority list.

The White House faced other problems as well. Throughout modern
U.S. history, every new administration has been bedeviled by a phe-
nomenon called, variously, "cozy triangles," or "iron triangles," or "issue
networks": the more or less permanent and ongoing alliances that
developed between congressional subcommittees, outside interest groups,
and the bureaucracies of government agencies. Presidents who have
wished to generate change in the status quo frequently have found their
desires thwarted by these ongoing iron triangles. But in the 1970s, with
more subcommittees, more interest groups, and more power vested in

bureaucracies through regulation, the problem for a new president was more widespread, especially the increased level of frustration over "leaks."

A Slowing Down

There is a temptation to imagine all these changes continuing to increase out of control, throughout the 1980s and beyond. Like most in U.S. political history, however, these changes are not linear but cyclical, and this cycle began to wind down by 1980. Inside Congress, a modest recentralization began, including a reduction in the number of Senate subcommittees, a slowing growth rate of the congressional staffs, and a decline in congressional activity from the peaks of the late 1970s. Under Speaker of the House Tip O'Neill and Senate majority leader Howard Baker, more assertive party leadership increased in both Houses. At the same time, the rate of growth of interest groups also began to decline, no doubt partly because a saturation point was near. Fewer trade associations established national headquarters in Washington, fewer corporations created new offices in the capital, fewer outside law firms moved to Washington—some even dismantled their Washington offices— and few new public interest groups established themselves on Capitol Hill. Concomitantly, the number of pages in the Federal Register began to decline from the peak of 87,012 pages reached in 1980; by 1983 the number had decreased by nearly 30 thousand pages.

Although we may see a cycle of change here, we are not returning to the political system that existed in the 1950s and 1960s. Rates of growth have slowed, and in some instances growth has leveled off entirely, or even declined, but levels of group activity and the congressional work load remain comparable to what they were in the mid–1970s and sharply above what they had been two decades earlier. Although a few congressional committee meetings and mark-ups now are being closed to the public and fewer roll-call votes are dominating the House or Senate floors, by no means is there the reemergence of the closed Congress. Mass media growth in Washington has slowed, but remains at a level unheard of in the past. And although the network news shows are covering Congress and Washington less these days and moving their stories out into the country a bit more, Washington is still receiving unrelenting attention from national and local news media. The new, open system of interest group activity, congressional behavior, and legislative-executive interaction, it appears, is here to stay.

Significance for Policy and Politics

We have much more uncertainty built into the policy process now than we did a decade or two ago. With more interest groups, a diffused Congress, tremendous media attention paid to the internal deliberations of political institutions, and a larger and more assertive White House, alliances shift regularly and in unpredictable ways, while key actors pop up in the most unusual places. As political scientist Anthony King described it in the book *The New American Political System*, contemporary politics means "building coalitions in the sand."[2]

This fluidity means, of course, political actors are less able to maintain control over the political agenda—what gets on it, what can be pulled from it, and when elements are considered. The embarrassments of this fluid and open political process—policy uncertainties and reversals as well as the exposure given to traditional logrolling, compromising, wheeling and dealing, and campaign financing—has increased public dissatisfaction with the political process.

Regardless of the cause, the consequence is greater pressure for political reform. The pressure to change public financing laws in reaction against the political clout of lobbying groups and the political action committees (PACs) and the pressure to regulate lobbying to eliminate or reduce some of the distasteful elements are greater than they have been in some time and are likely to increase in the next several years. Broader public dissatisfaction also means additional pressure for structural, including constitutional, reform to insulate the U.S. political system from the effects of politics and "special interest pressure."

Perhaps the most important consequence of the new Washington is the increased tension between the president and Congress. There are several reasons for this:

- An increasing number of interest groups attempting to achieve policy goals in Washington find it easier to use one branch of government, or one branch of Congress, against the other, as they search for an opening or a lever to assert their will. If a goal cannot be achieved inside the White House, there will always be a sympathetic subcommittee chairperson or other key figure in the House or Senate to carry the battle forward. If things do not work in Congress, there is always somebody with a connection inside the White House as a court of appeals. Today there are more courts, more judges, and more litigants in the political process than ever.

- The expansion in interest groups also means that there are more issues that get into the public agenda. Established groups in Washington are more wide ranging than at any time in U.S. history. In an open and fluid process, with hundreds of points of access, they have greater ease getting their pet issues onto the public agenda in some fashion. Although success within the government institutions may be limited, a clever group can find ways to get extensive publicity through media campaigns or stunts. The more issues that are on the public agenda, the more opportunities there are for conflict within and between branches of government, which is more true today than ever because the open presidency exerts pressure on the White House to take positions on almost every issue that is on or near the policy agenda.
- The newer, more decentralized Congress, combined with the expansion and multiplicity of group pressure, has made it more difficult in the past half dozen years to pass any legislation. Although legislative activity has expanded dramatically, legislative output concurrently has declined. The number of bills passed by Congress and enacted into law in the 1970s and early 1980s is only half of the output of the 1950s and 1960s. Yet Congress has expanded dramatically the length of the bills that do get enacted into law, so although there are fewer bills passing through Congress, those that do are longer and more complex. They now tend to be omnibus and, to overcome the objections of every member of Congress and multiple interest groups, they tend to be vague. More leeway is given to the executive branch. Although lawmakers in Congress may, of choice and necessity, pass the buck to the executive branch, they do not shrink from then pointing the finger and blaming the president and his agencies for misinterpreting their intent or inflaming the passions of affected interest.

The executive-legislative tension, and presidential-congressional tension, caused by these changes has been exacerbated by the Supreme Court *Chadha* decision removing the legislative veto mechanism by which Congress could cope with the open system and negotiate some discretion for the executive branch.

- These changes have brought a greater level of dissatisfaction within Congress as well. Members are upset by enhanced interest group activity and their openness and vulnerability to it. Many members of Congress remain bitter over the lobbying campaign conducted by banks, for example, to repeal withholding of earnings on interest and dividends. Many, although they openly and directly exploit campaign-financing laws, are unhappy with PAC activity and the need to raise campaign money from interest groups. Members of Congress often resent the multiple pressures and the lack of insulation from them built into the open Congress. This no longer is resulting in mass retirements or voluntary departures from Congress, but still it serves to increase the level of tension surrounding the policy process and enhance the environment for additional reform.

Conclusions

As one examines these consequences, it would be easy—even compelling—to conclude that all of these changes have been entirely bad for the political process. Yet it is not clear that the move from a closed political system to an open political system and a dramatic increase in interest group activity in that system have necessarily had pernicious effects.

Although an open system means more disappointments and unexpected reversals, it also means new opportunities for presidents, lawmakers, and other actors in the policy process. The stereotype of the old political process was that of a president sitting down with a couple of congressional leaders and working things out to his satisfaction, accomplishing what he wanted to accomplish. Far more typical was that of the president sitting down with congressional leaders and being told what he could not do—because chairperson X of the Rules Committee would not let something through or chairperson Y of the Ways and Means Committee was opposed.

Today, a president can bypass chairperson X or Y and mobilize outside interest groups to achieve a goal that might not have been possible in the old Congress. President Reagan discovered this when he used outside interests to mobilize public support for his economic package in 1981. A savvy president can take advantage of the open system, using his ability to affect timing in the political process and his access to outside interests, the mass media, and the mass of lawmakers to achieve goals that otherwise could not be met.

Second, these changes have created an explosion in interest group activity that, by the standards of the founding fathers, may be salutary. More groups active in pressure politics can mean balkanization and deadlock; they can also mean, in Madisonian terms, the best route for curing the mischiefs of faction. The great increase in PACs and in group lobbying activity in Washington has not meant "business" getting the upper hand and holding sway, rather it has meant that on most issues, one formidable business interest is opposed by another or others. In the old Washington, AT&T held sway; in the new Washington, AT&T is counterbalanced by ITT, GTE, MCI, and other three-lettered giants in the telecommunications industry. One cannot help but believe that James Madison would feel some satisfaction with the changes that have taken place in the past two decades.

The expansion of groups has not been entirely uniform. The greatest expansion has occurred among corporations, businesses, and trade associations, with less growth among groups lacking resources. As Sen. Bob Dole has pointed out, there are few PACs representing poor people or welfare mothers. But the expansion of interest groups and the decentralization of Congress and the executive branch have provided more clout than ever before for those groups that do represent the interests of the less well off. Not only are business interests counterbalancing one another, but the decentralized Congress inevitably provides a number of key lawmakers to champion the cause of the disadvantaged and who are able to block action that would further disadvantage them.

Despite all the obvious and significant costs, in the new, open political system, we have come closer to making our federal government the "forge of democracy" that the founding fathers hoped it would be by forging the multiplicity of narrow interests into something that approximates a national interest. It takes longer, it is more distasteful, and it involves great frustrations—but it is not all bad.

Notes

1. Atlee E. Shidler, *Local Community and National Government* (Washington, D.C.: Greater Washington Research Center, 1980), 19.

2. Anthony King, ed., *The New American Political Systems* (Washington, D.C.: American Enterprise Institute, 1978), 371.

Commentary: On Interest Groups and Lobbying

Kenneth M. Duberstein

The new system in Congress, as defined by Norman Ornstein, takes longer, is more distasteful, and involves greater frustrations—but is not all bad. In fact, I believe, it is very good and has worked exceedingly well, especially in the last few years, in contrast to the transition period that marked the start of the Carter administration.

The transition period in the executive branch was similar to the one in Congress and with interest groups, and the problems occurred for many of the same reasons. Certainly, the changes of the 1960s and 1970s helped precipitate an administration like that of Jimmy Carter. In the midst of tremendous fluidity it was difficult to determine what was going on, and the Carter administration, as a result, did not understand fully the congressional process and how to make it work. The Carter administration's experience—coupled with the slowed pace of change by the end of the 1970s—made it easier for the Reagan administration, as it moved through the transition, to design a series of techniques that could operate under an open system.

After the 1980 election, everyone assumed that the deadlock between the executive and legislative branches that occurred under Carter, the fact that Ronald Reagan was a newcomer to Washington, and the split control of Congress would dictate more of the same, if not worse. But it has not worked out that way at all. The Reagan administration has demonstrated an exceptional aptitude for manipulating the process generated by the new system and for achieving its legislative goals.

It is interesting to compare the manner in which Lyndon Johnson, the last great presidential master under the old system, dealt with Congress and the demands of the current process. Johnson knew Congress and was able to work it, by himself, out of the Oval Office. He was, essentially, a single-operative president who relied on Senator Everett Dirksen (D-Ill.) and three or four other old cronies from the Hill. They gave him information on what was going on, what could be done, and

Kenneth M. Duberstein is currently vice president of Timmons and Company, Inc. He served in the Reagan administration as assistant to the president for legislative affairs, prior to which he was deputy assistant for legislative affairs. He has also served as vice president and director of business-government relations of the Committee for Economic Development, deputy secretary of labor during the Ford administration, and director of congressional and intergovernmental affairs for the U.S. General Services Administration from 1972 to 1976.

what could not be done. Johnson's presidential modus operandi simply would not work in the 1980s. Even if a president were willing to devote 100 percent of his time to congressional management—and no president can come close to doing that—he could not do the job single-handedly. Today, he still would be forced to rely on a small group of individuals in Congress, but Congress is no longer controlled by the three or four most powerful members. Under the present system, a president has to have congressional contacts that can further extend his reach. Just as Jimmy Carter was beset on the Panama Canal Treaty by a freshman Democratic senator from Arizona named DeConcini who had nothing to do with canals or foreign policy, Lyndon Johnson would have a similar set of problems. He would be blindsided constantly by people he would have paid no attention to 20 years ago because then they were not factors in the congressional power equation.

Managing the process now requires more work from a greatly expanded staff. It is necessary to maintain ties to 535 representatives and senators, plus their sizable staffs. This means that the White House has to give consideration to a tremendous number of people to whom it never would have had to pay attention in the past. The Reagan administration has effectively mastered the required transition in the executive branch. Even the split control of Congress has been used to good advantage. President Reagan cleverly has played off one House against the other, and the leverage that the administration has gained from Republican control of the Senate has been fundamental in putting together coalitions in the House.

Still, the process can be distasteful and frustrating. For example, in the struggle to pass the FY 1985 budget, especially in the closing days, neither branch of government was at its best. The failure to reach prompt compromises and the temporary shutdown of some government agencies and departments caused many to question the soundness of the system. Admittedly, the legislative process does not work exceptionally well in a presidential election year, but the budget impasse was resolved, which indicates that the process is working, although perhaps not in the manner desired.

In the final days before passage of the FY 1985 budget, what happened was not an instance of the process falling apart but a complex match of end-game poker involving highly sophisticated and knowledgeable political actors trying to get what they wanted out of the process. The Reagan administration was the major player, and at the core of the dispute was the defense budget. The administration was attempting to extract the maximum amount possible from Congress and started with a firm figure, but in the final weeks realized that if it delayed any longer it would get less than what it wanted. The resulting compromise opened up the final budget settlement. It was neither pretty nor particularly edifying, but it was the political process in action—and it was the political process functioning more or less as it should. Instances such as these testify that things are indeed working.

The system is strong, therefore, and both branches of government have adapted themselves to the changes of the past 25 years. But what impact does this have on executive-legislative relations? What salient points can be made about the effective conduct of executive-legislative relations under changed circumstances? There are several observations that should be made.

First, it is impossible to overemphasize the importance of coalition building. Coalition building always has been a critical Washington activity, but it is even more so given the current process in which one is, as Ornstein quotes in his paper, "building coalitions in the sand."

Many people come to work in Washington without recognizing the importance of coalition building. Certainly, when one wins the presidency, the natural inclination is to turn to partisan rhetoric and the formation of partisan forces on the Hill. Yet, once the honeymoon is over, it is exceedingly difficult to put together a coalition just on one's own side of the aisle, regardless of whether one controls the House or the Senate. Witness the Carter administration: Democrats controlled the presidency and both Houses of Congress, but the Carter administration still could not mount an effective legislative program. Nor has the Reagan administration been entirely immune to the problem.

The Nixon administration, with its infamous "enemies list," is perhaps the foremost example of the dangers of partisan coalition building. One of the hallmarks of the Reagan administration has been that it does not keep an enemies list, which means the administration can go back time and again to representatives and senators who have previously voted against the administration. The ability to forgo vindictiveness and work with all potential allies has been fundamental on some of the big votes that the Reagan administration has had, such as the vote on social security. Unlike the first year in the Reagan administration when there were partisan votes and the administration picked up the boll weevils, it is usually necessary to shift constantly and build coalitions.

President Reagan has recognized that it is sometimes necessary to sacrifice on the far right in order to pick up moderate Democrats. The budget and the tax bill in the House in the second year are examples. The importance of reaching out and building coalitions has been a crucial factor in effective executive-legislative relations. Without a doubt, coalition building will be increasingly important over the next several years.

Second, closely related to the significance of coalition building is the need for increased attention to bipartisan cooperation. When I was assistant to the president for legislative affairs, many people accused me of being "Mr. Bipartisan." The accusation was well placed, but it is also true that the only way to run a congressional relations organization successfully in the executive branch is to focus on bipartisan cooperation. An administration certainly needs to build on its base, but also it needs to reach out and build a bipartisan coalition.

Bipartisanship is significant not only for crucial votes but also for scheduling and procedural matters. Looking back to 1981 and the bills that were the crucial first tests of Reagan's economic program proposals—Gramm-Latta I and Gramm-Latta II—many commentators fail to remember that the key breakthrough for the administration was the early negotiation with the speaker of the House concerning the timing of the votes, and the procedures that would govern their consideration. Negotiating this in a bipartisan fashion gave the opportunity for the administration to put together the coalitions to win.

Third, one of the keys to sound executive-legislative relations is early and frequent consultation between the branches. Under the old, closed political system, consultation was more regularized and the outcome more predictable. In the 1950s, for example, Senate Majority Leader Lyndon Johnson and Speaker of the House Sam Rayburn, both Democrats, would discuss with Republican President Eisenhower what could and could not be done. President Johnson followed essentially the same procedure, but, with his more intimate knowledge of Congress, he followed a more activist course.

With the dispersal of power in Congress, the ranks of those who need to be included in executive-legislative consultation have increased dramatically. The executive branch has had to become involved at the subcommittee and junior member level as well as at the committee and leadership level. It is commonplace to refer to executive consultation with Congress as lip service, but certainly it is more. It is essential if harmonious and effective relations are to be maintained between the two branches. The executive branch must give increased attention to the necessity for consultation.

Fourth, the executive branch has demonstrated a fundamental misunderstanding of the congressional mind-set. This failure has been fairly rampant in all administrations. It is most readily visible in the executive branch's ineffectiveness in dealing with Congress. With all the crosscurrents in Congress, with the dispersal of congressional power, and with the multiple outside interests, an administration often sends out conflicting signals when it decides what it wants out of Congress. Witness the Carter administration: early on it sent to the Hill 50 to 75 major legislative proposals. As a result, it jammed the system. No one in Congress knew what was most important to President Carter, and the legislative outcome was therefore disappointing.

The Reagan administration fared better in this regard. Entering office, it stated that the one thing of fundamental importance to President Reagan in the first year was economic recovery. The administration riveted Congress's attention on the budget votes and the tax votes. It was more effective not to clog the system, to tell Congress what was important, and to set out a priority list to keep Congress focused on the priority items.

The Reagan administration has tried to continue this policy so that Congress would be aware of the key votes ahead—whether on the MX, social security, or the jobs bill in the third year. Congress has to know the pace that is expected of it, and it has to know what is important to the executive branch. The Reagan administration's procedure has been significantly more effective than the practice of sending numerous proposals to the Hill and declaring that all are important. Understanding how Congress works and what will work with Congress is central to the successful conduct of executive-legislative relations. Too many administrations—and too many executive branch officials—lack this understanding.

Fifth, on the outside, consensus-building organizations are immensely important to the smooth functioning of the process for both the executive and legislative branches. Congress simply does not do a good job of educating the public on the issues for which a genuine public consensus is needed. Business groups, labor groups, and public policy research groups are important to building consensus. They cut away some of the brush and, by educating on the outside, give Congress a jumping-off point to start the policy and the legislative processes. Congress is not likely to act on an issue without an informed public. More needs to be done to encourage the work of these consensus-building organizations.

One of the ways to build an outside consensus that has come to prominence recently is through the national commission. The Reagan administration used the Scowcroft Commission on the MX and the bipartisan Social Security Commission, headed by Alan Greenspan, to build a consensus on these issues. The consensus formed was perhaps not the consensus the administration would have preferred, but it did form the basis for workable solutions. If Congress had acted on social security without having the umbrella of the bipartisan commission, it undoubtedly would have acted less responsibly.

Sixth, related to the significance of consensus-building groups is the need to recognize the increased importance of the media on the grass roots throughout the country. During the Reagan administration the mobilization directed by the White House Office of Public Liaison was strategically important on many key votes. The only thing that can compare to the personal intervention of the president with a representative or senator is input from the voters back home. Time after time a representative or senator would say to the administration: I really want to vote with the president, I really want to vote on his side, but I am not hearing from back home; or, I am hearing on the opposite side of the issue from back home, so if you can help me out there and if I start hearing some things, that will give me the flexibility to help you. The Office of Public Liaison often was able to coordinate that help back home and thus win congressional support.

The Office of Public Liaison had its genesis in the Nixon administration. It was not necessarily conceived as a lobbying tool or as a way of propping up the legislative strategy, but much more as a way for President Nixon to move to consolidate electoral power and develop ties to electoral groups to which he had not had strong ties in the past. Nor did the Carter administration initially see much lobbying value in the office. It was not until Ann Wexler was appointed assistant to the president for public liaison that the office was used explicitly to achieve legislative priorities. She was an insider who understood the changes that had taken place in the system. The Reagan administration, following Ann Wexler's example, used the office with great efficacy almost solely to consolidate its legislative goals.

Seventh, central to the success of the Reagan administration's legislative program was the establishment of the Legislative Strategy Group (LSG) inside the White House, a group that should be made a permanent fixture of this and all future administrations.

The LSG is the Reagan administration's most significant mechanism for promoting executive-legislative relations. Chaired by the White House chief of staff, it brings together all of the major officers inside the White House as needed. The tasks of the LSG are many. First, it plans strategy. Early each year it outlines the presidential and the departmental priorities for the next session of Congress. It establishes strategy alternatives and spends a large amount of time analyzing obstacles and how to overcome them. The LSG coordinates how to use the Office of Public Liaison and how the media program strategy is to be put together—whether, for example, the president is going to communicate the administration's viewpoint by television or through various speeches around the country. The LSG allocates the president's time for seeing representatives and senators on a specific vote. It determines whether or not a cabinet official, rather than the president, gets involved with a specific issue.

Secretary of Commerce Malcolm Baldrige's push within the Reagan administration for a Department of International Trade represents a prime example of how the LSG operates. The opinion within the LSG was that a Department of International Trade had no chance of success. There was, therefore, no need to put the president out front advocating its implementation. It was decided that Baldrige would spend one year, or however long it took, working out the jurisdictional questions among the various committees in the House and Senate and determining if there were a way to fashion a proposal that then could become a presidential priority.

The LSG learned that when it spoke and made a recommendation to the president it could deliver. No other White House has concentrated so many officials in so many meetings—15-minute or half-hour meetings three times a week or sometimes three times a day. The important thing was that meetings would put together all of the resources of the administration behind what the president wanted.

The success of the LSG in the Reagan administration has been attributable largely to the nature of President Reagan, who was willing to listen to what the LSG said and to devote a significant amount of his personal resources if the LSG thought it was necessary. Had the LSG been instituted while Jimmy Carter was president, the group would not have functioned nearly as effectively, because President Carter would not have been as willing to devote his own resources to the legislative process. The effectiveness of the LSG depends to a certain extent on the president in office. Even so, it is vital to bring together a White House and an administration when dealing with the legislative process. The LSG has done this for the Reagan administration, and the work needs to be duplicated regardless of who is president.

One argument against the institutionalization of the LSG might be that in its current low-profile status it has been sheltered from interest group pressure. The business community has failed to focus on the LSG, but then the White House has not announced the agenda or the times of the meetings. Certainly, the White House staff in their daily contacts with business interests have picked up their comments and views, but there has not been any direct lobbying of the LSG.

In addition to the LSG in the White House, several of the individual cabinet departments now have established their own LSGs. The cabinet-level LSGs consider both departmental and White House priorities, and they keep close tabs on how these priorities are being followed up within the department. Usually either the assistant secretary for legislative affairs or the top assistant to the secretary chairs the departmental LSG.

Ad hoc legislative strategy meetings also occur frequently. At the State Department, for example, if the issue is of some significance—on the level of the nuclear freeze resolution, Central America, or, in some cases, the Middle East—it is not just a problem for the State Department, it is also a White House problem. Such issues are taken to the LSG, and State Department officials participate in the LSG. But the State Department also has, on middle-level issues, its own legislative strategy meetings involving various interested parties within the department.

The Reagan administration instituted an ad hoc group to focus on these middle-level issues as well. Representatives from the Departments of State and Defense, the CIA, and the NSC meet once a week to discuss national security and legislative strategy. This innovation, too, is constructive, and coordination of this type needs to be formalized.

Executive-legislative relations thus have adjusted to the new and more open system described by Ornstein. Many of the factors that prompted effective executive-legislative relations under the old system—such as the need for consultation and bipartisan consensus building—are equally essential in the new. New procedures, however, also have been necessary, and responsive changes—such as the LSG—have been implemented. Certainly the experience of the Reagan administration in its first term has proven that successful executive-legislative relations can be achieved given the current structure.

That structure is here to stay for the foreseeable future. There has been, as Ornstein notes, some retrenchment, but there is no possibility of going back to the system that existed before the 1960s. There is no need to, because the system is working.

Of course, changes could be made in the process that would make it perform better and more smoothly. Congress needs to involve itself more in oversight. A two-year authorization and appropriations process would free badly needed congressional time. The number of subcommittees, the proliferation of which has been harmful to the process, could be cut back. And because, as Ornstein points out, it is easier to stop legislation than to pass it, there needs to be more positive legislative action by Congress.

There are no structural panaceas. What makes the process work is the combination of capable individuals acting within the system. Effective executive-legislative relations is more a matter of intelligent management than of massive structural reform.

8

Steering Committee Report: Policy Paper on Legislative-Executive Reform

edited by
Robert E. Hunter and Wayne L. Berman

Introduction

In writing the Constitution, the founding fathers ensured competition between Congress and the executive branch. This competition for power and the ensuing tension over policy directions are at the heart of the checks and balances that were designed more to protect U.S. liberties than to ensure the efficient functioning of a pluralistic democracy. The division of power was understood to impose added burdens and to make governance more cumbersome. Indeed, at times the power to obstruct or to delay can be important for the effective working of either the legislative or executive branch in the broader national interest. Furthermore, there is nothing new about serious tensions between the legislative and executive branches, nor about complaints that the system of governance is not working effectively.

Significant changes, however, have been taking place in Congress, the executive branch, and in the country at large that have made legislative-executive relations more difficult and complicated. Checks and balances that benefit a strong and independent Congress and executive seem to be achieved increasingly at the expense of the degree of efficiency and coherence that the government needs to deal promptly and effectively with critical issues facing the nation—whether in managing

Reprinted from Robert E. Hunter and Wayne L. Berman (eds.), *Making the Government Work: Legislative-Executive Reform* (Washington, D.C.: The Center for Strategic and International Studies, Georgetown University, 1985).

the economy, setting levels of spending and taxation, serving general interests rather than parochial ones, crafting and executing foreign and defense policies, or meeting other requirements of a society facing the stresses of technological, demographic, and social change.

The current difficulties in legislative-executive relations are unacceptable. We share the frustration found in both branches—frustration that cuts across party, ideological, and institutional lines—with the delay and difficulty in resolving critical policy issues.

Public esteem for both branches also has been seriously eroded. Elected officials may be able to defend their personal records in Congress, yet find it difficult to defend an overall record of congressional inaction or ineptness when challenged by their electoral opponents. "Running against Washington" has become possible in part because of widespread views that both Congress and the executive branch fall short in meeting national needs. Indeed, the political consequences of current failings in legislative-executive relations are perhaps the most significant driving force behind the search for means to reform these relations.

There is little dispute that many problems exist in legislative-executive relations. The task, however, is to identify which problems are most important in terms of permitting the U.S. government to function more effectively. Why do they exist? And what can be done to alleviate them?

We have divided the discussion and recommendations that follow into those functional areas most in need of reform if legislative-executive relations are to meet the demands of the times.

What Is the Problem?

Problems with Congress

The problems in legislative-executive relations that most concern us affect both branches and reflect criticisms leveled by one against the other as well as self-criticism. In recent years, for example, administrations of both political parties have expressed frustration with Congress— chafing at congressional straitjackets on executive authority and flexibility. Executive branch leaders are increasingly hindered in discharging their duties because of the detail in which Congress legislates, while Congress often seems unable to provide broad policy direction to the executive branch. These administrations also have been frustrated by the dispersion of power within Congress that inhibits the latter's effective leadership and collective judgment on some of the most difficult issues, both foreign and domestic, facing the country.

In domestic policy, frustrations have mounted as Congress is increasingly unable to meet even its own self-imposed deadlines. The congressional budget process limps along with the aid of the crutch of "continuing resolutions"; the budget process also severely restricts the ability of Congress to exercise its reponsibility of overseeing executive branch actions. It is becoming commonplace to see the federal bureaucracy grind to a halt as Congress struggles to pass even stopgap funding or to raise the national debt ceiling.

Problems with the Executive Branch

Congress, of course, has its own criticisms of the executive branch. A persistent complaint, for example, is that the executive branch has difficulty in either planning policies for the long term—in both foreign and domestic areas—or in coordinating policies in some especially difficult but important areas—in particular, that of international economics.

In addition, all recent administrations, whenever possible, have exploited the dispersion of legislative branch power to divide Congress politically and to achieve specific objectives. Various departments of government involved in the formulation of either foreign, domestic, or economic policy have become highly sophisticated in playing parts of Congress off against others. For example, various administrations have chosen to place their emphasis on working either with appropriations or authorization committees, depending on which at a given time and on a given issue seems more sympathetic.

Meanwhile, administration officials have become more resourceful in bypassing congressional restrictions and in averting effective oversight or legislation that would seriously limit administration actions, especially in foreign policy. Of course, at times these techniques have been self-defeating as Congress has reacted by reasserting its authority to block any action at all.

In foreign policy, particularly, congressional frustration with the executive branch abounds. Since the Vietnam War, Congress has attempted to assert its influence and to play a greater role in foreign policy, especially concerning the projection of U.S. military power abroad. Yet the response from various administrations—whether on the War Powers Act, genuine consultations, or modifications to policy in light of congressional criticism—has at times been less than forthcoming.

Common Problems

Problems—but also challenges—in legislative-executive relations have been intensified by some recent developments: These include the Supreme Court's decision in 1983 to eliminate Congress's use of the so-called legislative veto to limit executive branch action, the growing range of foreign policy issues subject to congressional action, and the increasing difficulties—plus polarization of the body politic—involved in issues such as Social Security and deficit reduction that entail especially hard choices.

Moreover, with the revolution in communications and in the instant availability of information, members of Congress sometimes find themselves swamped by information from the executive branch, from outside and competing interest groups, or from the world at large—information that must be mastered for the Congress to play its proper role effectively. Both branches have undergone an explosive growth in the size of their staffs and bureaus, adding complex layers of management; and both suffer from deficiencies of organization, making it harder for reasonable individuals to make sense of the whole.

In analyzing legislative-executive relations and the demands for reform, we have concentrated on the four most important areas.

Planning and Coordination in the Executive Branch. Consideration of legislative-executive relations should begin with the basics—what an administration is trying to accomplish and how it sets about achieving its goals.

The executive branch seeks mandates from Congress in domestic, economic, and foreign policy; however, it often does so without a clear sense of what it can achieve or a coherent strategy for doing so. In part this reflects a general inadequacy of planning within the executive branch—both for long-term, and sometimes even for short-term, policy coherence—that long has been endemic to administrations of both political parties.

Furthermore, few recent administrations have been particularly adept at systematically requiring policy choices to be resolved among different departments and agencies, especially prior to submissions to Congress. The internal budget process helps, but it still does not provide an administration and a president with sufficient control over the means of policy-making.

In addition, among the most difficult problems faced by recent administrations—both in making policy and in dealing with Congress—has been that of coordinating approaches to issues such as energy, agriculture, and trade. These issues cut across old distinctions between "foreign" and "domestic" policy. In organizing the executive branch to make policy, presidents have tended to pay inadequate attention to this intersection, particularly in the area of economics—that is, in those resource issues that compose most of both policy and legislative-executive relations. In recent years, the executive branch has experimented with a number of institutional solutions designed to deal better with international economic policy, yet none has worked particularly well. This is true in part because of the congeries of federal agencies, issues, and interests that are involved.

In approaching legislative-executive relations, all administrations must also grapple with the coordination of legislative strategy, both within the executive branch and between it and Congress. Yet the exercise of this responsibility has often fallen short of the minimum required for effective governance. When this happens, the cause is often less a matter of differences of viewpoint, interest, or attitude on policy—legitimate and even necessary aspects of political struggle—than of problems either with internal executive-branch decision making or with the ties between the two branches. Indeed, a significant part of the difficulty in legislative-executive relations reflects confusing or uncoordinated signals sent by an administration to Capitol Hill.

At the very least, the administration's intentions need to be perceived correctly by the Congress. To this end, presidents need to ensure that there is coordination in the way that both substantive policy and legislative strategy are made within the executive branch. Among other reasons, this coordination is needed to increase the chances that, once decisions are taken, officials of the administration will speak with one voice on Capitol Hill. Given the nature of the U.S. government bureaucracy, the "end run" to Congress by competing bureaucracies will never be halted entirely by any president, no matter how determined. Yet presidential discipline and an effective policy-making, priority-setting, and legislative-relations process within the executive branch can help to blend the cacophony of voices that has sometimes created such confusion as to stymie even the best efforts to conduct the nation's business.

There is also the question of the appropriate role of interest groups in the formulation of policy. It is a truism that few, if any, major issues exist in a political vacuum without strong advocacy on various sides from the nation at large. In legislative-executive relations, however, all too often the effort to bring to bear the ideas of different constituencies is done haphazardly or without policy coherence.

Finally, as part of developing effective strategies for legislative-executive relations, there has been a growing place for the bipartisan commission. Three commissions have stood out: Social Security, strategic modernization and arms control policy, and Central America. The first produced agreement that was sustained by Congress; on the second, consensus has emerged on some specific issues, while others continue to be debated; and the third was most important in defining the terms of debate on Central America and in suggesting approaches for U.S. policy. These commissions can be valuable, but it must be recognized that the convening of bipartisan commissions in legislative-executive relations is an extraordinary step for handling extraordinary issues or circumstances. Their use means that the regular procedures of governance have not proved sufficient in some way. There may be occasions on which such commissions are the only practical alternative, given the seriousness of issues, their urgency, and the strength with which opposing views are held—with opposing advocates each having the ability to veto the issues' resolution. When a common understanding of the need to decide something overrides differences of view, this mechanism can work and be valuable.

At the same time, however, the risk arises that the bipartisan commission will come to be seen as a panacea—a means for evading responsibility within either Congress or the executive branch. If that happens, the system will begin progressively to atrophy, and the basic principle of accountability will be increasingly violated to the detriment of the entire government. Thus the use of these commissions must be sparing and highly circumscribed. General rules are needed if their use is not to be abused, and if they are to be a last, and not a first, resort in developing legislative strategies.

The Sharing of Information and Consultations. The second key area of concern regarding legislative-executive relations relates both to the sharing of information by the executive branch with Congress and to consultations between the two branches.

Every administration seeks to control information—a coin of political power—but then often finds that Congress will either not act or will bring to bear vastly different perspectives on particular problems. Congress, meanwhile, spends a good deal of its time trying to elicit information or—lacking it—makes decisions without an adequate basis for judgment.

Consultations with Congress, involving the president and other members of the executive branch, is an idea as old as the republic, as seen in the "advice and consent" provisions of the Constitution. In recent years, however, the growing complexity of issues, the loosening of the congressional leadership structure, and the greater likelihood of political one-upmanship by individual members of Congress seeking media attention have changed much of the role of consultations. Consultations are now often narrowly based and designed simply to inform congressional leaders of the president's intentions rather than to solicit a genuine congressional role in the administration's policy deliberations. This approach may strengthen a president's short-term leverage, but it can cripple his long-term ability to form alliances and gain congressional support on both sides of the aisle.

Foreign policy presents a special problem. The officials of the executive branch charged with the conduct of foreign and defense policy testify ad nauseum before congressional committees, but this does not necessarily mean that members are provided with sufficient access to information they need to make their own judgments. Indeed, frustration in obtaining this information helps to explain the widespread use of formal hearings—to some administration minds, excessive use.

In general, presidents and their officials have wanted to keep as much control as possible over information relating to foreign policy, particularly in regard to sensitive intelligence. In recent years, however, the intelligence committees of both the House and the Senate have helped open the door to greater sharing of information by achieving admirable success in preventing leaks of secret information from Capitol Hill.

Cross-Fertilization. A third key concern in legislative-executive relations relates to the basic knowledge each branch has about the other. Indeed, a significant obstacle to improving the overall climate of these relations derives from the general lack of understanding in each branch about how the other actually works. Simply put, few policy-level individuals in either branch have any deep understanding of the other's motivations, problems, and modes of operation. Few members of Congress or congressional staff have ever served in the executive branch and thus have not had to grapple seriously either with the difficulties and dilemmas of making policy or of requiring the bureaucracy to act.

So, too, few people with responsibility for developing policy in the executive branch have ever served on Capitol Hill. Indeed, it is often true that many administration officials in the executive branch who must formulate policies with an eye on congressional opinion will understand the substance of the issue under consideration—tax reform, military readiness, or relations with a specific country—far better than they understand even the basic workings of Congress.

Improving the Capacity of Congress to Act. Finally, improvements in legislative-executive relations will require some changes in the ways in which Congress does its legislative business.

To assert its role in the face of frustrations, Congress has used a variety of weapons. For example, the legislative veto, now ruled unconstitutional, was used to provide Congress with a means for deciding, not just basic policies, but the specific ways in which they would be implemented—that is, congressional intrusion in the management of policy and program by the executive branch. In the process, however, the legislative veto often became an excuse for Congress's not debating and deciding at the outset what it wanted. Through this mechanism, Congress could require the administration to return to Capitol Hill for a second look. This increased congressional leverage, but it also became a way to avoid difficult decisions.

In addition, the legislative veto potentially provided Congress with its most effective tool in asserting a strong role in the making of the nation's foreign policy. It was designed to block individual and specific arms sales, to impose requirements on various agreements with other nations, and to provide continuing congressional oversight on the use and placement of military forces in high risk situations abroad.

The fact that Congress rarely used the authority it awarded itself through the legislative veto—especially in foreign and defense policy—did not mean that it was devoid of significance, especially in cautioning the executive branch against flouting congressional will.

The issue of the legislative veto illustrates a deeper question about the organization of Congress. In particular, are its processes and procedures now so cumbersome that it sometimes becomes next to impossible for Congress actually to deliberate? Does it thereby lack the ability to take enough time to give thorough consideration to important matters? Congress is also hampered in exercising one of its other primary functions—namely, to oversee what is being done in the executive branch. It can be argued that the legislative veto came into fashion as a shortcut for Congress to gain review authority later, because it was unable or unwilling, institutionally, to give issues the time and attention they deserved initially.

We believe, therefore, that the loss of the legislative veto is a blessing in disguise: it provides both a challenge and an opportunity for Congress to put its own house in order. Thus, Congress is challenged to develop ways of operating that will bring decisions to the fore on a timely basis, during initial consideration of policies and programs rather than during their implementation by the executive branch. In addition, the loss of the legislative veto also focuses attention on the need for both Houses of Congress to strengthen the oversight function, especially that of the authorizing committees.

The Congressional Budget Process

In considering Congress's challenge to reorganize itself so that it might better discharge its mandated responsibilities, we believe that no part of its activities is more important than the budget process. Indeed, probably no other reform in Congress would do more to increase its effectiveness—both in its own terms and in dealing with the executive branch—than streamlining the budget process.

In theory, Congress was supposed to gain immeasurably from its most important recent reform—the creation of the budget committees and budget resolutions in 1974. The reform was designed to assure that legislating on matters of taxation and spending—the core of most activity by the two Houses—would be conducted responsibly, with an awareness of the balance (or imbalance) between revenues and expenditures. In fact, however, this reform has made the job of legislating more complex, slower, and at times less effective than before.

Today's procedures have added another layer of complication: instead of two basic considerations of the same issues (authorizations and appropriations), there are now three. Budget resolutions have been passed later in the year, leaving less time for authorizing and appropriating legislation, as well as for the other legislative business of Congress, especially effective oversight of executive branch activities. Stopgap continuing resolutions have become more important, thus at times reducing the yearlong process of deliberation to a truncated effort to reach compromises at the end of each session.

Every participant in the process of appropriating and spending money—the executive branch, the budget committees, the authorization committees, and the appropriations committees—uses a different set of economic assumptions, accounts, baselines, and functional listings. The result, as Senator Sam Nunn told the Quayle Committee, is an "accountant's nightmare" that certainly keeps the budget process from performing its functions effectively.

A final complication that derives in large part from today's budget process is the fact that Congress still has not been able to come to grips with a central problem of governance: planning for the future—concerning allocation of the nation's resources—beyond the time horizon of this year's authorizations and appropriations. The cycle of elections and the quality of political responsibility involved make any real forward fiscal planning from one Congress to the next—with settled decisions—difficult to achieve politically. But today's situation, in which there is little fiscal foresight or continuity, is also not an answer.

The Budget Act. As is often the case with landmark legislation, the 1974 budget act was the product of a diverse coalition made up of members of Congress with disparate expectations. Some saw the budget process as a mechanism for restraining federal spending. Others viewed it as a means for making more effective use of the federal budget as a tool for allocating resources and thus setting national priorities. Still others saw the budget process as a means of reasserting congressional control over the nation's purse strings. Each of these viewpoints was forcefully advocated by key members in the debates leading to passage of the budget act; each in its own way contributed significantly to the budget process that finally emerged.

Despite current criticisms, in many respects the congressional budget process has served the nation well since 1974. Aspects of that process that have yielded considerable advantage to Congress and thus to the nation as a whole include the following:

1. the integration function, the absolutely essential aspect of the process that, for the first time, allowed Congress to look at the budget—both revenues and expenditures—comprehensively;
2. outyear projections, which, however imperfect, provide some sense of forward planning beyond the annual appropriations cycles; and
3. technical expertise, as the Congressional Budget Office and related support staff now provide the professional economics and accounting expertise that Congress must have to be engaged seriously in federal budgeting.

In addition, even when the act and its processes have been used to delay or to obstruct congressional efforts, that has sometimes been of benefit to the national interest. The issue lies in the inadequacies of the procedures even when there is common desire for greater efficiency and expedition.

Because of these and other real contributions, the budget process is here to stay. As Senator Howard Baker put it, "Someplace you will find a role for a budget function. There must be a budget function [in Congress]." How, then, should Congress assimilate and adapt these and other positive aspects of the 1974 act? How should it learn the lessons of its experience with the act? Perhaps most important, how should recommendations be designed so that, in the present congressional and political climate, they can actually be implemented?

Fiscal Responsibility. Fiscal responsibility is perhaps the most difficult area: It has changed most in recent years, from a time of rapidly expanding government to one in which, by political choice, it is more constrained; from a time of relative fiscal plenty to one of relative fiscal scarcity. The area of fiscal restraint is also the one least directly amenable to solutions based on the manipulation of process. Decisions about restraints on spending—including those involving the raising of taxes, cutting spending, and restricting entitlements—are inherently difficult and controversial, political not procedural.

Although few would argue that the current budget process has succeeded well in restraining federal spending, the problem is more a failure of political will in the face of difficult political choices than the need to revamp any particular structure or organization. No budget process can compel Congress, in the absence of political will, to take these difficult decisions. Once that political will is there, however, the current process could work effectively.

Moreover, without the current budget procedure to focus attention on aggregate revenues, expenditures, deficits, and the overall allocation of resources, the federal budget deficit could become much greater than it is now. Even so, the current congressional budget process should be tightened in ways described below to help Congress gain the capacity to restrict the rate of growth in federal spending.

Macroeconomic Tool. As noted above, many of today's difficulties with the congressional budget process, both on Capitol Hill and within the executive branch, stem from a degree of duplication and overlap among the three layers of fiscal consideration—budget, authorization, and appropriation—that was never intended by supporters of budget reform in 1974.

Rather than duplicating existing procedures and thus facing the executive branch with yet a third set of essentially the same hearings and committee considerations, the budget process was supposed to provide Congress with the necessary macroeconomic tools to help it set aggregate fiscal policy and national economic priorities more effectively.

Even Chairman John L. McClellan of the Senate Appropriations Committee, who was otherwise an opponent of the budget process, acknowledged in 1974 that this was worth doing.

> First, the attempt to analyze the budget in reference to the Nation's macroeconomic setting is very useful. For too long the Congress, and I must include the Committees on Appropriations, has been passing the budget one piece at a time. By looking at the budget in macro terms as a whole and then relating it to economic indicators of employment, inflation, and Gross National Product, it may be possible for the Congress to work closer toward a budget which best meets the existing economic situation in a given year.

But the budget process has begun to miss the forest for the trees and to become hampered by a welter of different and frequently inconsistent accounts and functional listings.

Other Key Congressional Inefficiencies

Meanwhile, there are some other functions of the Senate and the House that—while dealing with its internal procedures—are especially important in shaping the ability of Congress to deal effectively with the executive branch. For example, Congress faces a growing problem in getting legislation passed—especially with the complications of the budget process—because of the general failure to enforce existing rules regarding the need for amendments to be germane to the central purposes of the bill under consideration. The opportunities for delay—often defeating wider purposes—are rife.

In addition, the proliferation of congressional subcommittees has provided Congress with several avenues through which to influence the direction of policy as it is being formed, debated, and decided. For example, an administration must run the gauntlet of 43 subcommittees in both Houses on energy issues and 49 subcommittees on defense issues. Yet this proliferation of subcommittees has certainly not contributed to efficiency in legislation and has tended to create an array of vested interests that further reduces the role of congressional leadership.

Furthermore, Congress has paid a price in legislative-executive relations. The proliferation of subcommittees has allowed successive administrations to play various congressional interests off against each other; it has also helped administrations to polarize certain elements of Congress in an effort to prevent the passage of initiatives opposed by the executive.

In sum, much of the frustration felt by Congress in its relations with the executive reflects its own difficulties in playing the role assigned to it by the Constitution. Yet we believe that those steps we recommend below can increase the opportunities that both Houses have to apply themselves to considering policy at a national level, instead of being preoccupied with details because of procedural deadlock. Thus, there would be fewer occasions on which Congress would legislate with such general lack of understanding of its own overall intentions that it has to impose requirements for further review—for example, as happened with the legislative veto. In addition, by streamlining the budget process— the core of most congressional action—Congress can become a more equal partner with the executive branch in this critical area. In addition, Congress would gain the time needed to tend to other legislative business that has a decisive impact on legislative-executive relations.

Recommendations

In light of the preceding discussion, we have weighted recommendations for reform within the legislative and executive branches toward five key objectives:

1. the better long-term planning and coordination of executive branch policy, including the organization and management of executive branch relations with Congress;
2. an improved flow of information to Congress and better consultations between the branches;
3. the improved cross-fertilization between the legislative and executive branches;
4. the reform of the congressional budget process; and
5. other key reforms in the way Congress does its business—reforms that will also contribute to better legislative-executive relations.

The implementation of these recommendations in both Congress and the executive branch would alleviate some of the frustrations and reduce some of the unwanted political tensions in today's relations between the branches.

Planning, Policy Coordination, and Legislative Strategy

The executive branch should institutionalize a White House-based legislative strategy system that will enhance effective coordination of policy and liaison with Congress.

The Reagan administration has made significant progress in this area by organizing the Legislative Strategy Group, centered in the White House and directed by the White House chief of staff. This group is charged with setting overall priorities for administration policies, coordinating the development of those policies, assessing the best uses of presidential time, and judging legislative realities. In addition, the Legislative Strategy Group is significantly more insulated from outside lobbying pressures than are similar groups in individual executive departments; thus it can act to help ensure that offsetting political factors are seriously considered when the administration sets and orchestrates its legislative priorities.

By and large, the White House Office of Legislative Affairs (OLA) should draw its staff from the professional lobbying community and Capitol Hill to provide a wide range of experience with both political groupings and substantive issues. This step will help the OLA to put together different permutations and combinations needed to achieve a majority and thus could be seen as part of the process of competing for power with the Congress. At the same time, however, organization of the OLA staff in this manner also increases congressional involvement in the administration's policy process through consultations. This means of organization can be a two-way street for the channeling of influence between Capitol Hill and the White House.

There also needs to be sustained and high-priority attention within the executive branch to the coordination of congressional relations among all departments and agencies. This coordination should be centered in the White House, though without such a rigid structure that stifles liaison between Congress and individual departments. Not unnaturally in bureaucratic politics, departmental liaison staffs often lobby for parochial positions that may be at odds with official administration positions or the desires of the president, thus sowing confusion. This practice, too, cannot be completely eliminated, but steps should be taken to reduce its extent on highest priority issues.

The organization and management of international economic policy should be further centralized within the White House through the creation of an International Economics Council.

Better policy coordination—and thus the beginning of better legislative-executive relations in this area—could be achieved by establishing an International Economics Council, acting in parallel with the National Security Council and based in the White House. This step would increase the ability of the administration to integrate foreign policy concerns with economic policy. This council should be composed of senior representatives of all the key agencies involved in economic issues, including the pertinent cabinet departments, the Office of Management and Budget, the Council of Economic Advisers, the special trade representative, the Domestic Council, and the assistant to the president for national security affairs.

The International Economics Council should include a number of permanent staff members, in part drawn from the career services, to provide for institutional memory. The chairmanship should be at the president's discretion: It could be the secretary of the treasury, thus making this council a natural outgrowth and upgrading of today's Senior Interdepartmental Group (International Economic Policy). The executive director of the council should be selected in part for an ability to be an honest broker and coordinator of policies among the various contending interests. This relative bureaucratic neutrality would help to compensate Congress for the creation of another White House official not subject to congressional scrutiny. The International Economics Council should also place strong emphasis on congressional relations and communication by including the assistant to the president for legislative affairs as a permanent member.

A senior national security planning staff should be established, as an arm of the National Security Council, to concentrate the long-range planning function in the White House.

Creating such a planning staff could increase the means available to the president to gain greater control over foreign and defense policymaking within the executive branch, to establish some basis for continuity of policy, and to present plans and positions to Congress in a more coherent, coordinated, and sustainable fashion.

This senior planning staff should be made responsible to the assistant to the president for national security affairs. It would be valuable to keep it formally separate from the NSC staff, however, to help it avoid the crisis mentality that tends to prevail in day-to-day workings of the NSC. The new planning staff should draw experienced personnel from the various agencies of government, be located in the White House, and have some members with permanent status—again, for institutional memory and a basis for continuity of foreign policy from one administration to the next. The mandate of the senior planning staff should include emphasis on gaining the benefit of congressional views through the White House OLA. Working with the International Economics Council proposed above, it could assist in coordinating economic policies with other foreign and defense policies.

Certainly, no planning mechanism will be effective unless the president and senior officials will take it seriously, but creating a mechanism such as described here is a first step in that direction.

The administration should increasingly provide Congress with long-range policy planning and budget forecasts in both domestic and foreign policy.

Both the functioning of the executive branch and relations with Congress could be improved greatly if the administration would place much greater stress on long-range planning, including budget forecasts. Although no planning process can fully commit the U.S. government several years in advance, the development of such management tools can provide guidelines, especially for the purpose of focusing national debate on critical issues. The Defense Department, for example, already submits five-year budget projections to the Congress. This practice should be made increasingly widespread throughout the government— to provide the administration with a long-range management tool, to increase the chances for thoughtful congressional deliberation of key issues, and to strengthen the basis for more effective legislative oversight.

We believe that the following recommendations also have merit:

Congressional relations staff and leaders should be fully engaged in the policy and planning process. The assistant to the president for legislative affairs should be included in all meetings of the National Security Council.

Cabinet and subcabinet appointees should increasingly be recruited from among individuals with experience on Capitol Hill.

Although the United States does not have a parliamentary form of government, with a natural overlap between the executive and legislature, any administration will benefit from increasing the proportion of its senior officers drawn from the legislative branch, including former members of the House and Senate as well as staff. There would be a risk of further strengthening links between parts of the Congress and parts of the administration—possibly at the expense of a president's overall goals, but judiciously employed, this cross-fertilization can pay dividends for both branches of government. At the same time and for similar reasons, members of Congress should increasingly select staff with experience in the executive branch.

Departmental assistant secretaries for congressional relations should be chosen by cabinet members in conjunction with the White House and, in particular, the assistant to the president for legislative affairs.

This step would increase the chances that legislative strategy throughout the government could be coordinated. It would also assist the White House and executive agencies in sending clear and consistent messages to Congress.

Regular meetings of all departmental liaison officials should be held at the White House to maintain a sense of teamwork on legislative priorities.

These meetings should be held in close coordination with the plans and priorities set by the Legislative Strategy Group. Of course, there will always be differences of interest and perspective among different departments and agencies that will also be reflected in their congressional relations staffs. It is also important that the White House retain the ability to keep its distance from dealing with the Congress on some issues; this places the political onus of not acceding to congressional wishes on the departments and agencies. But the White House also needs to gain information from within the bureaucracy and to increase the chances of presidential control over at least the general directions of administration policy as it is being presented to Congress.

The White House Office of Public Liaison should engage interest groups in the coordinated lobbying process.

As the most successful efforts to gain agreement between the executive and legislative branches indicate, the least amount of stress is placed on the system when various interests groups are consciously brought in from the beginning. This represents an effort, where possible, to reconcile differences and to produce workable legislation. Of course, individual departments and agencies will continue to have their own ties to interest groups. Presidential leadership, however, can be enhanced—along with the clarity of signals sent to Capitol Hill—if the outreach efforts of the Office of Public Liaison are fully coordinated with the Office of Legislative Affairs in support of the president's legislative priorities.

The two branches should make limited but appropriate use of bipartisan commissions, with representation from Congress, from the administration, and from outside the government.

The use of these bipartisan commissions, as a last resort technique in legislative strategy, should be subject to the following three rules, in addition to the general rule of circumspection to prevent misuse:

- The issue in question should have reached a level of maturity at which decisions are both necessary and possible. This means that the issue should command urgency, that the range of alternatives for national policy should be well-developed, and that there is awareness of the political difficulties for all concerned in reaching any particular conclusion. In short, the issue must be ripe for a bargain.
- Appointments to the commission must be on a strictly bipartisan basis, with each political party in effective control of its own representation.
- The commission should apportion fairly the political burdens of taking decisions that, although necessary for the nation, are likely to be politically unpopular with one or another sector of U.S. opinion. Both the benefits of reaching agreement and the pain of the bargain struck must be shared by both branches of government and both political parties.

Information-Sharing and Consultations

The executive branch should consult Congress more systematically—especially on a bipartisan basis. It should also share more foreign policy information with Congress.

Both the administration and Congress can benefit from regular, informal meetings between the president and, separately, various cabinet members with bipartisan groups of congressional leaders, both on specific issues and on more general programs. This greater regularization of present informal procedures should also be seen as a valuable adjunct to the executive branch planning and coordinating processes recommended above. To be most effective, consultations should take place throughout the policy process rather than near the end to give members of Congress a stake in the outcome.

On foreign policy, the times, the nature of issues, and the authority of congressional leadership are sufficiently different from what they were in the early postwar years so that presidents can no longer expect to gain congressional support for foreign policy initiatives simply by meeting with senior leaders of both Houses. Nevertheless, presidents and senior officials should meet frequently with congressional leaders on a bipartisan basis to discuss foreign policy issues. The better part of wisdom for presidents is to take congressional leaders and other key members more, rather than less, into their confidence on foreign as well as domestic policy matters, instead of using consultations as a pro forma means of presenting settled lines of policy and action.

This practice can be especially valuable when an administration is preparing for actions such as arms control negotiations. The lesson of Woodrow Wilson's failure to take Senate Republican leaders to the Versailles Conference is worth relearning, as is that of Dwight Eisenhower's consultations with congressional leaders before he decided not to intervene in Vietnam. This need not—indeed, constitutionally it cannot—imply a diminution of presidential authority for the actual conduct of negotiations. Rather, such confidential consultations, which can normally be done through the committee structure, can increase the chances that a president will be able to sustain U.S. agreements with other countries after they are presented to the legislative branch. Of course, the same process of prior consultations is also invaluable in the domestic field, for example, in shaping tax reform.

The executive branch also often faces a trade-off between controlling information and gaining congressional support for its actions. Yet here, too, an administration should err on the side of being too forthcoming rather than too little. At the same time, members of Congress must be willing to take advantage of access to information that already exists; for example, few make the effort to review the annual intelligence report provided to Congress by the executive branch. The requirements of exercising discipline in respecting information that must remain secret should rest with the congressional leadership and the chairmen of appropriate committees.

The passage of the Trade Expansion Act of 1979 is an excellent example of the system's working through appropriate use of consultations. In advance, Congress had increased the chances of success by mandating (1) that the administration should create, during the negotiations within the General Agreement on Tariffs and Trade, a series of committees comprising interested parties in the U.S. private sector, and (2) that the implementing act itself could not be amended—it would have only an up or down vote.

Under the leadership of the special trade representative, the Congress—as well as a wide variety of constituencies in the nation—was deeply and continually involved in the process of negotiating the trade agreement. Congressional staffs as well as members were thoroughly and regularly engaged. The enacting legislation itself was written jointly by administration and congressional representatives. By the time the act was presented for debate and vote, it was truly a product of both branches of government and of both parties, earning broad approval of private-sector groups. Lopsided majorities in both Houses testified to the value of these procedures. They entailed, first, recognition that power and pain had to be shared for there to be a productive result and, second, the primacy of consultation and involvement. These majorities validated the basic principle that the political craft of individuals in government is critical to effective legislative-executive relations.

Cross-Fertilization

The two branches should develop a major congressional-executive branch staff exchange program.

The relative lack of knowledge that many individuals in each branch of government have about the other can be ameliorated in part through a sustained program of personnel exchanges between Congress and the executive branch, building upon what is done presently through the Congressional Fellows Program and the Pearson Amendment. This step, modest in concept but profound in implications, can provide broader experience for congressional staff members, foreign service officers, military officers, and civil servants. These exchanges should be undertaken on a one or two-year basis. Provision should be made for equivalence in compensation and benefits, and executive branch officers taking part in the program should be rewarded, not penalized, in career advancement.

Reforming the Budget Process

In considering the congressional budget process, we judge that it is no answer simply to recommend that Congress revert to practices prevailing before the 1974 budget act: The problems it was designed to solve would still remain. We also considered and rejected—as politically unworkable—the suggestion that one of the three sets of fiscal committees be abolished, perhaps through the merging of authorization and appropriations committees into program committees. That step might seem to be a logical solution to the budget problem, but it does not account for the different functions played by the different committees. Nor does it account for the role of internal checks and balances—or for the strong institutional resistance there would be in Congress to eliminating committees, chairmanships, staffs, responsibilities, and oversight: in short, real congressional power.

By contrast, some more modest, specific steps could help to improve the budget process and to break the recurrent logjam that now characterizes consideration of money issues within Congress—a logjam that reduces congressional effectiveness in checking the executive and complicates relations between the two branches. In the main, however, these steps should derive from attempts to make the Congressional Budget and Impoundment Control Act of 1974 more effective.

Congress should adopt a biennial budget cycle.

We believe that some "stretch-out" of the existing three layers of committee consideration of fiscal issues—budget, authorization, and appropriation—is imperative. This is particularly essential

1. if Congress is to be able to devote more of its time and attention to necessary oversight, and
2. if all participants in the process, including the executive branch, are to be kept from becoming hopelessly mired in budgetary considerations.

To make this basic recommendation effective, two other steps need to be taken.

With the biennial budget cycle, super majorities should be required to pass supplemental appropriations in the second year of the cycle.

Converting to a two-year budget cycle, while allowing for extraordinary consideration of additional spending measures by 60 percent or higher majorities, would allow sufficient flexibility for Congress to consider genuine emergencies. (It might also restrict overall spending growth, by permitting more careful consideration of each part of the budget process.) Some areas will need special rules to permit some added flexibility, however. This is true of defense, for example, since this area is most subject to a need for changes in spending in response to external or unforeseen circumstances.

Congressional reprogramming authority should be increased.

In addition, a flexible system of managing the two-year budget cycle would require greater delegation of authority to appropriate congressional committees for reprogramming monies between selected budget categories.

Of course, many problems concerning a two-year budget cycle remain to be solved. For example, rapidly changing political and economic circumstances may at times make it difficult to adopt realistic budget resolutions for a two-year period. "Turf" struggles among the different types of committees would also make specific phasing difficult. Furthermore, with any two-year cycle for budget, authorization, and appropriations, virtually any method of dividing the tasks over the full period will lead to the foreclosing of some major national decisions before a new Congress—and on occasion a new president—assumes power. No political figure can be satisfied with this relative loss of control. Thus there will need to be creative compromising about the timing of a two-year fiscal process. In addition, the creation of a budget process carried over from one Congress to the next would, in effect, alter procedures laid down by the Constitution.

Nevertheless, we believe that the benefits to the governing process from the adoption of a two-year budget cycle are significant. The results would mean

- greater congressional control over the nation's spending and allocation of resources;
- more effective capacity in Congress for serious deliberation of key policy questions;
- greater continuity of policy;
- the creation of some genuine capacity for Congress to begin forward planning;
- greater availability of time for Congress to oversee executive branch activities.

Thus we strongly support this recommendation despite the difficulties of its practical implementation. Indeed, the added time made available to Congress to discharge its other legislative responsibilities could make this reform its most effective response to the loss of the legislative veto.

There are many ways in which the two-year budget cycle can be structured, in terms of the timing and methods of handling budget resolutions, authorizations, and appropriations.

The Beilenson Task Force, referred to earlier, has set out a specific calendar for the budget process based on the adoption of a biennial budget with only one binding resolution. The Task Force also made several recommendations that would tighten rules regarding the timing of the consideration of any revenue or spending bill, as well as the introduction of "budget busting" legislation.

For its part, the Quayle Temporary Select Committee proposed the formation of a select Senate committee to analyze the two-year budget process more thoroughly. This procedure would be more likely to bear fruit than entrusting this review to the three Senate committees that now have statutory jurisdiction over budget reform. The Quayle Committee noted that "testimony before [it] on the need for a two-year budget process was overwhelming." Apparently, both groups rejected on political grounds, as did we, the idea of combining all fiscal legislation into one "super bill"—a bill that would include all budget, revenue, and expenditure legislation and would be brought to each House floor for a single vote.

We believe that Congress should give careful consideration to the alternatives presented in the Quayle and Beilenson reports. Most important, however, is that Congress, in its own judgment, develop a set of procedures that it finds to be most congenial. To that end, Congress should form a bipartisan committee drawn from both Houses to develop a biennial budget process that is both procedurally workable and politically acceptable. This committee should include members from the Senate Budget, Government Affairs, Appropriations, and Rules Committees, as well as from their House counterparts.

In addition, as a necessary adjunct to this reform, the executive branch should adapt its own budgeting procedures and schedules to conform to the two-year cycle as adopted by Congress.

We also endorse the following steps for a reformed budget process:

Congress should provide for expedited consideration of appropriations bills to curb excessive reliance on continuing resolutions.

Continuing resolutions stymie effective consideration of spending measures and also undercut executive branch fiscal planning because of attendant delays, uncertainties, and at times plain sloppy draftsmanship. They also short-circuit those controls and restraints that do exist to limit federal spending.

Because of the institutional and economic costs of continuing resolutions, Congress should place a premium on expediting consideration of regular appropriations bills to help discipline the process. For example, the Beilenson Task Force has suggested that the House be prohibited from considering a resolution for the July 4th recess and the Senate be barred from going out for Labor Day until all 13 appropriations bills have been passed.

Congress should provide for a single, binding budget resolution, with the possibility of later updating, to enforce top-down discipline early in the budget cycle.

As the Reagan administration demonstrated in 1981, difficult spending restraint decisions are best made early and imposed comprehensively, rather than made late in the session and in piecemeal fashion. In view of the fact that Congress has not recently been able to pass a second budget resolution, despite the requirements of the budget act, the Second Budget Resolution should be abolished and the Congressional Budget Act of 1974 should be amended to include the necessary enforcement powers in a single binding resolution. In short, if Congress will mandate adherence to its own existing procedures regarding the first budget resolution, some of the difficulty in the present system can be alleviated.

Achieving this goal, however, is basically a matter of leadership and political will rather than of procedural adjustment.

Budget subfunctions should be abolished and functions should be consolidated into broader management categories. The Rules Committee in the House and the Senate leadership should limit program-oriented or line-item amendments in floor debate on the budget resolution.

Encouraging the budget committees to stay away from consideration of detailed line items and specific programs would have a double benefit. First, it would eliminate the duplication inherent when all three types of fiscal committees focus on essentially the same questions. Thus, it would save both Congress and the executive branch the endless frustration of constantly refighting the same issues. Second, it would free the budget committees to do what they are supposed to do—to set overall fiscal policy for the nation.

The current accounting nightmare should be ended by creating uniform accounts and functional categories for all participants in the process.

Regular meetings should take place between the tax-writing and budget committees.

This step would enable both sets of committees to operate from the same basic information. It would also provide both with a better sense of levels of income and expenditure likely to emerge from the overall congressional process.

There should be increased use of joint hearings between authorization and appropriations subcommittees.

Increased use of the practice of joint hearings between authorization and appropriations subcommittees charged with specific governmental functions would lead to a greater sharing of information. Both types of subcommittees would also begin their deliberations from the same starting point. Furthermore, such hearings would permit executive branch personnel to spend less time giving essentially the same testimony before different bodies. Most important, the greater use of joint subcommittee hearings would help reduce the amount of time lag in the present budget process. Appropriations committees could carry out their work at the staff level simultaneously with the authorization committees; also, the latter could finish their work before appropriations were enacted, thus ensuring the importance of the authorization process.

Where possible, Congress should authorize long-term programs on a multiyear or even permanent basis.

Because much congressional time—especially in committees—is devoted to annual consideration of continuing programs or accounts, less controversial items like personnel should be authorized, where possible, on a permanent basis. Furthermore, some programs—like general revenue-sharing and the farm program—are already authorized on a multi-year basis: a practice that should be expanded. In defense authorizations, for example, major noncontroversial weapons should be authorized in terms of milestones, rather than on an annual basis to facilitate forward planning. These steps would increase the time available to the appropriate committees for in-depth consideration of central issues.

Congress should also consider other budgetary measures to increase its capacity to discharge its responsibilities regarding the budget.

Steps to be considered include integrating federal credit activity with a unified budget, incorporating the off-budget federal entities, and creating a capital investment budget.

Other Congressional Reforms

In a number of other areas, changes in the procedures and practices of Congress would help it deal more effectively with the executive branch. We believe that the following recommendations would be the beginnings of a "code of conduct" for congressional business:

Germaneness rules should be enforced and tightened in the Senate.

Stricter enforcement of the rules prohibiting nongermane amendments to appropriations bills would be a significant step in avoiding the use of continuing resolutions and government by deadlock. In addition, the Senate should adopt the long-discussed proposal to provide a rule under which a two-thirds majority of those senators present and voting would be required to overturn a nongermane ruling from the chair. This proposal would greatly increase the Senate's ability to act on major legislation while protecting the legitimate use of nongermane amendments.

House and Senate committee membership should broadly reflect both partisan and substantive divisions present in each body as a whole.

We believe that the House and Senate work most effectively when their committees produce draft legislation that is likely to enjoy broad support in each body as a whole. When committees report legislation that fails this test, it either does not pass the full House or Senate or it does so only after extensive and contentious floor debate and amendment.

Committee assignments and the number of subcommittees should be limited.
With fewer exceptions than it now grants, the Senate should enforce its rule limiting committee assignments for each member to a total of two major committees and one other committee. In addition, no Senate committee, with the exception of the Appropriations Committee, should have more than five subcommittees. By the same token, House committees should be limited to six subcommittees each with the exception of the Appropriations Committee.

Conclusions

These proposals for reforming legislative-executive relations do not exhaust the subject. We have chosen them, however, because they meet several tests: They are practical, relatively modest, and bipartisan— criteria related to the chances for their adoption. They are timely: They should be effective in a period when the same party controls both the White House and one House of Congress. And they do not necessarily imply any major shift in the balance of political power between the branches. Their implementation, however, can aid in the overall formulation and implementation of U.S. policy and programs. They can help the U.S. government function to the best of its ability.

In the final analysis, however, the functioning of the U.S. government is a matter of people. The procedural reforms suggested here can be only as good as the nation's leaders will make them and as the people of the United States will demand.

Bibliography

Books

Abshire, David M. *Foreign Policy Makers: President vs.Congress*. Washington Paper 66. Beverly Hills and London: Sage Publications with The Center for Strategic and International Studies, Georgetown Univ., 1979.

Andrews, William G. "The Presidency, Congress, and Constitutional Theory." In *Presidency in Contemporary Context*. Edited by Norman C. Thomas. New York: Dodd, Mead, 1975.

Baker, Robert G., with Larry L. King. *Wheeling and Dealing*. NewYork: W. W. Norton, 1978.

Bibby, John F., and Roger H. Davidson. *On Capitol Hill: Studies in the Legislative Process*. 2d ed. Chicago: Dryden, 1972.

Binkley, Wilfred E. *President and Congress*. New York: Random House, 1962.

Cassidy, Robert. "Negotiating about Negotiations." In *The Tethered Presidency*. Edited by T. Franck. New York: New York Univ. Press, 1981.

Chamberlain, Lawrence H. *The President, Congress, and Legislation*. New York: Columbia Univ. Press, 1946.

Cheney, Richard B., and Lynne V. Cheney. *Kings of the Hill: Power and Personality in the House of Representatives*. New York: Continuum, 1983.

Collier, Ellen C. *Strengthening Executive-Legislative Consultation on Foreign Policy*. Washington, D.C.: USGPO, 1983.

Crabb, Cecil V., and Pat M. Holt. *Invitation to Struggle: Congress, the Presidency, and Foreign Policy*. Washington, D.C.: Congressional Quarterly Press, 1980.

Destler, I. M."Executive-Congressional Conflict in Foreign Policy: Explaining It, Coping with It." In *Congress Reconsidered*. 2d ed. Edited by Lawrence C. Dodd and Bruce I. Oppenheimer. Washington, D.C.: Congressional Quarterly Press, 1981.

———. *Making Foreign Economic Policy*. Washington, D.C.: The Brookings Institution, 1980.

Edwards, George C., III. *Presidential Influence in Congress*. San Francisco: W.H. Freeman, 1980.

Egger, Rowland, and Joseph D. Harris. *The President and Congress*. New York: McGraw-Hill, 1963.

Fisher, Louis. *The Constitution Between Friends: Congress, the President, and the Law*. New York: St. Martin's Press, 1978.

———. *The Politics of Shared Power*. Washington, D.C.: Congressional Quarterly Press, 1981.

————. *President and Congress: Power and Policy.* New York: The Free Press, 1972.

Franck, Thomas M., and Edward Weisband. *Foreign Policy by Congress.* New York: Oxford Univ. Press, 1979.

Gallager, Hugh. "Presidents, Congress, and the Legislative Functions." In *The Presidency Reappraised.* Edited by Rexford Tugwell and Thomas Cronin. New York: Praeger, 1974.

Green, Mark J., James M. Fallows, and David R. Zwick. *Who Runs Congress?* New York: Bantam, 1972.

Hargrove, Erwin K. *The Power of the Modern Presidency.* New York: Knopf, 1974.

Henkin, Louis. *Foreign Affairs and the Constitution.* Mineola, N.Y.: Foundation Press, 1972.

Holtzman, Abraham, ed. *Legislative Liaison: Executive Leadership in Congress.* Chicago: Rand McNally, 1970.

Huitt, Ralph K. "White House Channels to the Hill." In *Congress Against the President.* Edited by Harvey C. Mansfield, Sr. New York: Praeger, 1975.

Hunter, Robert E. *Presidential Control of Foreign Policy: Management or Mishap?* Washington Paper 91. New York: Praeger with The Center for Strategic and International Studies, Georgetown Univ., 1982.

Javits, Jacob K. *Who Makes War: The President Versus Congress.* New York: Morrow, 1973.

King, Anthony, ed. *Both Ends of the Avenue: The Presidency, the Executive Branch, and Congress in the 1980's.* Washington, D.C. and London: American Enterprise Institute for Public Policy Research, 1983.

Leiper, J. *The Political Process: Executive Bureau-Legislative Committee Relations.* rev. ed. New York: Random House, 1965.

Livingston, William S., Lawrence C. Dodd, and Richard L. Schott, eds. *The Presidency and the Congress: A Shifting Balance of Power?* Austin, Texas: Lyndon B. Johnson School of Public Affairs, Lyndon Baines Johnson Library, 1979.

Moe, Ronald C., ed. *Congress and the President: Allies and Adversaries.* Pacific Palisades, Calif.: Goodyear Publishing Co., 1971.

Mullen, William F. *Presidential Power and Politics.* New York: St. Martin's Press, 1976.

Neustadt, Richard E. "Politicians and Bureaucrats." In *The Congress and America's Future.* 2d ed. Edited by David B. Truman. Englewood Cliffs, N.J.: Prentice-Hall, 1973.

Nogee, Joseph L. "Congress and the Presidency: The Dilemmas of Policy-Making in a Democracy." In *Congress, the Presidency, and American Foreign Policy.* Edited by John W. Spanier and Joseph L. Nogee. New York: Pergamon Press, 1981.

Ornstein, Norman J., ed. *President and Congress: Assessing Reagan's First Year.* Washington, D.C. and London: American Enterprise Institute for Public Policy Research, 1982.

Pious, Richard. "Sources of Domestic Policy Initiative." In *Congress Against the President.* Edited by Harvey C. Mansfield. New York: Praeger, 1975.

Polsby, Nelson W. *Congress and the Presidency.* 2d ed. Englewood Cliffs, N.J.: Prentice Hall, 1976.

———— . "The Washington Community, 1960–1980." In *The New Congress*. Edited by Thomas E. Mann and Norman J. Ornstein. Washington, D.C.: American Enterprise Institute for Public Policy Research, 1981.

Pyle, Christopher H. *The President, Congress, and the Constitution*. New York: Free Press, 1984.

Richard, Gary. *The Reaffirmation of Republicanism: Eisenhower and the Eighty-third Congress*. Knoxville: Univ. of Tennessee Press, 1975.

Ripley, Randall B. *Congress: Process and Policy*. 2d ed. New York: W.W. Norton, 1978.

———— . *Kennedy and Congress*. Morristown, N.J.: General Learning, 1972.

Rourke, John. *Congress and the Presidency in U.S. Foreign Policymaking: A Study of Interaction and Influence, 1945–1982*. Boulder, Colo.: Westview, 1983.

Schlesinger, Arthur M. *The Imperial Presidency*. Boston: Houghton Miffin, 1973.

Shull, Steven A. *Domestic Policy Formation: Presidential-Congressional Partnership*. Westport, Conn.: Greenwood Press, 1983.

———— . "An Agency's Best Friend: The White House or Congress?" In *The Presidency: Studies in Public Policy* . Edited by Steven A. Shull and Lance T. LeLoup. Brunswick, Ohio: King's Court Communications, 1978.

Spitzer, Robert J. *The Presidency and Public Policy: The Four Arenas of Presidential Power*. University, Ala.: The Univ. of Alabama Press, 1983.

Sundquist, James L. "Congress and the President: Enemies or Partners?" In *Congress Reconsidered*. Edited by Lawrence C. Dodd and Bruce I. Oppenheimer. New York: Praeger, 1972.

———— . *Decline and Resurgence of Congress*. Washington, D.C.: Brookings Institute, 1981.

Travis, Walter Earl, ed. *Congress and the President: Readings in Executive-Legislative Relations*. New York: Teacher's College, 1967.

Twiggs, Joan E. *The Tokyo Round of MTN: A Case Study in Building Domestic Support for Diplomacy*. Lanham, Md.: University Press of America and Institute for the Study of Diplomacy, 1986.

Wayne, Stephen J. *The Legislative Presidency*. New York: Harper & Row, 1978.

Wilcox, Francis O. *Congress, the Executive, and Foreign Policy*. New York: Harper & Row, 1971.

Wildavsky, Aaron. "The Two Presidencies." In *Perspectives on the Presidency*. Edited by Aaron Wildavsky. Boston: Little, Brown, 1975.

———— , ed. *The Presidency*. Boston: Little, Brown, 1969.

Wilson, Woodrow. *Congressional Government*. Boston: Houghton Mifflin, 1913.

Periodicals

Andrews, William G. "The Presidency, Congress, and Constitutional Theory." Paper delivered at the American Political Science Association meeting, Chicago, 1971.

Arnold, Peri E., and L. John Roos. "Towards A Theory of Congressional-Executive Relations." *Review of Politics* 36(July 1974): 418–429.

Black, Charles L. "The President and Congress." *Washington and Lee Law Review* 32 (Fall 1975).

Bonafede, Dom. "White House Report: Ford's Lobbyists Expect Democrats to Revise Tactics." *National Journal* 7 (June 21, 1975): 923–927.

———. Daniel Rapoport, and Joel Havemann. "The President Versus Congress: The Score Since Watergate." *National Journal* 8 (May 29, 1976): 730–748.

———. "Carter's Relationship with Congress—Making a Mountain Out of a 'Moorehill.'" *National Journal* 9 (March 26, 1977): 456–463.

Buck, J. Vincent. "Presidential Coattails and Congressional Loyalty." *Midwest Journal of Political Science* 16 (August 1972): 460–472.

Cohen, Richard E. "The Carter-Congress Rift—Who's Really to Blame?" *National Journal* 10 (April 22, 1978): 630–632.

———. "Legislative Veto Battle Escalates—Should Congress Have the Last Word?" *National Journal* 12 (September 6, 1980): 1473–1477.

———. "The 'Revolution' on Capitol Hill: Is It Just a Temporary Coup?" *National Journal* 13 (August 29, 1981): 1537–1541.

Cross, Mercer. "Carter and Congress: Fragile Friendship." *Congressional Quarterly Weekly Report* 35 (February 26, 1977): 361–363.

Destler, I.M., and Thomas R. Graham. "United States Congress and the Tokyo Round: Lessons of a Success Story." *The World Economy* (June 1980): 53–70.

Edwards, George C., III. "Presidential Influence in the House: Presidential Prestige as a Source of Presidential Power." *American Politics Quarterly* 5 (October 1977): 481–500.

———. "Presidential Influence in the House: Presidential Prestige as a Source of Presidential Power." *American Political Science Review* 70 (March 1976): 101–113.

Felton, John. "Hill Weighs Foreign Policy Impact of Ruling." *Congressional Quarterly Weekly Report* 41 (July 1983): 1329–1330.

Hager, Barry M. "Carter Seeks More Effective Use of Departmental Lobbyists' Skills." *Congressional Quarterly Weekly Report* 36 (March 4, 1978): 579–586.

Hammond, Thomas H., and Jane M. Fraser. "Faction Size, the Conservative Coalition, and the Determinants of Presidential 'Success' in Congress." Paper presented at the American Political Science Association Convention, Washington, D.C., August 28–30, 1980.

Hart, John. "Congressional Reactions to White House Lobbying." *Presidential Studies Quarterly* 11 (Winter 1981): 83–91.

———. "Staffing the Presidency: Kennedy and the Office of Congressional Relations." *Presidential Studies Quarterly* 13 (Winter 1983): 101–110.

Houston Chronicle, August 13, 1978. "Carter's Courtship of Congress."

Jackson, John H. et al. "Implementing the Tokyo Round." *Michigan Law Review* 81 (Dec. 1982): 267.

Johannes, John R. "Where Does the Buck Stop? Congress, the President, and the Responsibility for Legislative Initiation." *Western Political Quarterly* 25 (September 1972): 396–415.

———. "The President Proposes and the Congress Disposes—But Not Always." *Review of Politics* 36 (July 1974): 356–370.

Kahn, Gilbert. "In Perpetual Tension. Executive-Legislative Relations and the Case of the Legislative Veto." *Presidential Studies Quarterly* 11 (Spring 1981): 271–279.

Keller, William. "Executive Agency Lobbyists Mastering the Difficult Art of 'Congressional Liaison.'" *Congressional Quarterly Report* 39 (December 1981): 2387–2392.

Kernell, Samuel. "Presidential Popularity and Negative Voting: An Alternative Explanation of the Midterm Decline of the President's Party." *American Political Science Review* 71 (March 1977): 44–66.

Kirschten, Dick. "The Pennsylvania Avenue Connection. Making Peace on Capitol Hill." *National Journal* 13 (March 7, 1981): 384–387.

Lanoutte, William J. "Who's Setting Foreign Policy—Carter or Congress?" *National Journal* 10 (July 15, 1978): 1116–1123.

"Larry O'Brien Discusses White House Contacts with Capitol Hill." Interview conducted by NBC Reporter Paul Duke. Broadcast as part of the series "The Changing Congress" over the National Education Television Network during the week of July 11, 1965. Partial text in *Congressional Quarterly Weekly Report* 23 (July 23, 1965): 1434–1436.

LeLoup, Lance T., and Steven A. Shull. "Congress Versus the Executive: The 'Two Presidencies' Reconsidered." *Social Sciences Quarterly* 59 (March 1979): 704–719.

Manning, Bayless. "The Congress, the Executive and Interdomestic Affairs: Three Proposals." *Foreign Affairs* 55 (January 1977): 306–324.

Mansfield, Harvey L., Sr., ed. "Congress Against the President." *Proceedings of the Academy of Political Science* 32 (1975).

Martin, Jeanne. "Presidential Elections and Administration Support Among Congressmen." *American Journal of Political Science* 20 (August 1976): 483–490.

Moe, Ronald C., and Steven C. Teel. "Congress as a Policy-Maker: A Necessary Reappraisal." *Political Science Quarterly* 85 (September 1970): 443–470.

Mohr, Charles. "Carter's First Nine Months: Charges of Ineptitude Rise." *New York Times*, October 23, 1977.

Newsweek, March 7, 1977. "Carter and Congress."

Ornstein, Norman J. "Something Old, Something New: Lessons for a President About Congress in the Eighties." Revised draft prepared for the Conference on the Presidency and Congress, White Buckett Miller Center for Public Affairs, University of Virginia. January 24–25, 1980.

Pika, Joseph A. "White House Office of Congressional Relations: A Longitudinal Approach." Paper presented at annual meeting of the Midwest Political Science Association meeting, Chicago, 1971.

Pressman, Steven. "Congress Considers Choices In Legislative Veto Aftermath." *Congressional Quarterly Weekly Report* 41 (July 1983): 1327–1328.

Roberts, Steven V. "Carter and Congress: Doubt and Distrust Prevail." *New York Times*, August 15, 1979.

Schultz, L. Peter. "Goldwater v. Carter: The Separation of Powers and the Problem of Executive Prerogative." *Presidential Studies Quarterly* 12 (Winter 1982): 34–41.

Shinn, Donald C. "Towards a Model for Presidential Influence in Congress." Paper presented at the American Political Science Association Convention, Washington, D.C., August 28–31, 1980.

Shull, Steven A. "Presidential-Congressional Support for Agencies and for Each Other: A Comparative Look." *Journal of Politics* 40 (August 1978): 753–760.

————. "The President and Congress: Researching Their Interaction in Domestic Policy Formation." *Presidential Studies Quarterly* 12 (Fall 1982): 534–544.

————. "Assessing Measures of Presidential-Congressional Policy Making." *Presidential Studies Quarterly* 11 (Spring 1983): 151–157.

Smith, Donald. "Turning Screws: Winning Votes in Congress." *Congressional Quarterly Weekly Report* 34 (April 24, 1976): 947–954.

Smith, Terrence. "Carter and Congress: The Last Picture Show." *New York Times*, September 9, 1979.

Tate, Dale. "High Court Decision Reopens Dispute Over Impoundments; Congress Loses Spending Tool." *Congressional Quarterly Weekly Report* 41 (July 1983): 1331–1334.

Tidmarch, Charles M., and Charles M. Sabatt. "Presidential Leadership Change and Foreign Policy Roll-Call Voting in the U.S. Senate." *Western Political Quarterly* 25 (December 1972): 613–625.

Tolchin, Martin. "Slow Improvement Is Seen in White House Relations with Congress." *New York Times*, November 9, 1979.

Wehr, Elizabeth. "Numerous Factors Favoring Good Relationship between Reagan and New Congress." *Congressional Quarterly Weekly Report* 39 (January 24, 1981): 163–165.

Witt, Elder. "Legislative Veto Struck Down; Congress Moves to Review Dozens of Existing Statutes." *Congressional Quarterly Weekly* 41 (June 1983): 1263–1268.

Zeidenstein, Harvey G. "The Two Presidencies Thesis Is Alive and Well and Has Been Living in the U.S. Senate Since 1973." *Presidential Studies Quarterly* 11 (Fall 1981): 511–526.

About the Editors

Robert E. Hunter is director of European studies and senior fellow in Middle Eastern studies at the Georgetown University Center for Strategic and International Studies (CSIS). He is also contributing editor of *The Washington Quarterly*. He was special adviser on Lebanon to the speaker of the House of Representatives and lead consultant to the National Bipartisan Commission on Central America. Dr. Hunter served on the National Security Council staff, as director of West European Affairs (1977–1979) and as director of Middle East Affairs (1979-1981). He was foreign policy adviser to Senator Edward M. Kennedy. Among his many publications are *The Soviet Dilemma in the Middle East* (London: Institute for Strategic Studies, 1969), *Security in Europe* (Bloomington, Ind.: Indiana University Press, 1972), *Presidential Control of Foreign Policy* (New York: Praeger with CSIS, 1982), and *NATO: The Next Generation* (ed.) (Boulder, Colo.: Westview Press, 1984). He writes regularly for the *Los Angeles Times*.

Wayne L. Berman is senior fellow in the public policy process at CSIS and is cofounder of the Washington lobbying firm of Berman, Bergner & Boyette, Inc. He is active in Republican politics and has served in both an advisory and fundraising capacity for members of Congress. In 1980 he was deputy director for President Reagan's transition team for the natural resources area. Mr. Berman has served as director of Corporate and Political Affairs for CSIS. At CSIS he was also coeditor of *Making the Government Work: Legislative-Executive Reform* (Washington, D.C.: CSIS, 1985), and contributor to *The Critical Link: Energy and National Security in the 1980s* (Cambridge, Mass.: Ballinger, 1982).

John F. Kennedy is staff director for the Commission on National Elections and deputy to the director of European Studies at CSIS. He served as executive secretary to the CSIS Legislative-Executive Relations Project. He was a development consultant before joining CSIS. Mr. Kennedy received a B.A. in political science from Holy Cross College and has done graduate work at Georgetown University.

About the Steering Committee Members

Bill Alexander (D-Ark.) has represented the first district of Arkansas in the U.S. House of Representatives since 1969. The chief deputy majority whip, he is cofounder of the Congressional Rural Caucus and serves on the House Appropriations Committee.

Stanton D. Anderson is senior partner in the Washington, D.C. law firm of Anderson, Hibey, Nauheim & Blair. He was deputy assistant secretary of state for congressional relations from 1973 to 1975 and staff assistant to the president from 1971 to 1973. During the 1980–1981 presidential transition for the Reagan administration, he served as director for the economic affairs group.

Les Aspin (D-Wis.) is chairman of the House Armed Services Committee and has represented the first district of Wisconsin since 1970. Prior to that, he was economic adviser in the Office of Defense Secretary Robert McNamara and a staff assistant to President Kennedy's Council of Economic Advisers and to Senator William Proxmire (D-Wis.).

Michael J. Bayer is counsel to the vice chairman of the U.S. Synthetic Fuels Corporation. He has served as associate deputy secretary of commerce, as deputy assistant secretary for congressional affairs at the Department of Energy, and was executive assistant and counsel to former Representative Clarence Brown (R-Ohio).

Douglas J. Bennet is president of National Public Radio. He was administrator of the Agency for International Development (1979–1981), assistant secretary of state for congressional relations (1977–1979), and staff director of the Senate Budget Committee (1974–1977).

Jeffrey T. Bergner is a partner in Berman, Bergner, and Boyette, Inc. He was chief of staff of the Senate Foreign Relations Committee (1985–1986). He has also served as legislative director and administrative assistant to Senator Richard Lugar (R-Ind.).

Wayne L. Berman (project codirector) is a partner in Berman, Bergner, and Boyette, Inc. and CSIS senior fellow in public policy process. He was CSIS director of corporate and political affairs (1978–1984). He has also served as a legislative consultant to corporations specializing in energy and taxation and was deputy director of the Resources Group for the Reagan transition team.

Clarence L. Brown is deputy secretary of the U.S. Department of Commerce. A former nine-term congressman from Ohio, he was ranking Republican on the Joint Economic Committee and served on the Committee on Energy and Commerce and the Government Operations Committee.

Horace W. Busby is president of Horace W. Busby & Associates of Washington and publishes *The Busby Papers*. He was a close associate of President Lyndon B. Johnson and served as special assistant to the president and secretary to the Cabinet in the Johnson administration. He was a staff assistant in both the House of Representatives and the Senate.

Richard B. Cheney (R-Wyo.) has represented the state of Wyoming in the U.S. House of Representatives since 1978. In 1975, he was White House chief of staff under President Gerald Ford following a year as deputy assistant to the president. Chairman of the House Republican Policy Committee, he serves on the Committee on Interior and Insular Affairs.

Robert Cole is vice president, Washington affairs, of the Kaiser Aluminum & Chemical Corporation and head of its Government Affairs Committee. A former legislative assistant to Representative Clark MacGregor (R-Minn.), he has also been senior Washington representative of the General Motors Corporation.

William T. Coleman, Jr. is senior partner in the law firm of O'Melveny and Myers. Mr. Coleman served as secretary of transportation in the Ford administration and has held advisory or consultant positions to six presidents. He is a member of the Presidential Private Sector Survey on Cost Control in Government and the Presidential Advisory Committee on Federalism.

Alvin Paul Drischler is senior vice president of Black, Manafort, Stone & Kelly. He has been principal deputy assistant secretary of state for congressional relations and executive assistant to Senator Paul Laxalt (R-Nev.).

Kenneth M. Duberstein is vice president of Timmons and Company, Inc. He was assistant to the president for legislative affairs (1981–1983), prior to which he was deputy assistant for legislative affairs. A deputy under secretary of labor during the Ford administration, he was also director of Congressional and Intergovernmental Affairs for the U.S. General Services Administration from 1972 to 1976.

Stuart E. Eizenstat* is a partner in the firm Powell, Goldstein, Frazer & Murphy and adjunct lecturer at the John F. Kennedy School of

---

*Stuart Eizenstat supports the basic thrust of the report, but not necessarily all of the conclusions.

Government, Harvard University. From 1977–1981 he served as assistant to the president for domestic affairs and policy and executive director for the Domestic Policy Staff.

Charles D. Ferris is a senior partner in the law firm of Mintz, Levin, Cohn, Ferris, Glovsky & Popeo. He was chairman of the Federal Communications Commission, counsel to the House of Representatives, and general counsel to the Senate majority leader (1963–1977).

Paul Findley represented the twentieth district of Illinois for the Republic Party in the U.S. House of Representatives from 1961 to 1982. During his congressional career, he focused on agricultural legislation, especially its international aspects, and on opening dialogue internationally as a means of resolving disputes. He has written *They Dare to Speak Out: People and Institutions Confront Israel's Lobby* (Westport, Conn.: Lawrence Hill, 1985) on the impact of The Arab-Israeli dispute on U.S. institutions.

Lee H. Hamilton (D-Ind.) has represented the ninth district of Indiana in the U.S. House of Representatives since 1975 and is chairman of the Intelligence Committee and of the Subcommittee on Europe and the Middle East of the Foreign Affairs Committee. He is also a member of the Joint Economic Committee.

Stanley Heginbotham** is senior specialist in international affairs, chief of the Foreign Affairs and National Defense Division, Congressional Research Service, Library of Congress. He was a research associate (1968–1971) and associate professor (1971–1976) at Columbia University.

Robert E. Hunter (project codirector) is director of European Studies at CSIS. During the Carter administration, he served on the staff of the National Security Council, first as director of Western European Affairs, and then as director of Middle East Affairs. He was also foreign policy adviser to Senator Edward M. Kennedy (D-Mass.) and served on the White House staff under President Johnson.

Rady A. Johnson is vice president of government affairs, Standard Oil Company of Indiana. A former assistant to the secretary of defense for legislative affairs (1971–1973), he also served as administrative assistant to Congressman David J. Martin from 1965 to 1968.

Michael T. Kelley is deputy assistant secretary of commerce. He has also been deputy assistant secretary in the Office of Congressional Affairs at the Department of Energy.

**Dr. Heginbotham does not associate himself with recommendations in the report due to the nonpartisan nature of his organization, the Congressional Research Service.

Peter G. Kelly is a partner in the firm of Black, Manafort, Stone & Kelly. Formerly national finance chairman of the Democratic National Committee, he was also national Democratic Party treasurer.

John F. Kennedy (project executive secretary) is staff director for the Commission on National Elections. He received his bachelor's degree in political science from Holy Cross College and has done graduate work at Georgetown Unviersity.

William A. Knowlton retired from the U.S. Army as a general in 1980. He served as U.S. member of the NATO Military Committee, allied commander of land forces in Southeast Europe, chief of staff of the European Command, and superintendent of the U.S. Military Academy, West Point.

Melvin R. Laird is senior counsellor for national and international affairs, the Reader's Digest Association. He has served as secretary of defense (1969–1973), counsellor to the president for domestic affairs (1973–1974), and as U.S. representative (R-Wis.) (1952–1969).

Paul J. Manafort (chairman) is a partner in Black, Manafort, Stone & Kelly. He held senior positions in the Reagan presidential campaigns. He was personnel director in the Office of Executive Management during the 1980 presidential transition and deputy political director during the 1980 Reagan campaign. Mr. Manafort also served as deputy director in the Presidential Personnel Office in the White House under President Ford.

Richard Moe is counsel to the law firm of Davis, Polk & Wardwell. He was chief of staff to Vice President Walter Mondale (1977–1981) and Senator Mondale's administrative assistant (1973–1977). He was also administrative assistant to the mayor of Minneapolis and to the lieutenant governor of Minnesota.

Powell A. Moore is vice president for legislative affairs for Lockheed Corporation. He has also been assistant secretary of state for congressional relations and deputy assistant to the president for legislative affairs. He served in the White House Office of Legislative Affairs under Presidents Nixon and Ford, was a deputy special assistant to the latter, and was deputy director of public information for the Justice Department and a Senate staff aide.

Lyn Nofziger is a partner in Nofziger and Bragg Communications. He has served as assistant to the president for political affairs (1981–1982) and was deputy assistant to the president for congressional relations during the Nixon administration (1969–1971).

John M. Nugent, Jr. is vice president of Global, USA, Inc. He was a vice president of Timmons and Company, Inc. During the 1980 election campaign, he was executive assistant to the deputy director of the Reagan for President Committee and was special assistant to the administrator of the Federal Energy Administration during the Ford administration.

Nicholas A. Panuzio is president of Black, Manafort, Stone & Kelly and president of Panuzio Associates. He also served as commissioner of the General Services Administration's Public Building Service and was mayor of Bridgeport, Connecticut.

Richard Rivers is a partner in the law firm of Akin, Gump, Strauss, Hauer & Feld. He served as general counsel of the Office of the Special Representative for Trade Negotiations, was international trade counsel of the Committee on Finance of the U.S. Senate, and served as a congressional staff adviser to the U.S. Delegation to the Multilateral Trade Negotiations.

Walter Slocombe is a member of the law firm of Caplin and Drysdale, Chartered. He has served as deputy under secretary of defense for policy planning (1979–1981), director of the Department of Defense SALT Task Force (1979–1981), and principal deputy assistant secretary of defense, International Security Affairs (1977–1979). He also served on the National Security Council staff (1969–1970).

Robert S. Strauss is a partner in the law firm of Akin, Gump, Strauss, Hauer & Feld. He was chairman of the Democratic National Committee (1973–1976), U.S. special trade representative (1977–1981), President Carter's personal representative to the Middle East peace negotiations, and chairman of the Carter-Mondale Reelection Committee.

William E. Timmons is president of the consulting firm of Timmons and Company, Inc. He served as assistant to the president for legislative affairs for six years during the Nixon and Ford administrations. He was also administrative assistant to Representative William Brock (R-Tenn.) and a staff aide to Senator Alexander Wiley (R-Wis.).

Ben J. Wattenberg is a senior fellow at the American Enterprise Institute in Washington, D.C., coeditor of AEI's bimonthly magazine, *Public Opinion,* and vice chairman of the Board of International Broadcasting. He is a newspaper columnist, has hosted television serials and specials, and has extensive political experience.

Clyde A. Wheeler, Jr. is legislative counsel for the firm Riddel, Fox, Holroyd & Jackson and has served as vice president, Government Relations, of the Sun Company, Inc., from 1974–1985. He has also served as Sun Company's Washington representative, director of Government Relations, and in both the executive and legislative branches.

Francis O. Wilcox*** (1908–1985) was vice chairman of the Atlantic Council of the United States. He served as executive director of the Congressional Commission on the Organization of the Government for

---

***Francis O. Wilcox, who died as this study was being completed, was an able participant in the work of the Legislative-Executive Relations Project and made invaluable contributions to this project's paper.

the Conduct of Foreign Policy (1973–1975). He founded the staff of the U.S. Senate Foreign Relations Committee and was its chief of staff for 10 years. He was also assistant secretary of state for international organization affairs and a U.S. delegate to the UN General Assembly.

R. James Woolsey (vice chairman) is a partner in the law firm of Shea and Gardner and is counsel to CSIS. He has been a member of the President's Commission on Strategic Forces (The Scowcroft Commission). He has served as under secretary of the navy (1977–1979), on the National Security Council staff, as an adviser to the U.S. SALT delegation, and as general counsel to the Senate Committee on Armed Forces.

Index